Day by Day

Emotional Wellbeing in Parents of Disabled Children

JOANNA GRIFFIN

FREE ASSOCIATION BOOKS

First published in 2021 by
Free Association Books

Copyright © 2021 Joanna Griffin

A CIP Catalogue of this book is available from
the British Library

ISBN: 978-1-9113835-3-6

Cover design and typesetting by
www.chandlerbookdesign.co.uk

Printed and bound in Great Britain by
Short Run Press Limited

CONTENTS

Dedicated to A., J., B. & O.

Part 1
Introduction

1

Why I Wrote this Book

The Beginning

When my son was born, he was as close to death as it is possible to be. His pale, limp body was seemingly lifeless. I watched, uncomprehendingly, as the doctors put a tube in his mouth and pressed repeatedly on his chest, so hard that it broke several of his ribs. I held my breath, willing his to come. A twenty-three minute resuscitation which I can barely describe. Lying like a slab of meat on the table as I was sewn up. Time suspended, my mind frozen.

The matron, tight-lipped and concerned, reminded the paediatricians as they started wheeling him out to Intensive Care, 'Mum hasn't seen the baby.' He was wheeled back in for me to see. Alive, but only just. I looked at him and smiled, despite knowing inside that this isn't how things are supposed to be. Denial and shock intertwined and misfired like a short circuit in my head. The idealised version I had imagined, long dead and forgotten. My womb ached. My stomach felt hollowed out. There was a silent primitive howl from my body.

When, shortly after birth, my son was diagnosed with cerebral palsy, I felt I had fallen into an abyss from which I would never recover. I can still hear the consultant's words, carefully chosen: 'unlikely to walk', 'signs of visual impairment' and 'I know this is not what a young couple like you want to hear about your first child'. I didn't know where to look, how to sit, what I was supposed to do in response. I didn't feel real. Unravelling, we were plunged into previously inconceivable psychic wounds, due to the number of invasive medical interventions. One of his first cries was a scream that echoed down a long, desolate corridor as they inserted another needle into his tiny foot. The juxtaposition of his beautiful, soft skin next to hospital tubes and machines attached to every limb. I felt such a deep heartache that it has taken a long time to make any sense of it.

Not for us the euphoric moment I had dreamt of when first meeting our baby. There was no happy release of emotion, after twenty-nine hours of labour, in the delighted embrace of our first child. Instead, there were ever more doctors filling up the room, and the horrific realisation that something was seriously wrong. Seeing his eyes rolled up into the back of his head due to the medication given to prevent further seizures. Being given a photo of him as if this would be the last thing we had of him. My inability to remember my parents' telephone number to tell them the news. Finally getting through and hearing myself say, 'you need to come and see him because he might not survive'; words no parent wants to use to announce the arrival of a first beloved and longed-for grandchild.

I can time-travel to these memories – easy to fly back to, but still so painful to recall. The thought of how things could have been different is faded but still present at times.

Our Story

My husband and I met at university and after a number of years of following our own paths met again, coincidentally, in North London where we were both living. We married soon after and our conversations about our future together always involved children. I wanted a large number, three or four, close together as I had been the youngest by eight and ten years in my family and liked the idea of the close-knit siblings all playing together. My husband, always the more rational one, preferred two with a good space between them. As both of us were keen on sports, me at running and him at football, we joked about how sporty our children would be and that we'd spend all our free time ferrying them around to different activities.

I had trained as a Counselling Psychologist for many reasons but it especially appealed to me because it was adaptable to part-time working and being self-employed at home, which would help with childcare. I wanted to be the main caregiver as children had been my life plan since as young as I could remember. I love seeing how children grow, develop, learn and become their own little personality. I'd received a first in my Psychology degree including in the Child Development Section so I (naively!) felt as ready as one could be for what lay ahead. Little did I know.

Unfortunately, I do not think my experience helped me much in what happened. I had worked in General Practitioners' surgeries in the National Health Service (NHS), charities and other settings with adults on the autism spectrum. Despite knowing the system and how services connected to one another (to a certain extent), when I needed to use those services as a parent I was absolutely bowled over by how complex, unhelpful and frustrating health, education and social services could be and where and how to get the support that you need. I didn't have the words or understanding of how I could be emotionally floored yet unable to find somewhere I could fully articulate how I was feeling. I needed someone to help me rediscover my own compass. I hope I can help you, in some way, by writing this book.

The Early Years

Our son's traumatic birth set the tempo for the next few years. Initially it was physical things that were a struggle, then as my son got older the behavioural and cognitive challenges became the biggest fear and worry. I sometimes wondered if I could take any more diagnoses or difficulties being thrown at us and our tiny, darling boy. Did the professionals giving these diagnoses have any idea how devastating they were to hear? Did they believe they were providing something useful or just a list of 'facts' with little understanding of their impact?

Over time my psychological strength was worn down and my ability to take on any more pain depleted. Just as we'd assimilated one bit of news and started moving forward we were hit with another. Being bombarded with ever increasing appointments and advice for supporting him felt like I was expected to be able to rectify the problems caused by his difficult birth. I held onto information I'd been told about the importance of brain 'plasticity' in children and hence believed that if I worked hard enough I may be able to overcome his brain damage. If only I could be a good enough physiotherapist, speech therapist or psychologist. I now realise there is a limit to what plasticity can achieve but this added to the pressure I placed on myself.

The frustrations with services – lack of joined-up working, chasing up delayed reports, inability to get through on the telephone to speak to relevant people, not meeting the threshold for services – were re-traumatising. Having to explain and justify yourself for the little help that exists involves a loss of control and power that can affect your self-esteem. Feeling demeaned and undervalued in society and suddenly realising that you are 'othered'. My eyes were opened to the challenges that many disabled people face: judgement, discrimination and lack of understanding. Seeing social injustices, such as disability hate crime, to which I had previously been oblivious, shocked me in a profound way. Partly horrified at my own ignorance, terrified that my own precious son could be viewed in such a negative light and trying to make sense of my inner turmoil was not a pleasant place to be.

I love my son with all my heart. Yet there have been days, particularly when he is ill or out-of-sorts, where his struggles pierce me to my core and there is a pain that takes time to subside. I also felt a sense of failure that I did not understand the system nor sometimes my own son. The expectation that if one just followed the advice of therapists then everything would be simpler and easier caused self-doubt; I now realise there are no easy answers and the struggles are real and widely-felt. One of the skills I believe many parent carers develop is not only a wider awareness of the world but also an enhanced ability to take another's perspective – to see and understand the world from their child's viewpoint. This helps on so many levels but it is not always easy to get there. Life is better once you get here though.

It soon became clear that I could not continue in my work as a psychologist in the NHS. The demand on my time for appointments, therapies and my son's constant illnesses caused by his weakened immune system meant that I was pressurised and stressed. It feels unethical to regularly cancel clients' appointments so as a psychologist I had less flexibility in work. I felt like I'd lost my hard fought for and long-studied profession and the status that often comes with being employed. 'Mum' is an underrated position in our society, mother of a disabled child perhaps even more so.

Understandably this affected my own mental wellbeing, with a reactive depression to the traumatic experience as well as anxiety in relation to all of the expectations on me, as his mother-carer, to complete his daily therapies. I had no time or space to process the emotional impact. It was rare if a professional, of all the countless ones that had suddenly arrived in our life, asked me how I was doing, or acknowledged that the situation may be difficult. I sometimes felt like I couldn't just enjoy taking him for a walk or cuddling together while we read a book. My mind was so full of correcting the tight muscles in his legs or the way he was holding his hand that it affected our time together.

Attending baby and toddler groups with other parents of non-disabled children was isolating and at times upsetting. Hearing other mothers bemoan the little things (that are important to new mothers but felt trivial in comparison) such as lack of sleep or their child not saying their words clearly made me wish that they were my problems and I could go back to being ignorant of how life can change direction so spectacularly. I remember attending a baby massage group and my son was curled round in a crescent shape because of the tightness on one side of his body being more severe than the other. The other parents noticed but didn't know how to react and the leader commented she'd 'never seen that before', again emphasising that he, and me by association, was different and unusual. I felt I should have known what to do but I was under a massive cloud of un-knowing.

I was oblivious to the fact that I was smothered in post-traumatic stress (PTS). It was not PTS *Disorder* as I believe it was a natural response to the shock that we had been, and were still going, through. It was an understandable response to an unexpected, challenging and ongoing situation. But even as a psychologist I did not recognise what was going on because there seemed to be a great Wall of Silence surrounding parent carer coping. I know I'm not the only one who has experienced this; parents grow to expect *not* to have their feelings considered by others and when it does happen it's significant and meaningful[1]. I believe, with all of my soul, that it is better to talk about these feelings and, in doing so, process and make sense of the situation in which you find yourself.

---

[1] Roos, S. (2002) *Chronic Sorrow: A Living Loss*, New York: Routledge, p. 36

I wrote this book to share what I have learnt over the last thirteen years in the hope that no-one else feels so alone in the confusion and heartache as I did. Although it can be hard to find other families, and living in a mainstream world can feel isolating, there *are* other families out there with a similar experience and it can be valuable and restorative to find them. I hope this book reassures you that you are not mad or bad for feeling a whole raft of emotions in relation to parenting a disabled child, often all at the same time. This is an ordinary response to an extraordinary situation. I also hope it offers you signposts and ideas on how to support yourself during the journey.

Other Families

Having worked with other families, through various roles at *Hemihelp* and *Hoffmann Foundation for Autism* and consultancy work for *Scope* and *Mencap* (on the parenting programme *Early Positive Approaches to Support, E-PAtS*), I realised parent carers could experience complex and profound emotions in relation to their child's disability and challenges they face in society. However, there was not always an obvious place for them to discuss and process these emotions.

For the last few years alongside my Doctorate researching 'Emotional wellbeing in parents of children with a learning and/or developmental disability' (i.e. autism, intellectual disability, Down Syndrome, global developmental delay). I have spoken to, or heard from, hundreds of parents on the emotional impact of parenting a disabled child and have been moved, though not surprised, by some of the very difficult feelings parents have been carrying, largely on their own. I include quotes from parents *in italics* throughout the book. It's important you know that you are not alone and that the parent carer voice is heard.

I found hundreds of academic studies outlining the extra pressure we are under and the negative impact this can have on our own mental wellbeing. There are similar feelings across different disabilities, including those with life-limiting conditions. However, this information rarely seems to get to the very parents it concerns, and the opportunity to normalise and de-toxify difficulties is lost. These are not necessarily mental health issues, requiring diagnosis; they are understandable and common reactions to the situation in which parents find themselves. I refer to many of these studies in this book.

Having the insight that you are not on your own – others feel these emotions too and it will get easier – can keep hopelessness and helplessness at bay and provide a light when things feel bleak.

> *'If I could go back in time, I'd love to be able to, because I was a very broken person ... when [my daughter] was born, and talk to me and say I know that you're really scared, that is normal to feel like that, and it is normal to be have so much shock that actually you can't even take in what's going on, it's normal, other parents have this too.'*

It is important to recognise the reality of your own experience when life is tough and you need someone to talk to. In my own experience, and through talking to other parents, I noticed there was a deficit of specific emotional support available. I therefore created the website www.affinityhub.uk to signpost to counsellors, therapists, psychologists and organisations who provide emotional support. It outlines common emotions and advice on wellbeing as well as providing words of wisdom from other parent carers.

Two Sides to the Story: Challenges and Growth

After a shocking event life begins anew. It follows a different trajectory that may include pain and awareness of life's fragility. But out of the uncertainty it is possible for something meaningful to emerge. Life is messy, nuanced and rarely all bad or all good. Parenting can be a complex mixture of both. Feelings change, adapt and surprise us. Humans are able to survive and thrive despite adverse life events. I have seen this in my own life and my development as a mother, practitioner and human being. I have witnessed the resourcefulness, strength and love that most parent carers inhabit and I am proud to be part of this community.

There are many things for which I am grateful. My lovely boy survived; things could have been very different. He is a big part of our family and our life. Once we found the right school, routines and leisure activities, he settled down happier, having found true peers and a place in society that understands him. I cannot imagine life without him and he has touched so many people's lives.

He has taught me so much about the world, my own views of disability and the long way we have to go before society accepts difference. I am now less concerned with others' views of me and my family; the experience has helped me put things into perspective. I am a strong believer that diversity is a positive and parent carers are valuable advocates for this. I do not believe in wiping out variance and am worried about society's obsession with so-called images of perfection.

I have learnt I can survive and that I am more resilient than I knew. Many parent carers report personal growth in different areas of their life, such as renewed confidence or recognising what is truly valuable and precious. I have met people along the way with similar stories and struggles and when I've felt this connection it has made my heart burst with joy. I'm not the only one. And it has helped me to find my voice.

But many of our day-to-day struggles endure and need work. When society accepts difference, it makes life so much easier and more fulfilling. On a recent trip to an autism-friendly cinema showing, I noticed that my anxieties about potentially 'socially inappropriate' behaviours were gone. I realised that the other people there would have similar experiences and, without even needing to speak to them, it was grounding and supportive. Some social rules are absurd and unnecessary; this realisation can help put life into perspective. In the future, hopefully the whole of society can adapt to being more accepting of difference.

I do, however, think it is important that parent carers' feelings are acknowledged, voices are heard and the complex array of emotional responses are understood. Parents should not be shamed or judged for how they feel. Then hopefully they can work through their feelings and adjust to their new future. It is in this spirit that I write this book and document the experiences of many parents in an attempt to encourage openness and healing for all parents (and, by extension, families) who may be struggling. It is a difficult tension to hold; both acknowledging the difficulties families face whilst also wishing to challenge the predominantly negative narrative that often surrounds disability. But it is possible.

You may be a parent who feels unfazed by Special Needs Parenting. If so, I take my hat off to you, but this book is probably not for you.

Instead, this is for the parent who, like me, has felt (feels) confused and overwhelmed at points in their parent carer path. It is for those who want to hear from others feeling the same way and gain ideas of how to support themselves; a form of collective self-care.

In a way this is the book I needed while coming to terms with a multitude of different emotions when my son was first born and over years of receiving new diagnoses and challenges. I needed to know that struggles to cope weren't because I was deficient, rather it was part of the context – learning a new language and way of being to enable me to connect to my son while navigating services that are often inadequate and frankly at times harmful.

> *'There was no one to you know hold my hand and say, these things might help you.'*

As a psychologist, I'm obviously a believer in the importance of emotions, and my emotions were clearly telling me there was something very limited about the support set-up for families, yet I did not have the power, confidence or knowledge to fully identify what it was. I needed help and signposting to new narratives as I found my way in the special needs world but always alongside compassion, patience and understanding.

I'm forever thankful to the practitioners, teachers, carers, support workers and others who have been supportive and 'got it'. Especially those who have provided consistency and dependability and spent time getting to know us as a family and how to best support us all as a unit. They have shown their humanity and understanding. They have also shown that it is possible.

Compass

This book attempts to provide a framework for your own personal disability journey. This is not a path that can be forced, or made by anyone but you. But hopefully this can give you a compass of sorts for you to see the lay of the new land when old maps are no longer useful. It's not totally alien though. There are recognisable landmarks.

Everyone will have their own personal experience and, of course, parent carers are not an homogenous group (we are all different). However, I hope that outlining many of the responses from other parents will help you find something that resonates with you. If you have just received a new diagnosis for your child then it may help provide a map to prepare you for things you may encounter along the way and ensure you have the support when you need it. If you are already some way into your parent carer journey then hopefully it can allow you to see things in a different light or affirm some of your experiences.

Parent carers are an amazingly adaptable group of individuals. Generally, parents manage – because they have to and because they find ways that work for them. This is what I want to share with you.

Day by Day: The Rollercoaster

The content of this book is based on my own personal and professional experience, academic research (my own and others), anecdotes, as well as the responses from the online survey I ran on www.affinityhub.uk[2]. The title 'Day by Day' is taken from one of the most common responses from other parents, which is the advice to take it day by day and acknowledge and accept that your emotions may change and fluctuate even over short periods of time. We can feel happy one day as our child has achieved something we didn't think possible previously. Then we can feel devastated and in despair after a poor night's sleep or an unsupportive response from a service or school. It can feel, at times, that we are buffeted along like a boat in a storm. This is the 'rollercoaster' of which many special needs parents speak.

Charmolypi – Emotions are Complex

It is overly simplistic to talk about parent carers feeling *either* negative or positive emotions with regards to their child's disability or diagnosis. I acknowledge the unrealistic simplicity of dividing up later chapters into such clear-cut definitions when of course human beings are a wonderful paradox of conflicting thoughts and feelings all at the same time. Very few parents report feeling only positive or negative emotions and often they reflect that their feelings can, and do, change, not only day by day, but also minute by minute in reaction to things

---

[2] Griffin, J. (2019) Report on the emotional impact of parenting a disabled child, *Researchgate* and on www.affinityhub.uk

that happened during their day. It's also possible to experience 'both negative and positive well-being simultaneously'[3]. So you can feel a positive and negative emotion *at the same time.* This is the true meaning of ambivalence – having mixed or contradictory feelings. I found the beautiful Greek word Charmolypi very useful in capturing this complexity[4]. It means 'happiness and sadness intermingled'[5].

- *'Feelings fluctuate between down and then fighting for something and then happy when I succeed. And pride when daughter manages things which no one thought possible.'*

- *'It is a completely mixed bag of emotions that go hand in hand with having a child on the autistic spectrum, but it is never dull!'*

- *'We have at least 10 different emotions a day. Worried and anxiety being the most common ones.'*

- *'It brings out the absolute best in you and it brings out the absolute worst in you.'*

Conflicted feelings can be tiring – for example, you may experience relief that your child has gone to respite (I know not everyone likes this term; I'm referring to having a break from your caring role while your child accesses other activities) and then guilty for feeling the relief. It can be discombobulating.

Although it is a journey there is no guarantee of a neat conclusion or resolution at the end and we may continue to feel an array of emotions until the end of our own lives. We are human after all. We may have ups and downs, back steps and progress and we will develop greater skills to manage along the way.

It is valuable to recognise this as all part of the package of parenting a disabled child. I hope by sharing this with you, you will realise you are not alone.

---

[3] Hastings, R.P. & Taunt, H. (2002) Positive perceptions in families of children with developmental disabilities. *American Journal on Mental Retardation.* 107, 2, 116-127

[4] Griffin, J. (2020) Supporting Parent Carers, *The Psychologist*, June 2020

[5] Lomas, T. (2019) *Happiness Found in Translation: A Glossary of Joy from Around the World*, London: Tarcher Perigree

A note on Covid-19

Much of this book was already written prior to the pandemic. Clearly the impact of Covid-19 has been massive and multi-layered: lives lost, families devastated, support decimated and the pressures on our mental health multiplied. Parent carers and families have seen their support networks disappear and we realise once again that it is down to us and us alone.

Whilst the effect has been widely felt I do not think it has changed the nature of the problems experienced by parent carers, or the relevance of the findings outlined in this book. Rather it has exacerbated existing problems, challenges and neglect already experienced by families.

The pandemic has made it even more apparent that parent carers' wellbeing is vitally important and that we need to take active steps to maintain our emotional wellbeing on a daily basis.

2

Emotional Wellbeing in Parent Carers

'I think that's what I've learnt really more and more over the years is that self-care, which many people think is kind of self-indulgent, but it's not, it's like you're going to be a better mother, a better husband, a better wife, a better whatever, if you look after yourself.'

So often parent carers focus all their attention on their child and that will probably be the priority of all of those around you, including professionals and wider family. If there is one take-home message from this book it is the recognition that you are in need of care and attention too. In this chapter we will look at what emotional wellbeing means for parent carers.

Definition of Emotional Wellbeing

Despite most people having an instinctive understanding of what emotional wellbeing is, it can be hard to pin down. Parents came up with a number of different aspects: *'emotional wellbeing is something about how I feel from in here [puts hand to chest] and it's different from how anybody else expects us to feel'*; it involves being *'able to deal with the highs and lows of life'* and feeling that *'life is heading in the right direction'.*

Others equate it with *'mental health'*, *'looking after myself'*, *'having enough support to be able to support the family'*, *'not letting things get too overwhelming and doing things to stop it becoming so.'* Recognising that *'it's better to put myself first at times'*, emotional wellbeing is also *'about enjoying my life, the journey, having a degree of resilience and I suppose knowing how to help myself'.*

One father commented *'it's almost like the good/bad acting thing... you only really should notice bad acting, good acting should be seamless. I suppose good emotional things should be me not even thinking about it. It's just getting on with it.'*

Although hard to define it is generally acknowledged that emotional wellbeing involves self-acceptance, purpose in life, positive relations with others, environmental mastery, personal growth and autonomy[6].

There is overlap with the term resilience but I think emotional wellbeing is more all-encompassing. In theory someone can be resilient and bounce back from life's struggles (as parent carers have to) but still not feel good about themselves or that their life is fulfilling.

Scales of Emotional Wellbeing

It is often suggested that wellbeing is about achieving a state of equilibrium or balance in life much like a see-saw[7]. Rather than the see-saw image though, which can never balance, I prefer the analogy of the weighing scales:

---

[6] Ryff, C. (1989) Happiness is everything, or is it?: Explorations on the Meaning of Psychological Well-being, *Journal of Personality and Social Psychology*, 57, 1069–1081

[7] Dodge, R., Daly, A.P., Huyton,J. & Sanders, L.D. (2012) The challenge of defining wellbeing, *Journal of Wellbeing*, 2, 3, 222-235

Parent carer life is dynamic and what we need may change day by day. Outside influences can cause disruption and imbalance or alternatively provide support and strength.

'If you have a child with additional needs your mental load is higher than a family who has a typically developing child... so when other things happen they have more of an impact... it's like my cup is already full.'

We may need to keep some extra resources, or spare capacity, within the scales. As parent carers we know that there may be surprises that come along the way such as services removed or reduced, new behaviours requiring consideration or equipment that needs to be sourced. There are also big life and world events that affect us – just look at Covid-19.

Wellbeing is an ongoing process of adjustment rather than an endpoint that is reached and completed. One father described a phenomenon he termed 'issue fatigue' illustrating the 'perpetual stream of things to deal with' and little time to recover in between[8]. All of these issues take up time and attention. By keeping some reserves for these moments we are less likely to burn out. Similarly, after a crisis or period of battling, we need to allow ourselves time to take a breath and recalibrate to re-gain a sense of balance.

---

[8] Cunniff, A., Chisholm, V. & Chouliara, Z. (2015) Listening to Fathers of Sons with Duchenne Muscular Dystrophy, *New Male Studies: An International Journal*, 4, 2, 5-23, p. 11

SPECTRA
7 Dimensions of Parent Carer Wellbeing

My research highlighted seven areas that support parent carer wellbeing. I have developed the term **SPECTRA** to give an overview of the different dimensions of wellbeing for parents of disabled children. These are listed in Table 1 and then described in more detail later on in this chapter:

- *Sense of Purpose and Meaning*

- *Positive Others*

- *Empowerment*

- *Child*

- *Time that is Mine*

- *Replenish and Recalibrate: Self-care Swiss Army Knife*

- *Awareness of Emotions*

Table 1

Sense of Purpose and Meaning	Finding something in our lives that is important to us and committing to that cause (however small or large) improves wellbeing along with making sense of our life as coherent and significant (Ch.9).
Positive Others	These are the people or communities in your life that help and support you. Those that 'have your back' – this can be informal (e.g. family, friends or special needs network) as well as professionals. We consider who they are and what they do to help as opposed to hinder your wellbeing in Chapters 6 and 7.
Empowerment	A process and outcome whereby you are supported by others, including services, to empower yourself by gaining knowledge and expertise. It also involves an internal change where you find your voice and assert yourself. This theme threads throughout the book.

Child	In many ways our most important relationship and the catalyst of learning and development. A focus of love and joy but sometimes the system around the child can be difficult and stressful. Learning to notice and celebrate their achievements and your own capacity to gain a new perspective – your child's – to help you in your parental role. Our child is a key influence throughout the book.
Time that is Mine	A crucial part of the parenting role anyway, but particularly important for parent carers. We need time to pause and reflect, in order to develop all the other areas in our life. This is relevant throughout the book – time to recognise our emotions, time to engage with positive others, empowerment to ensure we protect our own time with appropriate boundaries, and time to commit to activities that replenish and recalibrate us.
Replenish and Recalibrate: Self-care Swiss Army Knife	An overview of self-care strategies to use – different skills at different times to flexibly support our own needs. I refer to it as a self-care Swiss army knife as it's important to always have it with us and accessible for whenever we may need it (Ch. 8).
Awareness of Emotions and the Human Condition	Awareness of our emotions informs how we can help ourselves. Acknowledging emotions, including those that are difficult, enables us to process them and move on. Ignoring them can lead to a negative build-up that comes out in other ways. Developing our emotional literacy to identify and name how we feel is a first step to emotional regulation. Chapter 4 looks at negative, and Chapter 5 positive, emotions. Awareness also includes greater insight into the human condition and parents describe how their eyes are opened to another world (Chapter 3).

Spectra is a useful framework for talking about parent carer wellbeing. Not only is the word 'spectrum' (of which spectra is the plural) often associated with different diagnoses, in particular, autism, it also identifies that our wellbeing can sit at different points on different spectra. We might not be on the positive end of all of them at the same time, for example we may feel empowered with our child and meeting their needs but not have managed to find some time for ourselves. The more spectra upon which we feel fulfilled, the more fully we are flourishing as human beings.

A worksheet is included in Appendix I which enables you to identify strategies, aims or achievements in each of these different areas as you move through the book. Looking at the different dimensions can also help you see how to gain more balance in your wellbeing both across, and within, the Spectra. Take the example of your child – if all your interactions with them are negative (or it's all therapeutic goals) then maybe you can look to bring in some positive interaction, such as doing something fun with them. It's about finding what works for you to ensure a more holistic, well-rounded life.

Multi-faceted

Emotional wellbeing involves many different elements which I address over the course of this book. Wellbeing is a personal thing and what works for you might not be right for someone else. What works for you at one point in your life might not work at another time. We bring our own learning needs, cognitive style and neurodiversity (differences in the way our brains work). There are, however, some broad themes which will be influenced by your personal, social and cultural experiences.

Emotional wellbeing involves the ability to be aware of our emotions, to notice how they change and what we can do to help. To recognise when we are lacking balance and to do things, or have strategies, that help us re-gain our equilibrium. That might be saying no to plans, chasing services or seeing friends. It might involve taking time to see a doctor about a recurrent back pain, asking family to have our child for the day or using mindfulness or meditation in our lives. It may be looking with fresh eyes at your connection with your child and the joy they bring. Chapters 4 and 5 look at the negative and positive emotions, respectively, that are commonly experienced by parent carers. Experiencing a complex array of responses to an unexpected situation is understandable. The negative and positive are embedded within one another.

There is a social element to wellbeing as how we feel is significantly affected by those around us. Our relationships, close community, as well as society in general all influence us. This means we need a multi-faceted approach to improving and maintaining our wellbeing – sometimes on our own and sometimes with others. We are interrelated and others affect us as we affect them. At times connections with those beyond ourselves are key to good mental health and stop us becoming stuck in a cycle of self-concern. Chapter 6 therefore looks at these relationships in more detail and Chapter 7 considers professionals, services and support and how these types of connections can help or hinder wellbeing. Empowerment, understanding and belonging are all key players in our wellbeing.

If services or professionals support and work with us, this helps our wellbeing. If family and friends understand what we need and connect with us in a way that is positive and helpful, this supports our wellbeing. If society is inclusive and accessible rather than discriminatory and judgemental then we have a positive grounding from which to launch our lives.

Practical Factors

Practical factors obviously play a part too, such as the social, political and economic structures that form our life landscape. For example, as well as disability discrimination, other forms of prejudice can intersect and research suggests that a disabled person from a Black, Asian or Minority Ethnic Group may face a double discrimination[9]. It is also recognised that there can be a 'double burden' when those families who face the most adversity are also less likely to have the financial resources to provide a buffer[10].

Lack of resources, a postcode lottery for services and austerity all have a massive influence on parent carers' wellbeing. However, this book is not specifically focusing on the practical aspects as I believe there are other resources better placed to support you in these areas,

---

[9] https://network.autism.org.uk/knowledge/insight-opinion/supporting-bame-autistic-people-and-their-families

[10] Institute of Health Equity (2014) *Local Action on health inequalities: building children and young people's resilience in schools*, London

such as the charities listed in Appendix III, lobby or campaign groups or your local Special Educational Needs and Disability Information Advice and Support Service (SENDIASS).

Instead, this book concentrates on what you can control and influence in your own life, which starts from within and the commitment to nurture and replenish yourself, despite what's going on around you. I consider what we can do to support ourselves while acknowledging that the world is far from perfect. We all face adversity along the way but that doesn't mean we give up fighting for a better and more socially just world; we just need to acknowledge our right to live a fulfilling and meaningful life alongside the challenges. If we wait for social justice to deliver equality before we can be emotionally healthy there will be a lot of people struggling with their mental health that need not be.

Chapter 8 considers ways in which we can direct our own wellbeing with activities and strategies that are shown to be beneficial. These ideas are based on talking to parent carers themselves as well as evidence-based research. In the final chapter I consider one of the key aspects of wellbeing – having a sense of purpose and meaning in life. Despite possible challenges (and I'll touch on some difficult subjects, such as future care and premature death), identifying this in our own life can enrich and strengthen us in whatever lies ahead.

Often the emotional impact of parenting a disabled child (and the factors that you have in your control to help you along the way) is neglected. A start is acknowledging that our emotional wellbeing is important. Then we need to take the time to develop awareness of our emotional landscape; we cannot help ourselves if we do not see that we are struggling. If we believe that unhappiness or chronic stress is just how life is, then we make no attempt to change it. As a parent carer you have a right to a life that is fulfilling and purposeful; where your needs, emotional and otherwise, are seen as important in their own right. A fulfilled parent raises a fulfilled child. But that should not be the sole reason for you supporting yourself and embracing self-compassion. To use a very over-used, but appropriate to parent carers, expression – you *are* worth it.

We'll now reflect further on what each dimension on the SPECTRA of parent carer wellbeing entails.

Sense of Purpose and Meaning

It is consistently shown that having purpose and meaning in your life is linked to wellbeing. Many of the parents I've spoken to reiterated this and their focus, rather than being on 'happiness' (the pursuit of pleasure and avoidance of pain), had developed into something deeper and more fulfilling (like the Greek word eudaimonia – suggesting living well, human flourishing or activity with purpose[11]).

The feeling of meaningful purpose in life is possible even in the depths of despair. In Viktor Frankl's[12] seminal work, *Man's Search for Meaning*, he describes how even in an unbearably traumatic and impoverished situation (he was a Holocaust survivor) it is possible to find meaning in life. We have freedom to choose our attitude towards life situations, even if we cannot change the situation.

By making sense of life events we can cope better. Your life purpose and meaning is personal – for some it is their child and for others it is totally unrelated to being a parent. It may be work, friends or another activity. There is situational (local and personal to you) and global (societal level) purpose and meaning. So it could be building good relationships with the team around your child or campaigning to improve national services.

Trauma and adverse events may trigger us to make new meaning and find purpose. Meaning-making is also a vital part of post-traumatic growth which we look at in more detail in Chapter 5. It is important to realise that having purpose and meaning is different from feeling positive and the carefree happiness for which people often strive[13]. So we may feel fulfilled but not necessarily 'happy'. But 'happiness' is a fleeting emotion that is hard to create and sustain. Rather it is through purpose and meaning that a longer lasting feeling of contentment occurs: a greater level of wellbeing. I will discuss this further in Chapter 9, 'Meaningful Futures'.

---

[11] Aristotle (1947) *Nicomachean ethics* (W.D. Ross, Trans.) in R. McKeon (Ed.) *Introduction to Aristotle,* New York: Modern Library

[12] Frankl, V.E. (1985) *Man's search for meaning*, New York: Washington Square Press (originally published in 1946)

[13] Wong, P.T.P. (2011) Positive Psychology 2.0: Towards a Balanced Interactive Model of the Good Life, *Canadian Psychological Association*, 52,2, 69-81, p. 76

Positive Others

Human beings are social beings and we are inescapably connected to others – our partner, family, friends, community, society and culture. This can bring positives and negatives and I explore in more detail the nature of these relationships in Chapter 6. I suspect that it is mainly through these connections that we grow and become more confident in our role as a parent carer (and a human being). It also helps us gain a broader perspective. We can link with others in many ways; with those in our immediate network – family and friends who can provide understanding and compassionate support. We connect with our community – both special needs and non-special needs – and this influences our capacity to engage in a full life. Schools, health care, leisure activities and local shops can all affect us, as we affect them in turn.

We can also connect in an abstract way with role models or 'movements' such as neurodiversity or disability activism. Even from our own armchair we can engage in a conceptual way, which influences how we make sense of our own life – even through social media or reading books. It can change our narrative.

When support from those close to us isn't forthcoming it can be hurtful and requires more resources on our part to manage day to day demands. It may then be that other special needs parents or networks become our most precious allies.

The theme running through positive others is the connection and belonging we feel that means we are seen, heard and valued as ourselves.

Empowerment

Empowerment is a key part of emotional wellbeing. Being empowered is a process as well as an outcome and there are internal as well as external influences.

Wellbeing can be supported by changing the world to match our expectations and hopes for life. It can also be improved by changing how we experience the world. Having a sense of control in our day to day interactions protects against depressive symptoms and feelings of helplessness[14]. This may be particularly relevant in the face of unhelpful services.

---

[14] Smith, A.M. & Grzywacz, J.G. (2014) Health and Well-being in Midlife Parents of Children with Special Health Needs, *Families, Systems & Health*, 32, 3, 303-312

By gaining greater knowledge and expertise, in order to meet the needs of our family, we become empowered. We are affected by others in the way they treat us, the information and skills they provide, and services and professionals who collaborate with us at appropriate times. We are empowered by knowing we have the law and a community on our side and in a similar situation.

Empowerment is also something we can take for ourselves, given the right conditions. It is the ability and capacity to assert our own needs, and recognise (and change) when others are not supportive. It is linked to agency and the belief, not only in our ability, but also that what we do makes a difference (or can). Just as with confidence, whatever your age or life-story you can increase your sense of empowerment.

There may be changes within ourselves that have to happen before we can become empowered. A first step is recognising our emotions and our needs – this requires time and space to reflect, to take a step back from our lives to enable us to see what is missing. We may then need to set boundaries and recognise we cannot say yes to all of life's demands.

As we know, other people in our lives can create positivity. But they can also bring conflict and tension. There may be times when we have to develop our assertiveness in order to avoid becoming overwhelmed by others or conversely ensure we can get what we need from others – including family, friends and professionals.

Challenging society's expectations of us – as parents, children, siblings – can be tiring and emotional. Fighting the hidden, insidious messages we receive from birth onwards takes resilience and perspective, for example, rejecting social norms about how children should behave, or an expectation to be a stay-at-home mum. We may need to develop a buffer against some expectations that are impossible or traumatic for us and our children, i.e. homework, school plays or navigating complex social obligations.

Once we've given ourselves space we gain clarity on areas of our life that are problematic. Is there an aspect of your life that causes you the most difficulties? If so you can begin to look for alternatives. This is a solution-focused, problem-solving empowerment. It starts with you and, if supported by those around you, can change your life. The more empowered we become the better able we are to deal with things in the future – it becomes self-fulfilling.

'I'm a lot less selfish, but then in other ways, I'm more selfish, so... I will say no to plans. I used to make myself go to everything but if I think, actually, I just need to be on my own, I will be on my own, I'll cancel plans.'

Let's imagine an example. A parent is struggling because their child wakes constantly due to feeling unsettled at night. Their behaviour is then often challenging during the day. The parent knows the strategies for dealing with behaviours that challenge, but is often too tired to implement them consistently. Everyone ends up tired, irritable and unhappy.

An empowered parent takes a step back, hopefully supported by friends or family. They recognise that a starting point is sleep. If everyone had more sleep they'd be able to deal with the daytime challenges. So the parent phones a specific helpline for sleep issues, or asserts their right to have an emergency paediatrician or specialist appointment. They also phone children's services to find out about short breaks or respite. They know they will have to be authoritative and may have to phone many times. They know that this will have a knock-on effect on their wellbeing and energy levels. They will need to have some time to themselves to recover because of the extra resources the fighting takes.

Over time, they receive advice on sleep which they can incorporate into their life. They apply the relevant aspects to see what works for their family. Hopefully, with better sleep hygiene, behavioural strategies or medication, the child starts to sleep and finally the parent gets a good night's sleep. As everyone is more rested the behaviour is better during the day and even when some issues arise the parent feels able, competent and well rested enough to put behavioural strategies in place. Even if sleep continues to be a problem, respite may be provided which means the parent can catch up on rest, ready to start again the next day. The parent feels more in control, more empowered and good about themselves. This causes a cycle of positive feelings and wellbeing that enables them to take part in other activities that make them feel happy, like seeing friends or engaging in a hobby they enjoy.

Of course this is a simplistic ideal but it can happen like this. There may also be obstacles along the way – lack of sleep support, not meeting the criteria for short breaks or the parent still lying awake at night despite the child sleeping. Change can take time to 'bed in'. The vital thing is that the parent manages to put together a plan, or a map, of what they can do to help their child and themselves. They have a sense of control and recognise their own expertise in their unique family situation.

Empowerment may also include activism and campaigning. On some level all parent carers become part of the disability movement. The personal becomes political because we want to make society better, not only for our child but for all disabled people. But this always needs to be balanced with engaging in activities we enjoy and that replenish us. So yet again we are back at the point of reminding yourself that you need and deserve time that is yours and you are allowed to assert your right to that.

Child

The relationship with your child is precious. Yet so often children with special needs come with so many additional pressures – fighting for services, discrimination and lack of resources – that we are distracted from the core love and joy of being a parent.

Parents talk about the amazing bond with their child, what they have learnt from them and how they have developed an enhanced perspective to see their child's point of view. Being able to create a new family narrative to incorporate these factors is important for supporting not only yourself but also protecting your child from the sometimes difficult attitudes that exist in society. By adapting our ways of thinking and seeing, we treasure little things that may be taken for granted by others. As one parent said, we *'celebrate the inchstones'*. Our minds are opened up to a new world.

Our own emotional wellbeing is affected by those around us including our emotions and those of our child often impacting one another; they are bi-directional. Acknowledging the additional pressures we may be under – as well as our child – ensures we give our self the time we need to re-group. Thereby enabling us to come back and be the parent we want to be and create the family life we want to provide for our children. This in turn makes parenting more rewarding and empowering, because we are able to manage the different demands rather than sink under them.

Time that is Mine

All parents feel short of time; it is part of having another 'being' to look after in our busy modern world. There is always adjustment when a new child arrives in a family and maintaining a sense of balance of your own needs and the child's is part and parcel of being a parent. It can take a while to find this but most people get there in the end.

Of course sometimes children with additional needs require more care and attention and may continue to need the level of parenting that a younger one needs well after they've passed that chronological age. Even if they are meeting milestones there may be certain anxieties or therapeutic input they require than means parents give more of themselves – practically as well as emotionally – to support their child.

All of this adds to our emotional load. Our resources need replenishing when they have become depleted by stress and additional safeguards need to be put in place to ensure we have time that is ours. It can involve time and space alone. As parents, we don't always get much time on our own and can feel bombarded by others' comments, questions and needs. So in a way it's not until we're on our own that we can fully engage in thinking about what it is that we want, or need, for ourselves.

What you want to do with your time may also depend on what you are trying to have time off *from*.

Time off from child and caring duties

It may be a specific need that we have – time off from our child with special needs and certain caring duties tied up with them. Doing the same thing all day, every day, inevitably becomes mundane – as humans we need some element of change and novelty in our lives. It is understandable that at times we just need a break from this.

> *[Benefit of short breaks] 'for us to have a break. And our own time. So emotionally we feel that we can re-set so that we're okay to manage him'.*

This also gives your child a chance to experience something new with someone else.

'At respite he's learnt that he can trust somebody, just like Mum, who can put him to bed.'

As with many of the issues raised in this book, the practical and emotional are intertwined. We can only have a break if we have someone else we trust to take on the caring duty. If this is not part of your life then it might be worth investing some time looking into possibilities – either through short breaks, children's services or family or friends.

Be aware, though, that it can take time to fully embrace your time off – time to build up a relationship with the person doing the caring, time for you to relax into your time alone. It's taken me about four months to fully relax when my son is at his overnight care as I needed to get to know the staff working with him, understand their procedures and framework for the day and get used to not having him in the house. It's been worth it – he loves and looks forward to it while we are able to do different activities as a family.

Time off from associated demands

Sometimes what we need a break from is not our child, but the rigmarole that can come with them. The appointments, the fight in perpetuity or the therapy regimes. There is a limit to our nervous system and how much information we can process at any given time[15]. By being aware of your limit you can put support in place, and assert your family's needs, before it becomes overwhelming.

'Sometimes when I feel like that [overwhelmed] I will take two weeks where I just don't deal with anything... not answering emails, not answering phone calls, obviously ordering her milk and her medicine but no contact with her therapists. I actually find that very helpful.'

Time off on difficult days

There are days when things are hard. It might be because of the number of demands on our time, it may be because of how you are feeling or it can be a culmination of things.

---

[15] Csikszentmihalyi, M. (2002) *Flow: The classic work on how to achieve happiness*, London: Random House

'Some days are just harder than others, emotionally,... things that he does... sometimes it's just too much, you just get exhausted... I don't feel I can give any more to that situation or to what he might do... it stresses me out, or dealing with him in a certain situation will stress me out or it'll stress [my partner] out and therefore it'll stress the family out.'

At times like this it's important to recognise that you need a time out. We are only human and we all need a break from things that are difficult. Ideally try not to let things build up until they reach crisis point when you just can't cope. Factoring in some self-care activities as a regular part of your day may prevent burnout. Keep this topped up.

If you have a day where everything becomes too much – believe me, we've all had those days – even if you can't take time away from the situation give yourself a break within your home. Watch a movie you've chosen. Take ten minutes' peace in the bathroom to read a magazine. Make tea in your favourite cup. Tell people you won't be available that day, or alternatively make the time to speak to someone you know will lift you up.

Replenish and Recalibrate: Self-care Swiss Army Knife

From talking to other parent carers it became clear that the strategies we use to look after ourselves may vary depending on how we are feeling in the moment as well as our context. We need to flexibly apply different psychological tools or support at different times. Change is the only constant and what we need at one point in our life may not be helpful at another. Life requires a repertoire of responses – what I refer to as a Swiss army knife of self-care – and it can help to monitor whether your go-to coping mechanisms still work. Or is it time to try something different?

We must start with the basics – getting sufficient quality sleep, exercise, eating healthily and drinking plenty of water. Simple but vital. Using calming strategies, such as breathing or mindfulness, can help at the most stressful times and remind us to focus on the here and now. At other times these may be less helpful, when past, present and future all need considering. Alternatively, engaging in a flow activity (where we lose ourselves in our focus), such as drawing, knitting or rock climbing, will help take our mind off other worries and provide a chance to re-set. Sometimes reflection, venting or consciously seeking out the positive will be what we need.

Scheduling in things that you enjoy throughout your day as well as allocating 'worry time' can help. This is when you delay thinking about something and then give yourself a certain amount of time, such as ten minutes, to focus on the problem. It can help prevent worry from spilling over into all aspects of life. But for some people this is not realistic and in the grips of solving a tricky problem it can be hard to focus on other things.

The important thing is that you find something that works for you, helps you in the longer term and enables you to live an emotionally satisfying and fulfilled life. Self-care is sometimes dismissed as meaning 'going to a spa'. It can mean this but it can also be going to your General Practitioner (GP) for your annual flu jab, saying no to friends you find draining or signing up for kick boxing classes. It can involve actively engaging in campaigning for social change. I discuss self-care ideas in more detail in Chapter 8.

Awareness of Emotions

Before we can recognise what strategies are supportive we need to tap into a greater awareness of our own emotions and emotional needs. These naturally go up and down over a period of time. Some people have a greater abundance of up or down days than others. It helps to know ourselves in this way, to see what our normal patterns and fluctuations are, in order to recognise when you may need a little bit of extra support. This is part of emotional intelligence.

'I'm getting better at recognising when my mood is beginning to sink a bit.'

We can become overly-comfortable and stagnant in our way of dealing with the world, such that we fail to notice that it's harming us. We need elements of change to shake up life and our ways of managing. It may be that taking time to acknowledge how you feel makes you realise that you've been suffering with anxiety without realising. Or it may be that someone else comments on how they've become better at doing something which in turn makes you stop and reflect and realise that you've developed all sorts of skills that help you in your life – you've grown but you hadn't taken time to notice it.

We don't always have to respond to our emotions as sometimes we need to sit with them. But being familiar with them can help us navigate our world. There are suggestions in Chapter 8 about how to hone your noticing skills as well as allowing your emotions to inform, rather than overwhelm, you.

Mind-body

Our mind and body are inextricably linked and how we are experiencing something may come out in feelings, thoughts, sensations or even ailments. . Parent carers often report poorer physical[16], as well as mental, health with a build-up over time. Chronic stress has been found to increase illness and suppress the immune system. Or we may have less time to get a physical ailment checked out so it's not until the problem has become chronic that we seek help.

Mind and body influence each other in both directions and positive emotional wellbeing is consistently linked to lower health risks[17]. Our responses to things are influenced by how we appraise a situation (how we interpret or make sense of an event or a bodily sensation)[18]; this in turn affects what we do to make ourselves feel better and return to a sense of equilibrium. If we believe we have personal control we may be less distressed by a negative situation[19]. Looking after your body *and* mind are fundamental to parent carer wellbeing.

---

[16] Bringing us Together (2018), Parent Carer Health: The impact of the caring role https://bringingustogether.org.uk/parent-carer-health-the-impact-of-the-caring-role

[17] Song, J., Mailick, M.R., Ryff, C.D., Coe, C.L., Greenberg, J.S. & Hong, J. (2014) Allostatic load in parents of children with developmental disorders: Moderating influence of positive affect, *Journal of Health Psychology*, 19, 2, 262-272, p.263

[18] Hefferon, K. (2013) *Positive Psychology and the Body: The Somatopsychic side to flourishing, Berkshire*, UK: Open University Press

[19] Cantwell, J., Muldoon, O.T. & Gallagher, S. (2014) Social support and mastery influence the association between stress and poor physical health in parents caring for children with developmental disabilities, *Research in Developmental Disabilities*, 35 (2014), 2215-2223

Awareness also includes a wider perspective on the human condition. Seeing that life can be fragile, some things are beyond our control and greater knowledge of disabilities all broaden our understanding. Although painful at times this viewpoint provides clarity and appreciation for what truly matters in life.

Being a Parent

Before we end this chapter I want to reflect on parenting in general.

Most new parents have myriad emotions after the birth of their child; the experience is life-changing and full of possibilities. Adjustment and adaptation can take time, patience and support from friends, family and wider community. It is useful to bear this in mind when considering the emotional responses we have to our child, particularly if they are disabled or in some way different to how we expected. There is always a sense of them being different from us, however closely connected we are to them. Children are never a clone or exactly how we imagined them to be. And this is how it should be; they are their own unique person.

Good enough is Great

Parenting can be hard. It asks a lot of us. Children deserve our care, thought, best effort and love, of course, but it can help to move away from the idea of perfect parenting and embrace the 'good enough parent'[20]. Winnicott believed that mothers (his focus was on mothers but this can be applied to all parents) made mistakes but were able to repair and readjust following these mistakes – what he called 'good enough parenting'. Children need at least one good enough parent or caregiver to feel emotionally safe and healthy. That is someone who does their best and gets things right most of the time while recognising and changing things that don't go so well.

The most important part of parenting is forming an attachment by providing warmth and nurture. This is the case with a disabled child as with any child. Parenting also requires a role modelling of self-nurture. Furthermore, at times you may need to say no to your child's demands or let them 'fail' at something so they can learn.

---

[20] Winnicott, D.W. (2006) *Playing and reality*, Abingdon, Oxon: Routledge

Perfection does not help anyone. It sets up unrealistic expectations for the child who then may struggle when real life lets them down (as it always will as life is not perfect). We all have to learn (within a safe framework) that when things don't go to plan or we make a mistake it is not a catastrophe, rather we learn and grow from it. Perfection also means that something is sacrificed as we cannot be perfect in all areas of our life. Often it is the parent's emotional needs that are neglected and this ends up causing a vicious cycle or resentment and exhaustion. Instead, think 'Good enough is great.'

Let go of Guilt

A common response from parents is that they feel guilty. We do not need to feel guilty for taking time for our self, for having interests or a sense of purpose outside of being a parent. These are necessities of living, not an indulgent luxury. They are requirements that enable us parent and care. If there was one thing I would remove it would be parental guilt. It is such an unhelpful and unwarranted emotion in the context of parent carers. Please let go of the guilt!

The Disability World

Before we explore the SPECTRA of wellbeing throughout the rest of the book, we need to take a little detour in Chapter 3 to look at the context of disability and how it can sometimes feel like we've woken up in another world.

Key points

- It is important that you look after yourself as a parent carer

- The SPECTRA is a useful framework for thinking about what helps your emotional wellbeing:
  - Sense of Purpose and Meaning
  - Positive Others
  - Empowerment
  - Child
  - Time that is Mine
  - Replenish and Recalibrate: Swiss Army Knife of Self-care
  - Awareness of Emotions

- Emotional wellbeing involves balance across different dimensions and areas in your life

- Different things will help at different times

- It can be helpful to keep some 'spare capacity' for when difficulties crop up unexpectedly

- The practical and emotional are inextricably linked. But even if you cannot change your environment, you can change your response to it.

- Good enough parenting is key

- Let go of guilt!

3

'Woken up in another world'

At first, the world of special needs and disability can feel like a very different and daunting place. In this chapter I will consider a number of factors that might help orient you in this new world.

Disability and Society

The reaction of others in our community may be wonderful and supportive or disheartening and ill-informed. Despite the improvements over the last century for those who are disabled, we still have a way to go. Scope's research shows that 87% of parent carers have felt judged by members of the public[21].

People rarely encounter serious illness, disability and death in their everyday lives. When we do it can make us confront our own frailty and mortality. We realise, first hand, that things can happen to people that make life difficult. Suddenly hospitals, interventions, medications, bodily functions and the limitations of the health, education and social services become part of life. Everyday things, like going to school, can be traumatic for our child. Sometimes when people are exposed to this harsh reality they withdraw, go into denial or become angry. Parents may react this way and it can also be the

---

[21] Scope, (2018) *Now is the time: Supporting disabled children and their families*, November 2018

response from sections of society. It may be the first time we have witnessed such prejudice and to see our own child judged through this lens can be shocking and heart-breaking. This may include stares, confused or judgemental looks or comments, as people make assumptions or project their own views, or fears, onto your child and you as a parent. We, as parent carers, may suddenly feel vulnerable to this social reaction combined with our desire to protect our child. It can be eye-opening and a huge learning curve.

Having to challenge negative assumptions or misconceptions can turn things upside down in our minds while we are also having to take care of, and understand, our child and their needs. It's a big ask all at once.

Although in general society is becoming more inclusive and accessible, sadly there can be backward steps, as seen by the fact that disabled people have been disproportionately affected by austerity[22]. Further, during the Covid-19 outbreak there were reports of some disabled people being asked to sign Do Not Resuscitate (DNR) notices[23]. Experiencing discrimination can have a detrimental effect on our health – physical and mental. It is clear that wellbeing in parent carers is not just influenced by personal factors; it is in part a public health issue due to factors such as stigma, both in the UK and beyond[24].

There can be differences in terms of whether your child's disability is visible or invisible. You may experience varied reactions from others, including family, friends and society as a whole. Developing resilience to these responses is fundamental to coping and avoiding social withdrawal. Society needs to become more accepting of difference.

Feeling prepared as to how you will deal with others' reactions can be helpful. Some people stop going out but this is harmful on so many levels. You do not need to hide away: it's important you connect with others as this is a crucial part of looking after your emotional wellbeing as well as being vital for your child to be out and about.

[22] Ryan, F. (2019) *Crippled: Austerity and the demonization of disabled people*, Verso: London

[23] Inclusion London, *Abandoned, forgotten and ignored: The impact of the coronavirus pandemic on Disabled People*, Interim report, June 2020

[24] Song, J., Mailick, M.R. & Greenberg, J.S. (2018) Health of parents of individuals with developmental disorders or mental health problems: Impacts of stigma, *Social Science and Medicine*, 217, 152-158

Sometimes you may not feel strong enough to deal with this aspect of parenting – perhaps take someone else along with you to help or share your worries. Your child is your priority, not the views of a stranger. Having a stock response ready for comments from others can help.

Finding places that are fully inclusive and welcoming to children with special needs, such as relaxed, autism-friendly performances at the cinema or theatre or Special Children's Days at zoos, help create a sense of community and acceptance. I notice my own stress levels, and that of other parents, being much lower when attending such events where my son is very happy. These days highlight the need for a more inclusive world as well as illustrating how little it takes from organisations or communities to make this inclusivity a reality for families.

In parallel to the societal changes required, we can also change our internal world, over time, to become more accepting of ourselves and our situation. A study corroborates the general trend that over time 'parents seemed to have become less sensitive to the reactions of outsiders and find stigmatizing behaviors less threatening to their self-esteem'[25].

We develop a thicker skin and gain a wider perspective of what is really important in life. This is part of a growing awareness, resilience and expertise that many parents of disabled children develop. We become our child's best advocate, as well as championing difference, tolerance and acceptance more widely.

Advocacy to Activism

You may embrace the role of activist. Parents have established charities, lobby groups, social media campaigns as well as taken the government to court for cuts to Special Educational Needs and Disabilities (SEND) budgets. Activism can provide a sense of purpose and meaning which I will come back to again in Chapter 9. The fight can also become all-consuming and take a personal toll.

'I just have found it very, very difficult to cope with. I don't really like upsetting people, I don't like conflict, and you can't be an activist or shake up a system without [it].'

---

[25] Gray, D. (2002) Ten years on: a longitudinal study of families of children with autism, *Journal of Intellectual & Developmental Disability*, 27, 3, 215-222, p.221

In the early stages, when everything still feels raw, try not to worry about this too much. Just focus on what you and your child need and ask for help and support from those around you. Education and awareness for all is a significant part of this journey but of course there are times when you do not want, nor cannot deal with, this increased burden. Take time to go home, re-group with your social network. Hopefully with time you will feel more able to take on this additional responsibility in a way that also protects your own mental well-being.

No one is a blank slate

No one comes to parenthood as a blank slate. Your own response will be affected by your prior experience of disability and personal histories. We come to this point in time with a significant number of assumptions, theories, beliefs and opinions. This will be influenced by our own upbringing, personality and culture[26]. Culture provides a set of guidelines (explicit and implicit) that inform how we make sense of the world and our experience within it. It will also be guided by our own attachment styles, family schemas (patterns and stories that exist in our family) and coping strategies we've developed over our lifetime.

At times if we've had difficulties growing up or as an adult we may be left with specific challenges or sensitivities. Such difficulties include experiencing abuse or neglect as a child, undergoing bereavement of a loved one or struggling with mental health problems. Any wounds that we have may be aggravated by further adversity in life although, for some people, knowing that they have come through tough times can help them cope in a new situation. Having a disabled child and the additional associated stressors may leave us vulnerable to further emotional upset. If the experience is re-traumatising extra support or time to work through our feelings and responses can help. You may need a professional to do this, such as with a counsellor or mental health team. Don't feel you have to cope alone.

All of these elements will have some influence on how you make sense of your current situation. Keep in mind though that feelings, attitudes and responses can change and develop with time, experience

---

[26] Whiting, M. (2012) Impact, meaning and need for help and support: The experience of parents caring for children with disabilities, life-limiting/life-threatening illness or technology dependence, *Journal of Child Health Care*, 17, 1, 92-108, p. 106

and greater knowledge. You are a work in progress, as are those around you, thrown into a new situation.

You are Not Alone

One of the most supportive factors that comes out of research time and time again is to find your own network of people who understand you and your situation. If you know of other families with a disabled child they may become a lifeline. If you don't, you can be put in touch with someone through the numerous national disability charities that exist (listed in Appendix III). When you find your community your life will generally be the better for it. If it isn't, then maybe you need to look for a new group.

Helplines and local support groups can also provide you with this connection to other families. The advice you receive from other experienced parents can be helpful as it's couched in the knowledge of the realities and complexities of the home environment. You need to be aware, though, that every family and individual is different so what works for one person might not work for another. Become your own expert and decide whether to take, or leave, advice you receive.

Even with the differences though it is important to recognise that it is our similarities as human beings that is the most striking of all. The shared experience can be affirming and poignant. By including quotes from other parents throughout the book as well as referencing the many research studies (that are unfortunately often inaccessible to families) I hope to emphasise that you are not alone in your emotional responses.

The Start of the Journey – Diagnosis (or not)

In general, the full realisation that there is something different about your child, or that there is a delay in development, will coincide with acknowledgement from an outside source. This may be at the point of diagnosis; however this is not always the case and some people never receive one. There are pros and cons.

Receiving a diagnosis for your child can feel shocking and upsetting. You may be overwhelmed with anxieties, questions and confusion. At times people jump to conclusions about what life will be like, assuming the worst case scenario and reading unhelpful information on the internet. We may not really understand what the terminology means and how it is presented to us can have far-reaching consequences. Realising that life does not always go to plan takes some adjustment and can make you feel vulnerable to the world, like a dinghy on a rough sea.

Conversely, diagnosis can help you understand your child, protect you from accusations of 'bad' parenting and may provide a framework of support to help you as a family. For those parents who suspected that their child was experiencing difficulties in an area of their life, there may be relief. To have had suspicions of your own, particularly if they were not taken seriously by others, can be a difficult and isolating place to be. Even if the diagnosis is welcomed, many uncertainties remain. The child needs to 'find their tribe' and where they belong – and so do the parents.

When there is no diagnosis you may be left with questions and continue through years of tests or searches for answers. Or you come to terms with uncertainty and not knowing.

Many parents I have spoken to worry that it is somehow their fault or feel like they will not manage. Alternatively, it may elicit a call to arms to fight for your child and you may turn into a super-researcher poring over the internet to try and find answers and support.

It is important to remember that a diagnosis does not tell you the whole story about a person, their life, or their experience. Your child is an individual with unique traits and a personality that is all their own. First and foremost, they are your child to be loved, treasured and enjoyed. Things may seem difficult right now but they will get easier as time passes and you will grow in confidence and expertise.

'People did tell me he would develop and grow and things would get easier but I didn't believe them, now I realise it did'.

How You're Told the News

The way in which diagnostic news is shared can be very different and have an enormous impact on how you process, and make sense of, the information[27]. As an illustration, I had two very different experiences.

---

[27] Langridge, P. (2002) Reduction of chronic sorrow: a health promotion role for children's community nurses? *Journal of Child Health Care*, 6, 3, 157-170, p.162

One consultant told me that my son had cerebral palsy and would probably be unable to walk or talk. My limited knowledge of cerebral palsy, and that it is a huge spectrum (that word again), meant I struggled to take this information on board.

In contrast the second consultant said 'he may well need some extra support from a speech and language therapist or physiotherapist when he is young'. The first consultant acknowledged that it was a big deal and made us feel the enormity of the situation. The second one, although maybe not acknowledging how difficult things could be, gave us some hope and strategies we could put in place. People will have a different preference, but for me the latter didn't make me want to give up and cry whereas the former did. I was not ready to hear that yet but perhaps, despite being floored, by hearing it a part of me was better prepared for what was to come.

It's unlikely you'll have had a choice about how a diagnosis is given but will be left to pick up the pieces with what you are given. There are guidelines for sharing such news with families but anecdotal reports show these are not always followed[28]. I believe that professionals need to communicate with parents with compassion, sensitivity and understanding over many years as it can take time to really come to terms with what it means. Diagnosis for parents is not necessarily a single event and should be influenced by what the parent needs to hear and what they are able to hear at that particular moment. Sometimes re-hearing the diagnosis at future appointments can be just as upsetting or traumatising.

Parents consistently report that good signposting to further information and support is of paramount importance. All too often, though, they feel that they are given the news and then left on their own.

> *'When we first got told her diagnosis we were rushed out of the room and left to it. Not knowing anything about our daughter, about what happens next, what to expect and how to cope. Thanks to a hospital appointment and speaking to someone else in the waiting room we found a support group.'*

---

28 Emerson, A. (2020) 'Room of Gloom': Reconceptualising Mothers of Children with Disabilities as Experiencing Trauma, *Journal of Loss and Trauma*, 25, 2, 124-140

As well as charities, parents commonly find online forums, blogs and support groups the most helpful means of becoming more informed and finding a new community to help assimilate the news.

Practical and Financial Impact

This book focuses mainly on the emotional aspects of having a disabled child. However, the practical, physical and financial impact cannot be overlooked and may significantly affect your emotional wellbeing. For example, having funds to buy special needs equipment (why is it always twice the price when the term 'special needs' is added to it?) can help you feel you are accessing what your child needs. If, however, you are fighting for services and your concerns are unacknowledged you may be left feeling angry and disempowered. There is a multi-directional impact.

Services

Across the country there are not enough support services to give families what they need, and what is provided (i.e. physiotherapy, occupational therapy and speech and language therapy) can vary enormously. The difficulties with accessing Child and Adolescent Mental Health Services (CAMHS) are well documented[29]. Short breaks and other respite services are not always able to deliver the support a family needs and often have very narrow criteria for accessing services. Many children remain without appropriate school places and the fight for Education Health and Care Plans (EHCP) is exhausting. Paediatric support can be hit-and-miss, with long waiting lists and often clinics that fall on days that are difficult for working parents to access.

On top of this, parents are having to familiarise themselves with health, social care and education systems at a time when they are most likely to be going through a huge process of adaptation. Worries about your child's education, health needs or who is going to look after them after your death may become all-consuming. Furthermore, it can be hard to see beyond the immediate state of worry, as even as one area of difficulty is resolved you move straight onto the next challenge.

---

[29] https://youngminds.org.uk/blog/what-parents-say-about-childrens-mental-health-services/

In terms of services, such as school or transport, parents are often aware that to be labelled the 'difficult parent' may be costly in terms of future support and relationships. This can add another layer of having to be politically and personally savvy about what you say, the battles you pick and how everyone else is feeling. It's quite exhausting.

'There's a long term thing in that, you know, we're going to need a relationship with the school transport team till she's 19. I don't want to go barging in.'

It's important to recognise the extra emotional burden involved in arranging certain activities or giving considerable thought to each and every action you take. That includes everyday requests that may seem inconsequential to other parents – such as notices from school or the Parent-Teacher Association (PTA). These can sometimes tip us over the edge.

Dealing with professionals

When you have a disabled child you will have increased contact with professionals, whether it is a paediatrician, social worker or therapists. You may have a portage worker, Special Educational Needs (SEN) support workers and nurses for medical needs. It can be overwhelming and sometimes unclear how to make the most of the support in a way that makes sense for your family. It is ok for you to ask a professional to clarify what they have said or ask for things in writing. It is not a failure to ask for support. Remember that they have (probably) been in the special needs world for longer than you so if there are things they know and you don't, that's to be expected. Sometimes they may need reminding about where you are in your disability journey and you can ask them for advice on how to access other services or if there's anything you might have missed. Chapter 7 considers professionals in more detail.

Becoming a carer

Parents do not always define themselves as a carer as they feel the support they give their child is part of what being a parent is all about. For some parents this is the case. For others it is important to recognise the role you have been placed in, which is over and above the typical parenting role. You may become a speech and language therapist, physiotherapist, occupational therapist, psychologist, special educational needs expert, nurse, care co-ordinator, finance and benefits specialist as well as someone proficient in medication and medical interventions. It may be that by naming yourself a 'parent carer' it helps you fight for the support you need, such as claiming Carer's Allowance, or a Carer's Assessment from social services.

It could also be that you don't feel ready to call yourself a carer as this, in itself, causes you to confront your situation. As your child gets older it will become clearer whether they will live an independent life or if your caring role will continue. Coming to terms with the latter can be a lengthy process; however, having it as a possibility in your awareness may help you in this journey.

Financial implications

The financial impact on families with a disabled child is well recognised[30]; it has been suggested that it costs three times more to raise a disabled, rather than a non-disabled, child. Examples of additional costs include: driving more as public transport is challenging; difficulties accessing informal childcare (and therefore having to pay); needing to buy equipment or specialist sensory toys or wearing out clothes or shoes more quickly due to wear and tear. Moreover, family income may be reduced due to restricted working patterns or having to pay for services that are not available via statutory services.

Living in poverty is commonly shown to have a detrimental impact on overall wellbeing. The stresses and strains are likely to filter through to family relationships and all aspects of life, including the child's wellbeing and development[31]. This includes poor and inappropriate housing.

Financial resources are shown to decrease, and protect against, stress. In other words, having practical and financial support can really help your emotional wellbeing. That's not to say that the stressors are removed, but financial support may provide a 'cushion'. Seek help for the practical things when and where you can, including getting advice on benefits and grants available to families. Appendix III lists organisations that may be able to assist you, and you may also wish to

---

[30] https://contact.org.uk/news-and-blogs/disability-and-poverty-in-the-news/

[31] British Psychological Society Research Digest (2019) The Psychological impacts of poverty, *Research Digest*, 3 December 2019

check the Local Offer via your Local Authority or speak to SENDIASS in your area. If finances are a worry for you then, alongside ensuring you can access funds, such as direct payments, other factors – such as social support – from friends, family or community, can also help reduce the negative effects of this stressor, including the impact on your physical health[32].

Work

Employment is consistently shown to be beneficial for our wellbeing and unemployment can markedly reduce a sense of life satisfaction. Sadly, many parents experience difficulties with work and need to rearrange, reduce or stop completely. *Contact* reports that 'only 16% of mothers with disabled children work, compared to 61% of other mothers'[33]. This obviously has a knock-on effect financially as well as (possibly) impacting the parent's sense of self and having a life outside the caring role.

> *'When I gave up my job I found that incredibly horrific,*
> *because I realise that you tie an awful lot of identity to*
> *yourself with your job title and self-worth.'*

Others have to reduce their hours or faced demotion due to the demands of their job. A difficult dilemma arises in that being employed can be good for our wellbeing but being torn in all different directions can have adverse effects on our stress levels. As one parent commented, *'I was spread too thin for work.'* This will very much depend on your situation and your role – is it something you enjoy and which makes you feel fulfilled? For those who found work rewarding and managed to make it feasible, it raised their self-esteem and provided a sense of satisfaction in their lives. It even provided skills that transferred across to other areas of their lives.

For other parents work becomes a source of stress and anxiety, adding to an already overloaded life. This might be because of the nature of the work or because of difficulties balancing home and

---

[32] Song, J., Mailick, M.R., Ryff, C.D., Coe, C.L., Greenberg, J.S. & Hong, J. (2014) Allostatic load in parents of children with developmental disorders: Moderating influence of positive affect, *Journal of Health Psychology*, 19, 2, 262-272

[33] https://contact.org.uk/media/773401/childcare_affordability_trap_research_june_2014.pdf

work life, including taking time off for appointments, illness or the challenges of finding appropriate childcare.

Parents who give up their job can end up feeling that it wasn't a choice; rather, it was a necessity. I felt this about my role in the NHS as it became untenable. If this is your situation it's important to find something that provides the same benefits that work did. Parent carers can be very inventive and entrepreneurial in the roles they find for themselves. It's worth seeking, if you have capacity, something that fits you and your family. In the final chapter we'll look in more detail at finding meaning and purpose in life and the benefit this has on our emotional wellbeing. Your life aspirations shouldn't disappear because you have become a parent.

It might be that at the moment work just adds too much pressure and you need to focus on family life right now – but that doesn't mean it will always be that way.

Terminology: What does 'disabled' *actually* mean?

Finally in this chapter I want to raise the tricky issue of disability terminology. Language can be powerful, particularly when fighting for services and limited resources, so it's important to set it in context. I give a brief overview of the social model of disability and further discussion on terminology in Appendix II.

Disability is a huge spectrum which may include learning, speech and language, social and emotional, sensory, physical health or medical difficulties or global developmental delays or differences[34]. In some ways the umbrella term 'disability' is so all-encompassing that it tells us very little about the person and what they need. It has been suggested that by grouping everyone together it may undermine the differences. However, I am using the term for this book as so many of the parent carers' experiences of wellbeing were similar despite the different diagnoses of their children.

For some parents, particularly those who have had little contact with the world of disability before, the term 'disabled' is rejected as it

---

[34] The Equality Act 2010 defines someone as disabled if: 'you have a physical or mental impairment that has a "substantial" and "long-term" negative effect on your ability to do normal daily activities.'

feels irrelevant to their child, or may be too difficult to initially consider. Special needs, additional learning needs or other terminology may be preferred. Take your time to come to some acceptance of this terminology as in the long run it will help you access services that you and your child may need. The term 'disabled' has political and social clout and throughout this book I am tending to use 'disabled person' as identified by the social model of disability.

It is also worth noting that terminology changes with time; 'It appears that no words or phrases remain acceptable in our culture for long, no doubt a symptom of our deeper difficulty in living with disability and all it conjures for us.'[35]

Conclusion

Crucially, as your child grows and develops so will you, along with your ability to make sense of your experience with increasing knowledge and mastery. You will gain a new perspective and understanding of your child and the new world you inhabit. The world is a richer and more interesting place for having a diversity of people in it with different diagnoses, ways of being, understanding and navigating the world. Despite this, it is important to acknowledge that certain impairments make the world a more challenging, confusing and sometimes painful place in which to be. As parents it can be hard to see our child struggle and be overwhelmed by things. A wound, physical or psychic, to our child can feel like a wound to us; it is a vicarious trauma. We cannot deny this reality for many disabled individuals and their families.

When I look back on my own journey I cannot believe how far we have come as a family, how I have grown as a person, learnt so much and come to a place of acceptance. But I do not, and cannot, deny that it has been extremely hard along the way. My son has found aspects of life difficult and upsetting. At times I have been so exhausted and depleted of all my inner resources and in these moments I could not have believed that I would reach the place I am now. Keep faith in your horizons.

---

[35] Bartram, P. (2007) *Understanding your young child with special needs*, London: Jessica Kingsley, p. 13

Sometimes we need help with these changes, as they can turn our world upside-down. If you are feeling like you need some emotional support, please speak to your General Practitioner (GP) or go to the website www.affinityhub.uk for signposting to organisations and private practitioners who can help you gain some perspective.

I end this chapter with some words of wisdom from other parent carers.

ADVICE FROM OTHER PARENTS

'Remember that a diagnosis is an opinion, not a prediction.'	*'It'll be ok you can do this.'*
'Make sure you find time for yourself so you don't get lost. Even if it's ten mins. Talking or just listening to others helps.'	*'Find support groups and others in the same boat as you. Ring helplines for advice on getting support.'*
'Don't be too proud to accept help. Asking for respite care doesn't make me a rubbish mother.'	*'Step into their world as soon as possible as early intervention and help is so important for their potential.'*
'It gets easier. You'll make friends. Better friends! You won't be alone.'	*'Own it!! Be proud! Sod what others think!! You will find a new normal.'*
'It's trite but true: be kind to yourself. It's not your fault if you struggle (and it's not your child's fault either). Some people will really come through for you, and some will let you down. Keep the good ones close.'	*'Take each day as it comes and find a time in the day to do just one thing that does not involve your child even if it is a five min break to read a page of your fave book make time to be someone other than a carer.'*
'Enjoy your child while they are little, and remember they are a child first and foremost and need your love.'	*'I wish I had shared more information with my mother, my brothers and sister-in-law... information about my son's disabilities, how they could help him and me more.'*
'I wish I had trusted my instincts more, been less embarrassed and self-conscious, and asked for help much earlier on.'	*[I wish I'd] 'asked more questions and asked the doctor to explain more.'*

Key points

- Entering the disability world, particularly if it is unfamiliar, can feel like you've 'woken up in another world'

- Seeing prejudice and discrimination can be shocking and sad

- We naturally become an advocate for our child and we may also become an activist for social change

- At times this is exhausting and we need to recognise when we need to step forward into action and when we need to step back to recalibrate

- People bring their own individual beliefs, opinions and experiences and it can be useful to reflect on these. Those around us will also have their own assumptions

- Diagnosis can be experienced in a number of ways – a shock or a relief and everything in between. It can take time to come to terms with what it means

- Practical factors will influence our wellbeing – including services, finances and work

- Terminology can be confusing – if you are unclear ask for explanations

- The social model of disability is a useful framework for understanding disability and the law

Part 2
Emotional Impact and Awareness

4

Emotional Challenges

[Parent carers] 'are really struggling... we need to start looking after carers so that they can care properly.'

In this chapter we will focus on some of the emotional challenges that parents can experience when they enter the special needs world. Despite being an understandable response to an unanticipated event they can feel negative and unwanted because the emotions are difficult to make sense of and painful to experience. We may feel guilty for feeling them in the first place.

We will also consider the diagnoses with most 'risk' to our mental health although I can't emphasise enough how your child and family are individual so sweeping generalisations need to be made with caution. I hope by sharing the research it will empower you in gaining the right support.

Emotions

Negative emotions are not mental health difficulties in themselves – it is part of being human to have negative and positive emotions and they are not always clear-cut or static. Yet even the way we talk about emotions is loaded – we aim for positives and avoid the negatives. But both are necessary for a well-rounded life. For example, emotions that are often considered negative, such as anger or regret, may lead to positive changes[36] in the same way that pain is necessary for gain in some sports.

There can, however, be a thin line between having a 'normal' negative emotional response and it becoming so difficult that you need some extra support. For example, sadness can be a typical response to difficult news but when it becomes all-encompassing, long-lasting and detrimental to your ability to take part in life then it is possibly turning into depression. You may wish to seek out additional support through your GP, counsellor or a support group. You certainly won't be alone in this. Contact[37] suggests that '72% of families with disabled children experience mental ill health such as anxiety, depression or breakdown due to isolation.' This is not a failure on your part. You need and deserve the right support to help you through this period.

At times it can be difficult to express negatives but if they go unprocessed they can fester. As well as causing depression or anxiety, lingering negative emotions can prevent us from engaging in behaviours that help us or our child. The negatives start to frame our whole life, including our relationship with our child. We need to make sense of our experience if we are going to move forward.

Emotions, feelings and sensations are part of our human ability to identify what we need, or that something requires changing. If we feel stressed it might mean there is something we need to do to, for example get through a difficult task, or reduce the demands on our time. If we are irritable it might mean we need more sleep. Emotions give us signals that need attending to. We don't always have to act on them but they provide useful information, or data, for us to reflect upon.

Emotions are complex and fluctuating based on a number of different factors. We therefore have to learn the language of emotions – our emotions – realising that at times we can do something to change them and at other times we have to learn to live with, or ride

---

[36] Griffin, J. (2019) Let's Celebrate Emotions: Our Evolutionary Allies, *Private Practice*, BACP, September 2019 https://www.bacp.co.uk/bacp-journals/private-practice/september-2019/evolutionary-allies/

[37] https://contact.org.uk/news-and-blogs/three-quarters-of-families-with-disabled-children-feel-so-isolated-that-it-has-caused-anxiety-depression-and-breakdown/

the emotion. We might know that a feeling is irrational or there's nothing we can do to change the situation but we may still feel the emotion and therefore have to develop skills that enable us to sit with it.

Research suggests that the more specific we can be in naming our emotions, the more we are able to deal with them. Language gives us a 'map' that enables us to make sense of our experiences in relation to the world and ourselves. This is the 'A' part of SPECTRA – Awareness of our emotions, which can help our wellbeing.

A note about emotions though – there is not always a clear definition and there is much debate about even defining what an emotion is. Sometimes it can be hard to find a word to express something that is hard to pin down and people differ in their ability to do this. So your experience and the way you describe it may vary. Hopefully what follows makes enough instinctual sense to resonate with your own experience, although I acknowledge the descriptions and definitions of something so personal, complex and intangible are sometimes inadequate.

Balance and Resilience

Human beings have a tendency to return to their usual set-point after highs and lows in life. This is referred to as hedonic adaptation. It is an amazing reflection of our adaptability and flexibility. The return path can be hard and take longer for some than others, depending on the context. The ability to bounce back following adversity is often referred to as resilience. It can involve recovering as well as flourishing. This is a bit of a buzz word at the moment. But it does depend on many factors and requires sufficient inner *and external* resources to cope with whatever life throws at us.

A number of parents I have spoken to have expressed a strong negative reaction to the word 'resilience'. I think in part due to how it is sometimes used to suggest a personal failure on behalf of the parent, i.e. if only they were more resilient then the situation wouldn't be a problem. When used like this it can be deeply shaming. It also places responsibility on an individual rather than acknowledging the system around the individual is failing.

'Up to now resilience to me has always meant how you are expected to tolerate poor services... So let's give you some resilience training so that you put up with this load of crap basically... And I always think well why don't you put this money into making your service better so I don't have to be so resilient in the first place.'

Individuals need community and social support in order to develop resilience in the face of continuous stressors. This can be referred to as 'community resilience'. There is also 'family resilience' which is the capacity of the family system to positively adapt to stressful life challenges; this includes making sense of adversity, providing mutual support and sharing emotions[38].

Although this chapter is looking at challenges and can therefore seem quite negative, this is not my intention. Acknowledging these may be a necessary part of the journey to the more positive elements of growth and adjustment that the majority of parents also report. That is not to say we only pay lip service to the difficulties in order to short cut through to the positive (if only that were possible). These feelings are intense, painful and often overwhelming. Do not feel you have to bear them alone. But please take heart that others have been there, and have come through to a place of greater acceptance, knowledge and awareness.

I will discuss post-traumatic growth in more detail in the next chapter; however it is worth flagging it up here too. When we go through adverse life events (which is nearly everyone at some point in their life) correlations have been found between those who experience the most stress and those who report the most post traumatic growth after they have made sense of the event[39,40]. We get to the positive by navigating the negative. You won't always feel the way you are feeling. I suspect that if, rather than the Wall of Silence many experience, there was more awareness and discussion of the difficulties parent carers face, then it could prevent longer term issues from developing and support emotional wellbeing for the whole family.

---

[38] Walsh, F. (2016). Family resilience: a developmental systems framework. *European Journal of Developmental Psychology*, 13, 313-324

[39] Calhoun, L. & Tedeschi, R. (2010) *Facilitating Posttraumatic Growth: A Clinician's Guide*, Routledge: Oxfordshire

[40] Janoff-Bulman, R. (1992) *Shattered Assumptions*, New York: Free Press

*'I needed someone to stop giving me the silver lining...
I think just being given the space to talk about it,
rather than anyone trying to minimise how you're
feeling, is really helpful.'*

You are not Alone

Partly what helps parents to deal with their negative emotions is the realisation **you are not the only ones to feel these emotions**. Being prepared and pre-warned about what may emerge helps parents not be taken aback by negative responses. It may be useful to be equipped with a 'go to' list of self-care strategies, people, organisations and services that can support you in times of need.

There are no right or wrong responses, and you may connect to some of what follows and less so in other areas. Many parents of non-disabled children also experience these. Everyone is different and unique and your own reaction will depend on many factors as already discussed in the previous chapters. My hope is that by naming these negative emotions they become manageable, understandable and cease to be overwhelming for those who experience them as such.

Common Emotional Responses

As there is no hierarchy of emotions or 'correct' order to experience them I have, for simplicity, listed some of the most common feelings identified in the research and my online survey in alphabetical order.

- **Anger and Frustration**
- **Anxiety, Stress and feeling 'on edge'**
- **Denial**
- **Depression and Sadness**
- **Disempowered**
  - *Confusion and Uncertainty*
  - *Helplessness or Feeling Stuck*
- **Grief and Loss**
- **Guilt**

- **Loneliness and Isolation**
- **Trauma and Shock**

Anger and Frustration

Many parent carers will go through a period of being angry. This may be aimed at themselves, other people or sometimes the diagnosis itself. It may even be directed at society, the universe or God. Sometimes parents feel let down by professionals, particularly if there are delays in getting a diagnosis or if concerns are dismissed. A lack of services or narrow support threshold criteria leave parents frustrated.

In rare, sad cases the child becomes the focus of the anger. If you feel like you may hurt your child it is really important that you seek help immediately. You can talk to your GP to explain your concerns; there are Mental Health Crisis teams across the country or the National Society for the Prevention of Cruelty to Children (NSPCC) will be able to signpost for support (listed in Appendix III). Sometimes when people feel like this they resist getting help because they are worried their child will be taken into care. More often than not this is not what happens. Instead support can be put in place to give you a well-earned break. At times shock, extreme pressure and a sense of helplessness can leave you feeling like you have no other options – please remember that you do.

Anger often covers another more painful emotion – sadness. When we feel hurt or upset we can rail against something else as a way of projecting out our unpleasant feelings. So, if we feel our child is not getting something that they need, it hurts us, and we get angry at the obstacle in the way. Recent statistics released by the Disabled Children's Partnership[41] show that only 4% of parent carers feel they get the right support to safely care for their disabled child. If showing anger is the only way to get what your child needs, no wonder parents feel like they have to go into combative mode.

> *'His school taught him two [Makaton] signs in five and a half years and I feel quite angry and hurt by their lack of performance.'*

---

[41] https://disabledchildrenspartnership.org.uk

Anger can come out as generalised irritability and an increase in loss of temper in situations not even directly connected with your situation. With repeated fighting and wanting to protect your child, professionals may come to view some parents as aggressive or difficult[42]. Unfortunately, being labelled a 'bolshie parent' may backfire and prevent us getting the help we need. It can help to try and turn the anger into assertiveness. This involves knowing your rights, trying to stay unemotional in communication with professionals and taking care of yourself behind the scenes in order to avoid becoming overwhelmed. There is an element of having to work with the system, on its own terms, to achieve what you need. It is a skill to regulate your own emotions in the face of bureaucracy that can often feel like it is against you. In the next chapter we will see that developing these skills can be a form of growth that can not only help you in your personal life but also transfer out to other areas, such as work.

What can help?

Remind yourself that you are human and feeling angry at certain elements of parenting is understandable. Self-compassion is crucial. I make sure I have a break and do something for me when I'm feeling particularly tested, including just going into another room to take some deep breaths. Talking to someone who understands can help offload the anger. Strategies such as exercise, distraction or channelling the anger into conscious constructive action can be useful. Anger is identified as an 'approach' emotion – that is, it can motivate and energise us to fight social injustices. At the right time and to the right degree it can mobilise social change. Try to listen to what it is telling you without acting in the moment. Hopefully you'll find some strategies that help you to harness this in Chapter 8 and among the other resources in Appendix IV.

Anxiety, Stress and feeling 'on edge'

Anxiety and stress are the most commonly reported responses. Although they are often experienced as similar they have slightly different definitions. Stress is a natural response to something

---

[42] Cunniff, A., Chisholm, V. & Chouliara, Z. (2015) Listening to Fathers of Sons with Duchenne Muscular Dystrophy, *New Male Studies: An International Journal*, 4, 2, 5-23, p.17

precarious or challenging – when external demands outweigh our resources. Becoming pre-occupied with problems and feeling unable to come up with satisfactory answers can lead to a 'pile-up of demands'[43]. Anxiety is what we feel when we are worried, tense or afraid, particularly about something that may, or may not, happen in the future or that has an uncertain outcome. Sometimes the cause isn't clear. In the short term these responses are normal and understandable but because of day-to-day pressures it can be hard to find time to make sense of things.

Over the longer term, though, stress and anxiety can be detrimental to your wellbeing – mental and physical. Symptoms can include headaches, raised heartbeat or breathing and grinding of teeth. Some studies report a greater risk of poor sleep, gastrointestinal problems and rates of infection[44].

There are different forms of anxiety diagnoses, dependent on how severe they are and what form they take: a generalised anxiety disorder (GAD) which involves worry about many things and not being able to stop worrying; panic attacks involve physical symptoms, for example feeling like you're having a heart attack; obsessive compulsive disorder, where we engage in patterns of thoughts or behaviours to try and gain a sense of calm but find that the patterns can take over our lives; and social anxiety, which is based on the fear of judgement by other people. There is also post-traumatic stress disorder which I consider further below.

Anxieties may lead to a ruminating about the 'what ifs' rather than staying with the present, being mindful and dealing with each moment as it comes. It can be helpful to consider the difference between reflection, where we need to go over something in order to process and make sense of it, and ruminative brooding where we get stuck[45]. We can become pre-occupied with the unanswerable or worry

[43] McCubbin, H.I. & Patterson, J. M. (1983) The Family Stress Process, *Marriage and Family Review*, 6, 1-2, 7-37

[44] Gallagher, S. and Whiteley, J. (2013) The association between stress and physical health in parents caring for children with intellectual disabilities is moderated by children's challenging behaviours, *Journal of Health Psychology*, 18, 9, 1220–1231

[45] Joseph, S. (2013) *What doesn't kill us: a guide to overcoming adversity and moving forward*. London: Piatkus

about things that have not happened, nor will not, but they take over our thoughts. This is our mind trying to come to terms with new and seemingly unfathomable information or circumstance. But anxiety can make it hard to think clearly.

I have been deeply concerned about the stress levels of many of the parent carers I have met over the last thirteen years. Many describe a constant, low-grade general anxiety running throughout the day that makes them feel 'on edge'.

> *'I always feel very, very stressed out to be honest and always like I'm running on empty.'*

It is understandable why parent carers feel this way. We are suddenly thrown into a confusing world of high demands (therapies, appointments, worries about the future) and low resources. I found it hard to accept being my son's carer and therapist, as I just wanted to be his mum. Additional pressures, such as when a child displays behaviours that challenge towards the parent or siblings, greatly heighten stress levels at home.

Part of the carer worry is that you are never fully off duty. Even when a child is at school or being looked after by someone else you are waiting for the call – if they're ill, had an accident or a seizure. And after school you may be on tenterhooks about what kind of day they've had, what mood they're in and the impact this has on the family home. It can feel like you're all walking on eggshells.

You need breathing space to digest and reflect on your situation and your responses. This will help you to not only cope with the day to day demands but also to move forward and develop other areas of your life.

What can help?

Most parents echo my own experience which is that, over time, they come to a place of acceptance, adjustment or adaptation. The stressors are not necessarily removed but our capacity to cope and respond in a healthier and more self-accepting way increases.

There are two over-arching themes in the ways in which you can manage your stress better: controlling external pressures, so that stressful situations don't happen too often; and building up your ability to deal with the difficult things in life. They can sometimes work in tandem. There are some things that are out of our control; therefore we need to learn to manage our response to them. And there are some things we can influence for the better, either in the short or long term, into which it might be worth investing some time and effort.

Stress and mental health problems can feed off one another. Ask yourself – is there anything I can do about this? If the answer is yes – take action or make a plan. If no, let it go or decide to think about it at another time – such as scheduling in some 'worry time' or write it all down in a 'brain dump' (Appendix I). Exercise and relaxation techniques can help as well as talking to friends and loved ones. There are more ideas in Chapter 8 and useful resources on anxiety listed in Appendix IV. If you need help understanding how to break this cycle you can talk to someone who is trained in helping unpick these tricky processes such as a counsellor or psychologist.

How we appraise (make sense of) the situation can also influence whether we see the environment as a threat, or something that we believe we can handle effectively. The meaning we bring to an event has a significant impact. Many parent carers talk about how they've learnt, through difficult circumstances, that they can cope with more than they thought they could. They've become more confident not only in dealing with day-to-day challenges, but also in their own ability to troubleshoot and problem-solve. To manage this though, we need space to reflect, to learn and to grow. If you have no spare capacity it's going to lead to burnout. Try not to just plough onto the next problem, as we cannot think clearly when we're constantly in crisis mode. Sometimes we throw ourselves into busyness or overload because we are avoiding negative emotions but there are more productive ways to cope with this imbalance.

At times we are overloaded because of the reality of being a special needs parent. Developing our assertiveness and ability to say no as well as finding trustworthy others to support us will help. At times the demands may not be possible, for example attempting to work and home school our children during the coronavirus lockdowns. Some things will not get done. That is ok; you are not superhuman.

For some individuals medication, such as anti-anxiety tablets, may be necessary to get the anxiety under control before you are able to tackle other strategies. Talk to your GP if you think this would be helpful. Bear in mind though that medication on its own is not always the answer without addressing some of the underlying issues, such as lack of balance, or the number of stresses in your life.

Denial

It is a natural reaction to go into denial in times of shock, and many parents cannot get their head around things straight away. My personal experience resonates with others who report denial as initially being useful. For the first eighteen months of my son's life I was not able to process the enormity of what had happened during a very traumatic birth, along with the ongoing emerging difficulties. Although I did his exercises and attended all appointments, by not fully acknowledging the situation, or thinking too much about the future, it enabled me to carry on with the day to day demands of having a baby and feel less overwhelmed.

People are different in how much information they want at a given point in time and how they process difficult news. For some, they want all the information straight away so that they can start to understand; for others, it needs to be given piecemeal in digestible amounts at the right time for them. We can't know what the other person needs and we don't always realise what we want for ourselves. Those who are in denial will, inevitably, not always realise it so it is useful to take a cautious approach. Sometimes well-meaning interventions from outside people can have a very detrimental effect if the timing is wrong for that person.

However, denial doesn't work in the longer term. It isn't always healthy and may impact your ability to take on board information or help that could be useful. It can make things worse or create additional problems.

Often we cling to denial because we realise, on some level, that to face our situation means that things, such as our long-held beliefs or imagined futures, will have to be re-imagined. Managing to 're-goal' where we give up an initial goal in life, if it becomes impossible or unachievable, is linked to improved wellbeing. It's not always easy and we need patience and empathy from others during the process.

Reality has a habit of catching up with you. There were a number of occasions when obvious difficulties kept knocking on my door and despite trying to mentally run away I couldn't escape the facts of my son's increasing list of diagnoses. A visit to the shoe shop with comments from other customers about the splints on his feet, the assumption from someone who had only just met him that he had autism, the absence of a party invitation from someone I considered his friend at mainstream school. They felt like a slap in the face. I realised my son was seen as different and 'othered'. Yet these awakenings also led to me making better, more appropriate, decisions about what my son needed. Such as realising he'd hardly spoken at his mainstream school and once he started special school his expressive language and friendships blossomed. I also developed a thicker skin.

What can help?

The difficulty with denial is that it happens at a level at which we are not always conscious or aware. To confront someone in this state is not always helpful and may cause them to dig their heels in further or become overwhelmed with anxiety, depression or despair[46].

Some things may help if we are at risk of being in denial. Try to ask for written information or take notes in appointments to help keep a record of what was said and any organisations you could contact for further support. You can then refer back to them at a later date, when you are ready. Professionals can help by providing clear information, time to process and check out parental understanding, always with empathy and sensitivity.

There is a difference in denial of fact (unhelpful) and denial of implication (which may help us focus on the here and now)[47]. Some parent carers develop a form of conscious prioritising of competing demands which can be an important coping strategy that I call a 'Worry Controller' (Chapter 8). This is when we deliberately switch off from something in our life, for a short period of time, so that we can focus on another task in hand. We may hope for the best but prepare for the worst as a means of coping with everyday life.

Denial of fact is less helpful though, and, in some extreme cases

---

[46] Hill, D. et al. (2014) Regoaling: a conceptual model of how parents of children with serious illness change medical care goals, *BMC Palliative Care*, 13, 9

[47] Lazarus, R.S. & Folkman, S. (1984) 'Coping and Adaptation' in W. Doyle Gentry (ed.) *Handbook of Behavioral Medicine*, New York: The Guilford Press, p.302

over long periods of time, denial can turn into dissociation and mental health difficulties. If you are struggling in this area it is vital you seek emotional support.

Depression and Sadness

While a short period of sadness (although unpleasant) is nothing to worry about, if it carries on for a longer period of time you may need some extra emotional support. Depression includes symptoms such as continuous low mood, difficulty finding joy in activities that were previously enjoyed, as well as lethargy and sleep problems. Depression is more common in parent carers than in the general population; in fact studies have suggested mothers of children with intellectual and developmental disabilities are about 1.5 times more likely than other mothers to experience depression[48]. Fathers are twice as likely to score above the cut-off on a psychiatric disorder screen[49]. This implies it is reactive to the situation in which parents find themselves.

Other researchers go further, stating 'when children are diagnosed with developmental delays, their parents may experience psychological turmoil similar to that experienced by suicidal individuals... [however] having a disabled child may help to strengthen adaptive characteristics and, possibly, reduce the risk of suicide'[50]. In other words, the child becomes a reason to live and this helps parents through the challenging times. While depression and low mood aren't experienced by every parent it is important to raise awareness of these emotional challenges, so that parents seek the support they require and don't then add another layer of guilt for feeling this way in the first place.

---

[48] Singer, G.H. (2006) Meta-analysis of comparative studies of depression in mothers of children with and without developmental disabilities, *American Journal on Mental Retardation*, 111, 3, 155-169

[49] Emerson, E., McCulloch, A., Graham, H., Blacher, J., Llewellyn, G. M., & Hatton, C. (2010) Socioeconomic circumstances and risk of psychiatric disorders among parents of children with early cognitive delay, *American Journal on Intellectual and Developmental Disability*, 115, 30-42

[50] Ellis, J.B. and Hirsch, J.H. (2000) Reasons for living in parents of developmentally delayed children, *Research in Developmental Disabilities*, 21, 323-327

What can help?

While this period of low-mood may be a common phase for many parents, it is most likely temporary. Over time the cloud will lift even though it doesn't always feel possible while we're in the middle of it. Although we can't always stop the emotions we can ensure we don't add to it by dwelling on the past or giving ourselves a hard time for feeling this way. Basic self-care activities can help, such as meeting up with friends, exercising, gaining a sense of control in an area of your life (however small) and getting a good night's sleep. Avoiding alcohol or drugs as well as watching your caffeine intake. Trying to re-engage in enjoyable and absorbing activities may lift your mood even temporarily.

In the next chapter I will reflect on how many parents come through a phase of feeling low to find a new perspective. If you are feeling down at the moment, please know that this is not how you will always feel.

If it does not get easier over time, though, you may find it helpful to speak to your GP about some additional support.

Disempowered

There are slightly different responses that I've grouped under the heading of feeling disempowered. This includes the confusion and uncertainty that parents may initially experience, as well as a helplessness or sense of being 'stuck' and feeling unsure how to get out of the quagmire.

Confusion and Uncertainty

Initially you may have only a vague notion of what a diagnosis means or you may have never even heard of the terminology before. The predicament of not knowing how to best look after your child can leave parents feeling de-skilled (I'm using this term to describe the feeling that you don't yet have the necessary skills) and incompetent. We often have to defer to professionals and feel like they know more about our child and their condition. This feeling of uncertainty can be exacerbated by having a glut of professionals all treating different parts of the child, or giving sometimes conflicting advice on what your child needs.

I remember feeling that I could no longer trust my 'mother's instinct' to know what my son needed. When he was in intensive care I was gently stroking his arm when the nurse told me that young babies with brain damage don't like being touched like that, rather it was better to use a firm, holding touch. It was helpful to receive this feedback but I could feel myself recoil with a sense of hurt that I did not know how to care for, and connect to, my son. The natural bonding process with your child can be interrupted because of the emotional upheaval of coming to terms with things and time taken to develop your new understanding.

Alternatively you may be met by a lack of support and advice and the ground you're under can suddenly feel shaky. We don't always know what we need or what we have a right to and can end up questioning our own viewpoint.

As well as trying to process the shock of the unexpected, you may also be uncertain about the future. What will it bring? And for some, more pressingly, will there be a future? For many parents the difficulty of wanting answers from those around you but the impossibility of anyone fully responding to your questions can be deeply frustrating. No one knows for sure what the future will bring. With time things will become clearer: what your child will be like, what they will manage to do on their own, how they will grow and develop, and how you, and they, will come to terms with their disability.

Some individuals may find it better not to plan too far ahead. I remember reading books, quizzing professionals and other parents in the hope of identifying how my son would be as a teenager and trying to imagine what our family life would be like in the future. No one could answer this. Like many parents before, I had to learn patience and become stronger and more resilient at tolerating a difficult situation.

Over time we do become the expert on our child and their best advocate but sometimes we need help to get there. This is not a failure. It is an important recognition of where our understandable areas of learning need are and then seeking out those that can support us.

Helplessness or Feeling Stuck

At times we can feel like our life is taken over and laid bare to outside scrutiny, much more than with other families. I lost count of the number of people we had visiting us at home. There was an expectation I placed on myself but which was probably also there from others, to keep the house clean and tidy, offer tea or coffee, make notes of the advice received and see through all therapeutic recommendations on a regular basis. At times both my son and I resented the intrusion into our private family life.

Over a period of time, loss of control can lead to 'learned helplessness'[51], referring to that feeling when, despite your best efforts, nothing you do changes the situation. Psychologist Martin Seligman undertook unpleasant experiments using electric shocks on dogs. By the end of his experiment the dogs just lay down and submitted themselves to the shocks. They had learned there was nothing they could do to escape them, they just had to roll over and accept it. The studies led to a recognition that helplessness can lead to depression and a feeling that future efforts to change things are unlikely to work. It is no wonder if sometimes we as parent carers – battle-weary - feel like giving up.

Unfortunately, the battle with the 'system' (health, education, social care and other wider influences) may continue even as your child gets older. Fighting for information, support and sometimes even a response from an organisation can leave you feeling powerless and frustrated.

We can feel helpless when life becomes less spontaneous and requires meticulous planning for our child. In turn this can crush spontaneity and our sense of play and enjoyment.

When we rarely get a break or chance to take a breath, there can be an overall feeling of 'stuck-ness' that we cannot escape. The responsibility is all ours and ours alone. Who will pick up the pieces if we are no longer here?

---

[51] Seligman, M.E.P. (1975) *Helplessness: On depression, developments and death*, San Francisco: Freeman

What can help?

Remember to be kind to yourself and realise that you are not expected to be the expert on your child's condition – why would you be at the beginning? You *will* learn about your child along the way and your child will teach you. By developing your knowledge and skills you will gain a new confidence and trust in yourself which counters early feelings of being disempowered. I think my drive to undertake doctoral research and write this book was in part a re-skilling to counter the early feelings of not knowing. You will find a way to re-gain expertise and empower yourself.

Asking questions of the professionals you come into contact with or other parent carers can help. Many parents consult charities, organisations or social media groups for support or training. Searching online can be a lifeline; however, be aware that the internet is a mixed bag. Knowledge is a powerful tool but reading too much negative, misery-inducing information or seemingly magical treatments that can 'cure' your child can be detrimental to your own well-being and the expectations you have of your child. Every child is different, every family is diverse. Although some things are common, no two experiences are exactly the same. Research, but treat your research with caution. Embrace your own expertise.

Changing our own attitude to the situation and requesting that appointments and advice are tailored to suit our particular needs may give us back some sense of control. Of course, there is a balance to be struck between following the advice of experts and our own instincts.

On reflection though, I think the best advice I could have been given by a health professional would have been 'here are some things/exercises you can do to support your child's development (which research has shown is helpful), but most of all they need love and you to enjoy being with them'.

By gaining a greater understanding of our child – something I refer to as 'enhanced perspective taking' in the next chapter – we become empowered in how to support them. It counters a sense of helplessness, develops our sense of mastery and in turn supports our (and their) emotional wellbeing.

Refocusing your attention on what you can do right now - tidying up, putting on clean sheets or, my personal favourite, organising the tins in the kitchen cupboard - can help even in times of uncertainty.

Small, yes, but significant because it provides a sense of control and achievement that may be lacking in other areas.

If there are times when you feel 'stuck' in the caring role, take a moment for yourself. Even a few minutes' break can help with this if you can find a friend or family member to help. Taking time to invest in other forms of support will help us, and our child, to develop and gain independence.

> *'I can feel very trapped by it sometimes because if you think too much about actually this is forever and I'll be doing this when I'm 85. Yes, it's good to know that there are people around... knowing that I'm not trapped is really helpful. Knowing that you know if I need an out and I need to go and spend 10 minutes on my own I can, is really helpful. It's just knowing that if you need it, it's there.'*

As with any job, you need downtime and something else in your life to fulfil and nurture you. Try to remember some balance, even when it feels like that is not possible.

Grief and Loss

People often use the analogy of grief for parent carers, moving through Kubler Ross'[52] different stages, namely denial, anger, bargaining, depression, before reaching a point of acceptance. Although this does resonate for some parent carers, I believe the analogy should be handled with care. Often the reality is more complex, showing closer similarities to chronic sorrow (discussed further below) or complex or disenfranchised grief, particularly where the grief cannot be named, for fear of shame or judgement. Parents have been told 'at least you still have your child' or suggestions have been made that they are in some way disloyal for expressing negative aspects of parenting a disabled child. Of course parents love, and are thankful for, their child but there may be a period of transition which they have to navigate.

As well as being construed as offensive by some, the risk with comparing a parent carer's experience to grieving is that people will expect you, at some point, to come to a place of final acceptance and

---

[52] Kubler-Ross, E. (2014) *On Grief and Grieving : Finding the Meaning of Grief through the Five Stages of Loss*, Simon & Schuster UK

closure. This may be the case for some people but many reflect on a circuitous experience, moving back and forth in response to the external world. There may be setbacks along the way at key points of transition, such as adolescence or moving into adult services and support. The oscillation of emotions continues and people can get stuck at different stages, which is when they might need additional support. It can sometimes feel that rather than one 'event' there may be many 'little deaths'[53] throughout a child's life.

'I don't recognise my life compared to pre-disability...
with each seizure I feel like a little part of me dies.'

Another parent described grief like a bungee jump cord, that extends and contracts over long periods of time. However, it may be a loss of control, spontaneity or independence that is mourned rather than the 'imagined' child per se.

In my experience, having to leave my job (and, as it felt at the time, my profession) in the NHS because of the challenges co-ordinating appointments (ironically within the NHS) and therapies added to a sense of life being irreparably altered.

I wonder if the word 'loss' may be more illustrative of some people's experiences which fits with a different model of grief – the Loss and Restoration model[54]. Acknowledging that some form of loss is part of everyone's life, this model reflects how we move between different positions – loss and recovery – and that is part of adaptation. New roles are developed yet a sense of loss may still intrude in between distractions. The idea of an ambiguous loss[55] may also be helpful; these are changes in life where it is not possible to reach a resolution or the outcome is unpredictable.

For some parents the term chronic sorrow[56] is a more accurate description of their experience. It is about living with loss. Holding

---

[53] Langridge, P. (2002) Reduction of chronic sorrow: a health promotion role for children's community nurses? *Journal of Child Health Care*, 6, 3, 157-170

[54] Stroebe, M.S. & Schut, H.A.W. (1999) The Dual Process Model of coping with bereavement: Rationale and description, *Death Studies*, 23, 3, 197–224

[55] O'Brien, M. (2007) Ambiguous Loss in Families of Children With Autism Spectrum Disorders, *Family Relations*, 56, 135-146

[56] Roos, S. (2002) *Chronic Sorrow: A Living Loss*, New York: Routledge

this emotional state can be exhausting and depress our systems for the necessary energy and motivation we need to parent our child.

But in direct opposition to the grieving analogy are the many parents who do not identify with grief or loss at all. This is powerfully expressed in the 'Wouldn't change a thing' campaign to challenge negative perceptions of Down syndrome.

Overall I think people should be wary of making simple comparisons with grief, using it as a shorthand for a very complex and personal experience. Professionals who expect parents to progress neatly through different stages and reach a permanent resolution are setting up an unrealistic expectation that does not always reflect parental lived experience. There may continue to be upsets throughout a child's life that bring up a well of sadness for a parent, particularly when making comparisons with others. I felt this when I saw my son's year group graduate from the mainstream primary school he had first attended before moving to a special school. I wasn't expecting my reaction and it threw me out of kilter for a couple of days.

What can help?

It is important for those around you to understand that profound changes in your life are not necessarily something you 'get over' within a set amount of time. We are all different and our pace of adaptation will differ. The words 'adjustment' or 'adaptation' are gross simplifications of what is often a complex, painful, and iterative, process.

Allowing yourself space for reflection can help make sense of any feelings you may have around loss and the need for adjustment. In the same way if you were mourning a loved one's death or had been through a traumatic event, such as a major illness, you wouldn't expect life to get back to normal straight away (if at all). You would give yourself time, acknowledging the transition. Furthermore, you would hope that those around you would be understanding and supportive. Sometimes they may need telling explicitly what support you need.

A sixth stage has been identified in the grief model which I believe *does* have relevance to loss or any kind of adaption – that is, finding new meaning[57]. We will look at that in more detail in Chapter 9.

---

[57] Kessler, D. (2019) *Finding Meaning: the sixth stage of grief*, London: Rider Books

Guilt

Many parents feel guilty over their child's disability for many reasons – their own struggle, not knowing how to best support their child, the state of the world and society's attitude to disability. Initially I had enormous guilt about my son staying overnight at respite, but when I rationalised it to see that my other sons were having sleepovers at the same age (and having the same amount of fun) I was left wondering what the guilt was about.

There may also be a genetic guilt – if you are the carrier of a gene, i.e. fragile x syndrome. But it is important to recognise that we cannot control our genes any more than we can choose our parents.

I suspect the feeling of guilt is in part because we have a primal desire to protect our children at all costs. On receiving news that our child is disabled, it can feel like we have failed to do this, however much we can see, logically, that it was out of our hands and not our responsibility. Talking this through with parents, they realise that there was nothing they did that caused the difficulties; however, emotions are not always rational.

> *'Guilt was massive – wondering if I'd been*
> *healthier in pregnancy maybe my child wouldn't*
> *have been premature.'*

The majority of parents do everything they can to help their child. (Of course, there are rare instances of a child being hurt but these are the exception.) Yet we still take on the mantle of guilt; feeling responsible for our child and the challenges they face. It may partly be in response to helplessness when something happens that is out of our power. By feeling guilty it takes back some control as if all things are under our influence (which they obviously are not) however inappropriate or illogical this may be.

Our realisation that we cannot always prevent negative things happening to our child – say pain, illness or seizures – means that we may end up handing over our role of being the 'expert' to other professionals, and the message is that we no longer know what is best for our child, or how to help them. This layers on the guilt again.

I wonder if there is an element of 'survivor guilt' at play here: a term that is usually applied to people who have 'survived a catastrophe that has not spared others'[58]. Something has happened to the most precious thing in our lives, namely our child, rather than to ourselves.

Guilt is also exacerbated by society's expecttations and idealisations of the parent role. This can be seen where parents are judged for their disabled child's behaviour if it is somehow deemed socially inappropriate. If there was greater tolerance of difference and disability in society at large, there would be less of a pressure on us as parents to be 'perfect' and have all the answers.

What can help?

Self-compassion and acceptance can help counter parental guilt. Recognising what is beyond our control alongside a forgiveness for mistakes made is important – no human is perfect nor ever can be.

Acknowledging that some of the behaviours or difficulties that children exhibit can be part of typical development. However, because parent carers already have a heightened sensitivity to their child's needs they try to protect against any unhappiness or additional struggle in life, assuming an excessive amount of responsibility[59]. All children need to make mistakes and be pushed to develop their independence. We may go over and above their care needs because of a sense of guilt.

I certainly recognise now that I found my son's discomfort unbearable and had an unrealistic determination to prevent him from ever being unhappy. It can be useful to focus on the 'ordinariness and not the "special-ness" of the child'[60] to gain some perspective. Some parent carers lose the sense of normalcy that other parents have, because often they have been through a traumatic time which triggers their sense of hypervigilance and alertness to danger.

Shame is slightly different from guilt but worth mentioning here. Shame involves feeling that we are in some way deeply flawed or worthless as a person, as opposed to guilt which may be about something we have done (or not done). Shame is strongly related to

---

[58] Calhoun, L. & Tedeschi, R. (2010) *Facilitating Posttraumatic Growth: A Clinician's Guide,* Routledge: Oxfordshire, p.7

[59] Barrett, M. (2010) *You and Your Disabled Child: A practical guide for parents,* West Sussex: Woodfield Publishing Ltd., p. 3

[60] Bartram, P. (2007) *Understanding your young child with special needs,* London: Jessica Kingsley, p.11

depression and finding ways to support yourself vital. Using techniques from Compassion Focused Therapy can be helpful and there is more information on this in Appendix I.

Loneliness and Isolation

When friends, family or society fail to understand our situation it can be both upsetting and disappointing. Everyone has their own way of making sense of the unexpected in life and sometimes that can involve taking over, blaming others, feeling anger, withdrawing or a whole host of different reactions. It can be isolating. Some parents report that their wider family deny the child's difficulties and blame problems on poor parenting or over-reaction, which can be very painful. This is especially hard for those parents who want to get the right help for their child and involve all the family in therapies and support.

The everyday aspects of raising a disabled child can sometimes exacerbate the feeling that you are outside the 'norm'. Accessing groups can be hard if they fail to be fully inclusive or accessible. Sometimes groups lead to painful comparisons and judgement. We may at times feel ashamed or embarrassed about things (our child's behaviour or our lack of knowledge) until we have re-gained confidence in ourselves.

Self-doubt can also creep in without a network around you. It may be that a special needs community comes to provide what you don't get elsewhere. Supportive others can make all the difference and provide extra (community) resilience to get through the good times and the bad.

What can help?

> *'I look back... and I'm like what was I doing, like the pressure I'd put on myself to do that [go out], but it was because if I'd just stayed at home, it would just overwhelm me. [I needed to be] getting out, seeing other people, having something to focus on, having a job to do, pack the bags, pack the car. Get out the door.'*

Withdrawing does not help us, yet choosing the right place to go and the right group of friends is important as, if misjudged, it can add to our sense of loneliness. Accessing special needs groups via local charities or mainstream groups that have an inclusive and accessible attitude is useful. If you feel nervous it can be helpful to go with other parent carers. We can't always assume, though, that just because someone is a special needs parent they'll be a lifelong friend – it depends on personal preference. However, it's worth persevering to find your community.

There may be times when you need to acknowledge when a particular activity is not going to be for your child and sometimes this can feel like a loss and re-adjustment all over again. I made errors in judgement about places to take my son because of my desire to have a 'normal' family experience. Visiting a large shopping centre at Christmas time was not my finest moment! My desire to do what I believed to be a 'typical family' thing prevented me from seeing that it would not be enjoyable for any of us, especially for my son. I had yet to develop the enhanced perspective taking that is so key to understanding our child – more of which in the next chapter.

Relationships between the parents can also be tested at times, although some people report that their relationship became closer as they navigated their new situation. Trying to keep communication open between parents can help reduce a sense of isolation.

For single parents the vulnerability to isolation can be greater and it is worth seeking out support through friends, family or single parent groups.

Trauma and Shock

'It just totally threw us as parents....It just... it took my legs away, if you like, it was quite profound.'

PLEASE NOTE: Post-traumatic stress is a common reaction to a shocking event or events in our lives. It only becomes a disorder when it goes on for a long time and affects our functioning. If you are experiencing flashbacks, intense memories of a traumatic event, heightened startle reflex or hypervigilance which are affecting your overall mood, making you avoid certain places or things, affecting sleep or your concentration for more than one month after the event please talk to your GP about a referral for psychological support – such as Trauma Focused Cognitive Behaviour Therapy (TF-CBT) or Eye Movement Desensitisation and Reprocessing (EMDR).

The experience of trauma is more than the anxiety or worry parent carers so often report. Many parents will have had a traumatic experience – seeing their child go through invasive medical interventions, a difficult birth, or even day to day cumulative traumas – and may show evidence of post-traumatic stress.

> *'I've seen my daughter have a lumbar puncture without*
> *any anaesthetic and they literally... held her down, it*
> *was a room full of doctors and they held her down like*
> *an animal and they shoved a syringe in her spine.*
> *I swear nobody wants to ever see anybody have that*
> *happen to them, but for a parent to see that to a five*
> *year old child, you know, that's brutal.'*

It may be small 't' traumas rather than big 't' Traumas that are difficult to cope with. For parents managing behaviours that challenge, there can be no let-up or chance to recover and it can cause post-traumatic stress disorder[61]. The personal toll can be huge for all involved.

Re-awakening previous trauma

For those who have unresolved past trauma it can be re-triggered by a new situation. Even if we have not experienced prior trauma it can awaken us to the fragility of the human condition. Freud adopted the term 'trauma' from the Greek word which means 'to pierce' as if the event pierces 'the psychic skin which most of the time successfully contains our subjective experience'[62].

As parent carers we usually come into contact with medical and other staff more often than other parents. Every experience of contact is potentially re-traumatising and the quality of the interaction is of utmost importance – it can literally make, or break, someone's day. Emerson suggests that 'UK services are not designed to support traumatized parents, and health practice may serve to compound distress'[63].

---

[61] Stewart, M. et al. (2020) Challenging child behaviours positively predict symptoms of posttraumatic stress disorder in parents of children with Autism Spectrum Disorder and Rare Diseases, *Research in Autism Spectrum Disorders*, 69

[62] Bartram, P. (2007) *Understanding your young child with special needs*, London: Jessica Kingsley, p. 20

[63] Emerson, A. (2020) 'Room of Gloom': Reconceptualising Mothers of Children with Disabilities as Experiencing Trauma, *Journal of Loss and Trauma*, 25, 2, 124-140

Something simple like my son's blood test can bring up all sorts of emotions for me. The combination of my stress levels about how he will cope, memories of all the other times we've been at the hospital along with frustrations about waiting times or lack of adjustments in the waiting room can lead to feelings of sadness.

Even when all goes well and my son has been fine, I often need some nurturing to recover afterwards such as going for a coffee (me) and chocolate cake (my son) to make a nice ending to the event. The feeling can linger though and makes me think how often parent carers rush from one appointment to work to another appointment without acknowledging the impact. We need space to re-charge. We need compassionate, understanding and timely help from others to enable us to continue in our caring role.

Symptoms

Traumatised individuals may have an exaggerated startle response; intrusive thoughts; constant concern for their child's health and, if the child has siblings, their health as well. Parents can go into hypervigilant mode and it can take time and patience to re-gain faith and trust in the world. Where there is a continual re-traumatisation from new diagnoses, problems and difficulties in our daily lives, there is little time to catch up, take stock and re-ground ourselves for the next hurdle. For those children who are medically fragile there may be many hospital visits, close calls and having to prepare for bad news.

It took many years for my hypervigilance to reduce back to pre-birth levels. I would jump out of my skin at passing ambulance sirens and would find the frustrations with services (such as being put on hold while calling a local orthotics service, appointments not being booked in, difficulties getting the relevant person at the Local Authority to call me back) led to a re-traumatising helplessness that brought me to tears on numerous occasions. Pinning my son down in A&E while he had his head sewn up after accidentally banging it on a radiator eviscerated me for several days. I felt I'd let him down and it re-awakened the old wounds of his birth and guilt at not being able to keep him safe from harm.

Severe shock can also lead to a pre-occupation with what I refer to as the 'pre-articulus stage'[64] (pre-traumatic incident) that occurs

---

[64] Griffin, J. (2016) Parenting a Disabled Child, *Therapy Today*, October, p.12

just before a devastating event. We may think about it constantly and become overwhelmed with questions of 'what if?' that prevent us dealing with the reality of our situation.

What can help?

If this is your experience then it is essential to acknowledge it. Consider how you would support yourself in any other traumatic situation, such as a road traffic accident – what would you want from others? What would support you? This may be what you need now too.

Parents report that understanding, compassion and empathy have a positive impact on their wellbeing. Providing the opportunity to have control and be empowered in a safe and trustworthy environment all contribute to services working in a trauma-informed way.

Whilst challenging and difficult to comprehend, the majority of people who go through adverse events in their life do come to terms with their new existence. Their levels of happiness return to what they were before the event and they find new meaning and purpose in their life. Rather than bouncing back this is sometimes referred to as bouncing forward.

Getting specialist support

If you remain in a traumatised state for a prolonged period please talk to your GP, health visitor or social worker about getting support as soon as possible. Caregiver Post-Traumatic Stress Disorder (PTSD) does exist, although it is not always recognised by untrained professionals, and it's important you get help.

Treatment for PTSD includes Trauma-Focused Cognitive Behaviour Therapy (TF-CBT) and Eye Movement Desensitisation and Reprocessing (EMDR). Both treatments are evidence based and available on the NHS[65]. If you need help in this area it is important to be seen by a mental health professional with the appropriate training as otherwise it may lead to further re-traumatisation.

Crisis can be a catalyst for change

Sadly sometimes it takes a person or family reaching crisis point before things start to get better. This might be that services support them

---

[65] https://www.nice.org.uk/guidance/ng116

or make the referral they need. Alternatively it may be that through reaching rock-bottom we develop skills that help us because we have had to in order to survive. This might involve changing our attitude to something (i.e. no longer seeking an unrealistic image of what family life is like; finding other ways of getting support), putting into place practical things that help us cope, such as saying no to demands or spending time doing something else.

Ideally, we would not leave it until 'crunch point' to then address difficulties in our lives. However, sometimes in life things creep up on us and suddenly we have fallen into an abyss. By developing our capacity to notice our emotions we can see how we are doing, check in with our energy levels or mood and then take action as necessary (i.e. have a break, see a friend, undertake relaxation strategies). Unless we are aware of our own needs it can be hard to implement our self-care strategies pro-actively rather than reactively.

We'll now look at research suggesting areas where there is an increased risk to our mental health and how this highlights the need for self-care and looking after our wellbeing as parent carers.

Increased risks to your emotional wellbeing

A NOTE OF CAUTION:

If there is higher risk of distress it does not mean that this is inevitable. This may not be your experience at all. Some parents with a non-disabled child may also experience these reactions.

In the next section I refer to some of the studies I came across that considered increased risk. You might not feel it is helpful to know this increased risk; however it may aid your arguments with professionals and social care for more support. It may also remove any guilt or self-blame for times of struggle. If you don't think this would be helpful for you then you can move onto the next chapter on Positive Change.

If you are feeling very low or anxious over a period of time you need to speak to a professional about accessing support, such as a Carers' Assessment, Short Breaks or other respite service. Finding someone to talk to about your problems may help you get through some of the toughest times. You can find organisations and professionals that provide emotional support on the www.affinityhub.uk website.

As we've already acknowledged, parents of children with intellectual and developmental disabilities may be at increased risk of mental health problems. This is sometimes due to the child's condition or behaviours or often can be related to the lack of support, resources and adaptations available to the family. It is therefore a mental health inequality that does not need to exist if all of the support was in place.

Whilst not wanting to worry parents who are in the newly diagnosed phase, I believe raising awareness of the potential risks to your mental health, particularly if you are surrounded by people who deny this for a multitude of reasons, will help you to fight for the support you need. In my personal experience I felt that some professionals avoided considering the impact my son's disability had on me ('Wall of Silence'). If someone had said to me 'this is understandable' or 'others have felt like this' and worked collaboratively with me to find solutions it would have been beneficial for my own emotional wellbeing.

How a parent feels will have an impact on others in the family and vice versa. Families are systems that affect one another, so a depressed member can affect the whole. Therefore a child's disability and the parental or sibling reaction to it can end up causing an imbalance in the family that is often hard to see from the inside as it becomes so ingrained and everyday. Sometimes it takes a professional or an outsider pointing out a different way to manage challenges that provides a different perspective. However, families with a disabled child already have a number of 'experts' telling them what to do that can be intrusive and seem judgemental so any such intervention needs to be handled sensitively and in a timely fashion.

Different risks

There is some evidence to suggest that different diagnoses can be connected to increased levels of stress. However, it can be overly simplistic to talk about the spectrum of difficulties that individuals may experience under one name. Within each diagnosis there are numerous ways people respond and behave; it is a massive umbrella. What might be more useful is to consider what every day life looks like for your child and the wider family, including their connection with those around them. It can also help to think about your own beliefs and expectations around parenthood and family life and how, at times, these may need to shift. Most of all remember that your child is an individual and your family unique.

I wonder if there is also a personal, individual element to what diagnosis or difficulty is the most challenging. For some people their worst fears may be around issues such as incontinence whereas for others being able to communicate with their child is the most important skill. It is not as simple as saying the more severe the disability the greater the negative impact on the family; instead it may be the 'perceived severity', complexity or number of problems that has more of an influence[66].

Autism

Some studies suggest there can be a greater risk to parental mental health when their child has autism, although the exact cause can be unclear[67]. It could be a particular aspect, such as hyperactivity, behaviour that challenges (see below), lack of support[68] or attachment-related anxieties[69] between parent and child that increases the risk.

There is a primal desire to connect with others that goes back to our own dyadic relationship with our caregivers. If there is a limited, or different to expected, connection then it may be harder to feel the rewards of parenting that can make other challenges more manageable. However, for many parents with an autistic child this is not their experience and they would dispute the suggestion that

---

[66] Brehaut, J.C., Kohen, D.E., Garner, R.E., Miller, A.R., Lach, L.M., Klassen, A.F. & Rosenbaum, P.L. (2009) Health among caregivers of children with health problems: findings from a Canadian population-based study, *American Journal of Public Health*, 99, 7, 1254-62, p. 1259

[67] Totsika, V., Hastings, R.P., Emerson, E., Lancaster, G.A. & Berridge, D.M. (2011) A population-based investigation of behavioural and emotional problems and maternal mental health: associations with autism spectrum disorder and intellectual disability, *Journal of Child Psychology and Psychiatry*, 52, 1, 91-99

[68] Bromley, J. (2004) Mothers supporting children with autistic spectrum disorders: Social support, mental health status and satisfaction with services, *Autism*, 8, 4, 409-423

[69] Keenan, B.M., Newman, L.K., Gray, K.M. & Rinehart, N.J. (2016) Parents of Children with ASD Experience More Psychological Distress, Parenting Stress and Attachment-Related Anxiety, *Journal of Autism and Developmental Disorders*, 46, 2979-2991

there is a limited connection with their child. They develop a greater understanding of their child. Some parents may even share similarities (or diagnosis) with their child which can help or hinder their wellbeing.

'There are a lot of parents who are suffering with conditions such as social anxiety which is brought on by the fact that they are parenting children with special needs, but actually it's deeper than that, it's because they themselves have special needs that... they haven't had help with.'

It could also be that having a lower household income (due to limited employment opportunities and higher cost of equipment) elevates the risk for parental wellbeing, rather than the diagnosis itself.

In contrast, studies looking at life satisfaction and positive affect have identified that parents of children with Down syndrome reported higher levels than those whose children had autism. It is worth noting that some research does question what is sometimes referred to as the 'Down syndrome advantage'[70] and it may be that socio-economic status is a protective factor rather than the diagnosis itself (parents of children with Down syndrome have tended, in the research, to be older and in a higher income bracket). Again it will vary by family.

Untangling the web of symptoms and diagnoses is complex, if not impossible, as diagnostic tools remain blunt and open to subjective interpretation by professionals. Everyone is an individual so even within the diagnosis there can be huge variation in behaviour and abilities. Trying to break this down into a coherent cause and effect is not always possible.

Because diagnoses don't always fall into neat boxes it also seems that once your child has one diagnosis, they can quite easily pick up others. As our son gained new ones along the way it felt like trying to shoe-horn him into a made-up set of tick-boxes. My attitude now is that I will use a diagnosis to access services and support but I realise it tells me very little about my son. We must bear this in mind when thinking about the link between diagnosis and increased parental mental health risk; the diagnosis is not the whole story.

---

[70] Dunn, K., Kinnear, D., Jahoda, A. & McConnachie, A. (2019) Mental health and well-being of fathers of children with intellectual disabilities: systematic review and meta-analysis, *BPsych Open*, 5, e96, 1-10, p. 7

Behaviour that Challenges

Unsurprisingly to many of you I'm sure, studies highlight that behaviours that challenge can be difficult for parents (and the child). Families who are subject to continuing difficulties in this area can be vulnerable to poorer mental health[71] and find their quality of life reduced[72].

> *'It's the shock and awe thing. It literally was like someone had decided to wage war against you.'*

Furthermore, social support may be harder to come by, including finding childcare or respite, thereby having a knock-on effect. We all need a break sometimes. If this is your situation it is of paramount importance that you seek help whether it is via your GP, paediatrician, Child and Adolescent Mental Health Services (CAMHS) or charities such as the *Challenging Behaviour Foundation* (Appendix III). Do not suffer in silence as it can seriously affect the wellbeing of the whole family. Ensure the support is specialist and they understand your situation.

When appropriate support is received it can assist parents in understanding what their child is communicating through their behaviour, and strategies can be put in place to help. However, some parents who have received behavioural support find the interventions stressful and time consuming so it is important that you are open with professionals about what is possible in your family life and that you work together to be creative in finding solutions. Some professional advice is not realistic in a typical family home and gaining suggestions and strategies from other parents in a similar situation can be helpful as they have 'walked the walk'. A home is not a clinic or a school and cannot be run as such. Therefore, things will inevitably be less structured, predictable and harder to control (e.g. someone unexpectedly ringing the doorbell). This is not the parents' fault; it is just the reality of running a home.

---

[71] Totsika, V., Hastings, R.P., Emerson, E., Lancaster, G.A. & Berridge, D.M. (2011) A population-based investigation of behavioural and emotional problems and maternal mental health: associations with autism spectrum disorder and intellectual disability, *Journal of Child Psychology and Psychiatry*, 52, 1, 91-99

[72] Gray, D.E. (2002) Ten years on: a longitudinal study of families of children with autism, *Journal of Intellectual and Developmental Disability*, 27, 3, 215-222

The image of the arousal curve can be helpful[73] as different interventions work best at different stages of an acute reaction to being overwhelmed or overstimulated (as opposed to a tantrum, when a child doesn't get their way). When in the overwhelmed state, it will be impossible to reason or implement new behavioural strategies. In that 'red' moment the priority is to keep everyone safe, even if that means you moving to another room.

The time to put behavioural strategies into place is before the problem becomes insurmountable, i.e. changing an overly stimulating environment or preparing your child for any changes. Being able to see what is upsetting your child, before it becomes overwhelming, and making adaptations at that point will bring about the best outcome. We as parents have to become detectives, looking for clues and being aware of the environment around us. For example, if sensory overload is the cause, what exactly is it – lights, sounds, touch, change of routine, or something else? Gaining advice about a sensory diet from a trained Occupational Therapist may help. Sometimes a child's own calming behaviours, such as repetitive or stimming activities, help them to cope with overwhelming stimuli and if this behaviour is prevented it can lead to further difficulties.

Be aware that an upsetting trigger doesn't always disappear even if the behaviour has dissipated. Sometimes aggravations continue to trigger the child and further upsets can follow soon after without appropriate calming or distracting interventions put in place. Working out what your child likes and dislikes will help to set up successes in future and avoid pitfalls. This involves developing your skills to take their perspective.

Identifying coping strategies that can help you in the moment are crucial. These may include focused breathing, mindfulness and recognising the causes of the behaviour. Unfortunately, we can feel judged by society if we are unable to control our child or understand their behaviour. Try to take the personal out of any behaviours; your child doesn't hate you, you are not failing as a parent. They are communicating their distress or wishes about something to the person closest to them, namely you. Remember this is not your fault: you

---

[73] http://www.challengingbehaviour.org.uk/learning-disability-files/02---Finding-the-Causes-of-Challenging-Behaviour-Part-2.pdf

are trying to make the best of a difficult situation. Likewise, it is not your child's fault either: they are trying to make sense of a confusing situation and do not know how to tell you what they need. Recognising that your child isn't defined by their challenging behaviour, and neither are you as a parent, can be helpful in gaining perspective. Setting up support and behavioural strategies are important when your child is young as it can become harder to deal with as your child grows.

It is also important to acknowledge that there may be times when behavioural support is not enough and you need a break to re-charge your batteries. Under the Children and Families Act 2014 parent carers have a right to have a Carers' Assessment. Social services may be able to offer respite but they will need to have a clear record of the behaviour and impact, so make sure you document incidents. Ensure you take time out to re-connect with something outside of your caring role.

Language

Many of the parents I have spoken to referred to the specific difficulties when their child was non-verbal - it may be harder to know how they are feeling or what has happened in their life, for example in their day at school. It can leave parents feeling as if they are having to second-guess things and ensuring good communication – such as a home-school book – is even more important.

> *[I don't know] 'what he really thinks about or what he really feels, you know, it's very difficult.'*

For other parents though they have a clear understanding of their child and their needs through other forms of communication – a smile, reaching for something, symbols, a look on their face or a position of their body that tells those that know them well how they are feeling. They become experts at interpreting the smallest look or gesture that others may miss. It can open up a whole world of communication. Again, how parents experience this is personal and individual.

Concluding Thoughts

This chapter has been a difficult one to write because, while I strongly believe that the negative feelings parent carers may experience needs to be voiced, it is important to place this within a wider context. We may feel negative emotions due to many factors: our child's difficulties, diagnosis, society, reaction of others or challenges to our own belief systems. It may be practicalities – changed relationships, work patterns, overload and lack of support. The responses need to be talked about and parents enabled to do so without judgement or guilt.

However, we will not always feel like this. Even those parents who found things difficult at first, when questioned ten years later, were able to identify positive developments such as gaining greater skills, being 'less sensitive to the reactions of outsiders' and reported 'improved relationships with their extended families'[74].

Positive and negative emotions are embedded within one another. Negative experiences may be a stepping stone to a more complex and nuanced life experience, one that has sorrow *and* joy, despair *and* hope, challenge *as well as* growth.

As I highlighted at the beginning of this chapter, where there is trauma there may also, over time, be the potential for growth for parent carers[75]. The path is rarely linear or smooth, mirroring the model of Post Traumatic Growth (PTG) that earlier pain is not removed, rather it morphs into something more manageable or even transformative. Many parents express what I refer to as a 'wisdom' – a realisation that the world isn't perfect, some things are out of our control and that we have more resources and resilience in us than we ever thought possible. The skills and sense of mastery that we gain may, over time, spill out into other areas of our life and we recognise that our life is forever changed. Our child changes us, our perspective, our assumptions, our knowledge base.

It is positive change that we will look at now in the following chapter.

---

[74] Gray, D.E. (2002) Ten years on: a longitudinal study of families of children with autism, *Journal of Intellectual and Developmental Disability*, 27, 3, 215-222, p. 221

[75] Cadell, S. et al. (2014) Posttraumatic Growth in Parents Caring for a Child with a Life-Limiting Illness: A Structural Equation Model, *American Journal of Orthopsychiatry*, 84, 2, 123-133

Key points

- Negative emotions are not mental health difficulties in themselves – they are part of being human

- At times it can be difficult to express negatives but if they go unprocessed they can fester

- You are not the only ones to feel these emotions

- Parent carers commonly report feeling anxious, stressed or 'on edge' as well as there being an increased risk of depression and low mood

- Some feel angry and frustrated, as well as guilty, lonely and disempowered

- Parents may be in denial or can express a sense of grief or loss, although this analogy needs to be handled sensitively

- Those parents who are traumatised need to recognise this and may need specific emotional support

- Studies suggest that autism and behaviours that challenge increase the risk of poorer parent mental health. However, untangling the web of symptoms and diagnoses is complex

- Positive and negative emotions are embedded within one another. These feelings are not static and will change over time

5

Positive Change

*'I'm not like I was at all. I'm a lot more resilient.
I think that could be my middle name.'*

There is often an assumption that having a disabled child has a solely negative impact on parents. Thankfully, studies are increasingly illustrating what parents themselves know, that this is far from the whole story. The majority of families report positives in relation to parenting a disabled child[76,77], if not at first, then as time goes by. There seems to be a naturally occurring arc of development that, with the right support, acknowledgement and understanding, can lead to positive change.

However, timing and context are crucial for this to occur. For those who are still in the blur of the early years, or struggling to survive day-to-day, emphasising the positives can be like rubbing salt in a wound. They are not ready to hear or see that it is possible. In contrast, for parents who are at the more positive stage of acceptance in their life, to hear comments such as 'I'm sorry to hear that your child has X'

---

[76] Hastings, R.P. & Taunt, H. (2002) Positive perceptions in families of children with developmental disabilities. *American Journal on Mental Retardation.* 107 (2):116-127

[77] McConnell, D., Savage, A., Sobsey, D. & Uditsky, B. (2015) Benefit-finding or finding benefits? The positive impact of having a disabled child, *Disability & Society*, 30, 1, 29-45

can be equally galling. Parent carers need sensitivity to where they are on their disability journey, acknowledging that we may continue to alternate between positives and negatives, such as joy and heartache, confidence and uncertainty, over many years.

Many of the issues we cover in this chapter can enhance our sense of empowerment and thereby our wellbeing. In addition, empowerment is affected by external as well as internal factors and others can support us in becoming more empowered by sharing information, collaborating with us and encouraging our agency. Over time we gain greater knowledge, awareness and understanding and recognise our ability to not only manage but also develop and grow. Realising we can influence aspects of our life (and let go of that which cannot be controlled) reinforces our belief that we can get our (and our child's) needs met. This is in contrast to the de-skilling (the discombobulation and feeling stumped) parent carers often feel when they first enter the special needs world.

As we've already alluded to in the previous chapter, post-traumatic growth (PTG) may be of relevance to parents of disabled children. Through stress and adversity we learn valuable lessons about ourselves and others, as well as realising we have a greater capacity to cope with difficulties than we previously thought. Paradoxically, in PTG studies often those who have experienced the most stress also report the most growth. People describe their experience of trauma as meaningful and often simultaneously negative and the point in their life and when they felt most alive[78]. These views are not new and the idea that good can come from suffering has been documented in 'the writings of the ancient Greeks, Hebrews and early Christians, and the teachings of Buddhism, Hinduism and Islam'[79]. Sometimes we will not notice the growth or positive change until someone points our attention in that direction. This is another aspect of the Awareness of Emotions in the SPECTRA of Parent Carer Wellbeing. Sometimes we have to stop and notice the positives. I hope this chapter can help you in this respect.

That is not to suggest the journey to growth is an easy one. It can be gut-wrenching, painful and slow. We cannot just jump to the

---

[78] Mearns and Cooper (2005) *Working at Relational Depth*, London: Sage, p. 67

[79] Calhoun, L. & Tedeschi, R. (2010) *Facilitating Posttraumatic Growth: A Clinician's Guide*, Routledge: Oxfordshire, p. 10

growth part without travelling along the arduous path. Transformation is complex and we may experience positive change but not necessarily feel 'happier'[80]. A meaningful, growthful life is focused on something more fulfilling and purposeful.

Does Change Always Equal Growth?

Not all parents report positives and identify with a sense of growth, though. For many, their lives have changed beyond all recognition and they do not necessarily see the changes as a good thing.

> *'I don't necessarily know if I've grown in a positive way,*
> *as opposed to maybe going sideways.'*

They have, however, developed a greater awareness of the fragility of life, seen that things don't always go to plan and a number of parents referred to having 'grown up'. Making peace with our new reality entails a certain wisdom – an opening of one's eyes to the wider world.

The Influence of Positive Others

It is often through connection with others (virtually or in reality) that we start to look with fresh eyes, or what psychologists call 're-framing', at our experience. We may find this connection in a special needs network, with a professional, a family member or through seeing disabled role models in public; representation really does matter. We may shift our perspective through inclusive and accessible services, or welcoming and ambitious teachers who expect the best for our child. This narrative makes our life fuller, bigger, better. It helps us to challenge potentially negative or restrictive views and see the world anew. People have paved the way for us if we are willing to follow on the sometimes uncomfortable or painful journey but one where our new perspective grows into something quite special.

In this chapter I will outline some of the positives parents report in their lives before looking at lessons we can learn from post-traumatic

---

[80] Ryff, C.D. (1989) Happiness is Everything, or is it? Explorations on the Meaning of Psychological Well-being, *Journal of Personality and Social Psychology*, 57, 6, 1069-1081

growth. As outlined in the previous chapter our feelings may vary over time, day by day, even minute by minute. This is normal and it's useful to remember that positives and growth do not mean that you do not feel distressed at times.

Areas of Positive Change

I have grouped the many positive themes parents experience under the following headings:

- **Acceptance and Adjustment**

- **Assertiveness**

- **Enhanced Perspective Taking – seeing your child's viewpoint**

- **Expertise and Sense of Mastery**
  - *Diagnosis or having a plan*
  - *Knowing you've done your best*

- **Inner Strength or Resilience**

- **Motivation or Fighting Spirit**

- **Putting Things into Perspective**

- **Pride and Joy**

- **Re-affirm Beliefs and Values**

- **Skills – transferable across life domains**

- **Tolerance, Empathy and Patience**

Acceptance and Adjustment

The majority of parents do reach a place of acceptance with regards to their new family situation – they adjust to, and grow from, it. Rather than a final destination it is a more fluid process that keeps needing to be assimilated as new things arise in our life. Perhaps it is better to refer to it as accept*ing* and adjust*ing*.

*'You have to just accept what's happening, accept how
you feel about it, accept that other people are going to say
annoying things about it and then with each step you kind
of have to unpick it and put it back together again.'*

There is something unconditional and expansive about accepting our life and child as they are. There is an openness to the richness and diversity of existence. For many of us it will involve changing our perspective; a (previously perceived) 'problem' declines in importance as we develop better strategies to cope and understand our child's needs. We harness greater knowledge and understanding which helps us.

We recognise that life is fragile and precious and does not always go to plan. We may begin to challenge the perfectionist representation of how life 'should' be that is often seen in society. Who is to say what life 'should' be? We can make our own decisions about the meaning and importance we bring to our life. We can decide for ourselves when we are a 'good enough' parent or citizen rather than chasing an impossible existence. There are possibilities for learning and growth in all of our so called 'mistakes' – that are part of being human. Don't get me wrong, of course I am not condoning neglect or abuse. What I mean is that we accept that life is imperfect and full of paradox. Recognising that change is part of life and there are some things we cannot control. Seeing difference as a strength gives us a new perspective enabling us to re-focus our attention on things we can influence and that really matter.

There aren't always easy or simple answers to challenges; we are all just muddling through and that's ok.

Assertiveness

Saying no

Finding, and asserting, your voice is often necessary as a parent carer. We learn how best to manage the demands on our time and inner resources. Gaining greater awareness of our voice and our rights can increase our confidence to say 'no' to things and set boundaries that work for you as a family. It is an act of self-care.

It may also lead to assertiveness in seeking the right support and information from professionals. Alongside a growing confidence in parents' knowledge of their child and their condition there is a realisation that other professionals may not have all the answers.

'I've grown. I'm more confident now. I would never have questioned a doctor before... And they are just human and they make mistakes and actually they don't know everything.'

The inevitable increase in appointments and other commitments that come with being a parent carer requires us to recognise when our resources and capacity are becoming depleted and to take action. Including being realistic about how much you can give – of your time, but also of yourself.

Growing a thick skin

As well as the ability to say no and assert their own rules and decisions, many parents grow a thicker skin in response to others' judgements or lack of support.

'Yes, there's judgement... I used to be really hurt by it, it used to really upset me, and then I would... try and avoid situations, but I've just grown a really thick skin... And it would be as a result of thinking I can't always feel this way, when we're visiting family... because the emotional cost to me was too high... And they weren't going to change.'

Motherhood in general may entail a rejecting of unrealistic, social expectations of mothers[81]. It may be more pronounced for parent carers as we need to reject particular 'social norms' that don't fit with us or our child's life. Our growing confidence and competence can have a positive impact on our wellbeing and allow us to leave some impossible goals behind, thereby escaping a vicious cycle of perceived 'failures'. Although the need to grow a thicker skin can be hurtful, several parents found that humour helped get their message across. Although humour can often come from a place of sorrow.

'When he was very young we had t-shirts made up which said 'Autistic' in massive letters and then underneath 'and bad parents', just as a kind of a defence.'

---

[81] Arnold-Baker, C. (2019) The Public-Private Paradox: An existential exploration of mothers in society, *Self & Society*, 47, 1, Spring

Enhanced Perspective Taking – seeing your child's viewpoint

When parents develop the skills to understand their child – to really see life from their perspective – this helps on many different levels. I struggled to find a word or phrase that fully encapsulated this ability that so many of the parents I've met demonstrated. The psychological literature on generic parenting often talks about 'mentalisation'[82] to describe the reciprocal mirroring between caregiver and child, but what I'm referring to here is an enhanced perspective taking which helps parents feel empowered, enables them to understand and support their child and has a positive effect on their own wellbeing and self-esteem.

This is more than knowledge. It may begin with training or information (for example, on sensory overload or Makaton) but it grows so parents can then apply what they've learnt to different situations. It includes empathy – both emotional (how our child feels) and cognitive (how they think) – but also develops beyond this into something instinctual. I recognise what mood my son is in just by a noise he makes. We just 'get' what is going on for our child, and in parallel to this gain a greater understanding of our self and others.

I summarise some of the examples of this skill below:

Developed skill	Quote
Deep understanding of your child Including their behaviours and communication.	*'I've found the key to him.'* *'The sensory stuff, like the stimming, I love it, I love when he does it, I find it really calming, it's almost like watching a lot of fish in a pool, back and forward, so he's taught me, he's teaching me.'*
Empowered and competent When you understand your child you can develop a 'plan' of how to support them – in turn you are empowered and feel competent.	*'I think now I've got these skills... I probably step in earlier and make it right quicker, so we're not having the unhappiness and I don't feel as anxious about the unhappiness because I pretty much know I've got more of an idea where it's coming from.'*

---

[82] Fonagy, G., Gergely, G. & Target, M. (2007) The parent-infant dyad and the construction of the subjective self, *Journal of Child Psychology and Psychiatry*, 48, 3-4, 288–328

Seeing through child's eyes	'I would like people to understand that as meaning that he's also as valid as the next person standing and maybe he's more right than the rest of us – he says things as he sees it.'
A new way of looking at things – taking your child's viewpoint and becoming more open to difference.	'[I] almost prefer my son's viewpoint on life, which is why do I have to be in this school play, if it doesn't suit me, and I don't want to dress up and I don't want to be a silly character, why do I have to.'
Confident to question normative assumptions	'They are like fantastic educators themselves, making you realise how you do for other people because it's expected of you, but is it actually the right thing to do?'
Consequently, it makes you stop and question socially accepted automatic 'rules'.	'[I gained] the confidence as a parent to pick and choose my battles so instead of choosing battles that society was telling me were really important, I could focus more on his emotional need... Rather than making him like a parrot to say hello when he meets people.'

Enhanced perspective taking also means parents don't take their child's behaviours personally and they can understand the communication behind them, thereby removing any sense of guilt. Some people can do this naturally whereas for others it's something they need to develop over time.

Research currently being conducted suggests that autistic people are better at empathising with others on the spectrum than those who are neurotypical[83], so this may be a benefit for some parents who are also autistic. Likewise other similarities between parent and child can help parents make sense of their child's behaviour[84].

It is often suggested that autistic people have difficulties with 'theory of mind' (understanding that another's point of view or perspective may be different from their own) yet there can also be a

[83] Crompton, C. (2019) http://www.thinkingautismguide.com/2019/05/the-problem-with-autistic-communication.html

[84] Pakenham, K.I. Sofronoff, K.& Samios, C. (2004) Finding meaning in parenting a child with Asperger syndrome: Correlates of sense making and benefit finding. *Research in Developmental Disabilities*, 25, 245-264

'double empathy'[85] problem where neurotypical people (those without autism) struggle to understand someone with autism. We may need to expand this model to develop a 'theory-of-a-mind-that-is-different-from-our-own' to gain our child's perspective. This is an important part of the up-skilling that parents need to go through in order to understand their child. This enhanced perspective taking can empower parents and improve the parent-child relationship.

I have learnt to understand when my son is able to bear physical touch and when he can't. When he was younger I would automatically go to cuddle him and he would sometimes recoil. It hurt (me emotionally and him physically). Over time I realised that touch involved a sensory overload for him and that it needed to be on his terms. Now when he does reach for me – often touching his fingers to mine – I know this is a deeply felt connection, but to the outside world it may seem distant or strange. I've developed a better ability to put myself in his shoes.

Realising that someone else's perspective is different from our own means we are less likely to confuse our own needs with theirs (i.e. 'does my son want a hug, or do I?'). This can be a transformational realisation and one that is so important for parent carers. We need to constantly check our biases, assumptions and viewpoint as parents and avoid getting psychologically stuck in a rut. It's not possible to undergo this learning unless we adopt a stance of openness and flexibility.

This deep connection reflects the 'I-Thou' relationship to which the philosopher Martin Buber[86] refers (as opposed to an I-It one which treats the other as an object). This involves really trying to understand the other, exactly as they are, and being ok with how they are. It is a true position of other-perspective taking. Adopting this stance is positive in a cognitive sense (knowing or thinking) – we want to know how to respond and have a plan for managing our life – as well as emotionally positive; it feels good to understand and support our child. Which leads nicely onto the next positive area – growing expertise and mastery.

---

[85] Milton, D. (2012) On the Ontological status of autism: the 'double empathy problem', *Disability and Society*, 27, 6, 883-7

[86] Buber, M. (2000) *I and Thou,* (Trans. Ronald Gregor Smith), London: Simon & Schuster

Expertise and Sense of Mastery

Parents can often find the early years overwhelming, with the sudden onslaught of professionals in their life giving advice, designing therapy programmes and sometimes commenting directly on their parenting style. This can be daunting and disheartening and undermines our instinctual knowledge of how to support our child. At times when you do not know the best way to help it can feel disempowering.

When receiving conflicting advice, or even no advice at all, there comes a realisation that we have to make sense of all the different views, competing pressures and practicalities of our own family life to find something that works for *us*. Moreover, parents can benefit from entering their child's world and developing new, improved ways of coping that are personal and individual to each family. This understanding, along with gaining the necessary knowledge and experience, can provide a sense of mastery and confidence which transfers over to other parts of your life. This includes gaining new employment in the field of Special Needs because of increased knowledge. This resonates with my own experience. A parent, having been 'in the trenches' with their own disabled child, often brings an element of authenticity to certain roles that may be lacking from professionals. Although I would not claim to be an expert on another's experience, as everyone is unique, there can be a depth of shared compassion and understanding. A sense of a journey shared.

Trusting your own instincts can enhance a feeling of agency and control which increases self-esteem and self-acceptance. Believing that we have mastery over life's challenges is associated with better psychological and physical health[87].

Diagnosis or having a plan

While diagnosis can be fraught for many, a number of parents reflected that receiving a diagnosis empowered them in the long run and had actually been a 'relief'. They had a label or a map that could provide a useful framework for understanding a child and their differences.

---

[87] Cantwell, J., Muldoon, O. & Gallagher, S. (2014) Social support and mastery influence the association between stress and poor physical health in parents caring for children with developmental disabilities, *Research and Developmental Disabilities*, 35, 2215-2223

It can validate parental concerns, which may have previously been dismissed by others as overly anxious parenting. Sometimes it gives the parent confidence to trust in their own parenting instincts, especially if they have long suspected that their child was finding something challenging. They can feel enabled to seek information, support and understanding from others.

Having a name to describe the child's difficulties can help the whole system around the child adjust and empathise. It may open up avenues of support and resources.

> *'As soon as I had that information the assessment was critical because then I could really focus my energy on one path, which was understanding autism, versus understanding an attachment problem, or a something else.'*

Admittedly, things don't always go to plan, even with a diagnosis; such as Education Health and Care Plans not being adhered to, lack of school places or the challenges that lockdown caused. Even in the face of continuing difficulties, though, the sense of having a direction or framework, however simple or broad-brush it may be, can help.

It is possible to have a plan of how to support your child even without a diagnosis – with the right training, information and knowledge. By having an idea of your child's strengths and areas of development, what the next target is and realising that you are able to support your child can all counter helplessness. It can protect us from depressive symptoms and other mental health issues.

Knowing you've done your best

Another aspect of expertise and mastery is that parents want to feel that they have done their best to support their child.

> *'As long as I know... I opened the doors for him [even] if it doesn't work, then we tried.'*

Learning the system and the language is a large part of this and helps us to advocate for our child.

The future is ever present in the minds of parent carers, and feeling like you are positively contributing to a brighter one for your child can bring a sense of reward and achievement.

> *'[Knowing] that many many many hours of research and reading up and trying to find the information paid off because you know that is actually a skill that I realise I have.'*

These moments of success can validate your efforts and renew enthusiasm and confidence to face future obstacles. It can make you feel confident and good about yourself thereby positively affecting your overall wellbeing.

Inner Strength or Resilience

When we go through adverse experiences, particularly those that test our ability to cope and manage, there can be a renewed sense of strength or resilience. Many parents reflect that they feel more competent to deal with challenges both now and in the future. We recognise that we are stronger despite, or because of, the difficulties we've been through.

> *'I think I've found inner strength I wouldn't have known I had.'*

Having been through difficulties in the past can provide us with experience and strategies to fall back on when we need to get through a new difficulty. Even knowing that we have managed can provide confidence that we will get through.

For some the capacity to cope is experienced as surprising, especially after feeling lost at sea in the early years. The new realisation that they are stronger than they had thought boosts their self-esteem. It can appear paradoxical that we feel more vulnerable, yet stronger. If I could go back to when my son was born I would want to share the hope for the future as a counter to the despair I felt.

Other parent carers told me their experience had made them face their fears. One mum was fearful of using the phone before becoming a parent, which led to developing the confidence she needed. Having to speak in large meetings or public places suddenly becomes a necessity that is achievable on behalf of your child.

'I'm not afraid of public speaking any more.
That was a really big deal for me back then. It's kind
of thinking I could. You know my heart broke but
I got a backbone.'

There may also be a growth of what I referred to earlier as 'family resilience'. This is when the whole family develop positive strategies to adapt to their situation and face any challenges together. Resilience breeds better coping mechanisms and there are benefits to our emotional wellbeing in realising one's capacity to cope.

Motivation or fighting spirit

Realising that our child needs extra support can inspire a strong motivation in us, as parents, bringing new energy and raison d'etre. The sense of purpose to fight and protect them takes us out of our own lives and connects us with something bigger.

'I don't know if it would be different if she'd been born
without disabilities, but she's just such a big motivation
to do everything in life.'

When my son was born I felt that I had been called to the most important cause of my life. To fight and keep on top of the appointments, targets and milestones can provide a sense of achievement, even pride. This drive can see parents through the initial difficult period and ensure that support is put in place via health or social services.

A word of caution

The need to fight for services, resources, as well as understanding from others can sometimes leave parents feeling as if they are forever putting on their armour, preparing to do battle. Resources seem scarce in the health, social and education services and we can be left with the sense that, unless we shout the loudest, or make the most fuss, we will be left without help. Being aggressive rarely achieves the desired ending but the frustrations caused when faced with a flawed system can bring out the worst in us all.

There is a risk of burnout if parents do not maintain some space for their own interests and relationships. Although we may develop new skills of assertiveness and motivation to fight a broken system this isn't always positive.

> *'So the system was wrong. I understood that and took it on. And won. But at great cost.'*

> *'Fighting for the EHCP (Education Health and Care Plan) that period of time, those two years, I think has put a lot of strain on myself, like I really got very sick, stressed... it was a really, really difficult time.'*

Every parent wants the best for their child but at times the move from worrier to 'warrior parent' can be exhausting and detrimental to the whole family. It is a pyrrhic victory if it damages our own wellbeing so ensure you keep some perspective, for example, losing a particular battle but winning a war. We don't always know how things are going to work out so, at times, taking the 'wait and see' position might be helpful. We cannot control everything in life and sometimes the act of letting go can become a challenge in itself. Recognise that we all need time to relax, switch off and just go with the flow. Referring to the image of the scales in Chapter 2, this relates to the 'spare capacity' parents need to keep as back-up. Over time the same motivation and energy you feel in supporting your child may blossom into personal growth for you in other areas of life.

I believe there is sometimes a link between the 'fighting spirit' and parents adopting what I call a 'carer identity'. It is as if their whole existence is taken over by their child's needs and in ensuring they get the support they require. Whilst understandable, this position does not allow for anything else in the parents' life. Use your fighting spirit when you need to but ensure there is a healthy balance of rest and other things in your life to replenish and recharge you. You are a person with interests, opinions and needs of your own – don't overlook them. It is also a skill to recognise when it's worth continuing to fight or work on something and when it's time to step back and take a break. If you feel like this, go for a coffee with a friend, do something different. A technique called temporal distancing involves picturing ourselves in the future looking back at our present. It can help give us perspective even in an uncertain and challenging time.

Putting Things into Perspective

Parents of disabled children are more likely than other parents to have seen their child nearly die, be in pain or go through invasive medical interventions. Upsetting situations will be more common in our lives and, compared to parents of non-disabled children, we can sit on the frontline of life, death and illness. To have been confronted with our own child's mortality or disability upsets the natural order of events and raises issues of our own impermanence and lack of control in life. Attending numerous clinic appointments can be stressful both on an emotional level, as seeing people in hospital who are unwell and infirm can be shocking and upsetting, as well as on a practical level, such as finding parking, co-ordinating appointments and liaising between departments. We will have faced things that most people generally manage to keep at arm's length.

Whilst difficult, these scenarios can make us more aware of what is important in life. Trivialities, such as inconsequential worries (a child not eating their broccoli or making the football team), may be less important to us. Although at times it is testing to hear others' woes, we can have a renewed sense of what is really important in life and appreciation of what we have. Our extraordinary experiences allow us to put things into perspective.

'I no longer sweat the small stuff.'

Change in life priorities or goals may include focusing on parenting or family above other competing demands on our time. For some parents there is a simple gratitude in their child being alive and 'having the opportunity to continue in the role of caregiving'[88] that re-affirms their belief in the preciousness of life. Bonds between family members can be greater and bring families together. We only have one life (maybe?) on this planet so we may as well make the most of what is important and valuable in our existence rather than getting caught up in superficial concerns. This positive outlook creates an upward spiral in our wellbeing.

---

[88] Konrad, S.C. (2006) Posttraumatic growth in mothers of children with acquired disabilities. *Journal of Loss & Trauma*, 11, 101-113, p. 106

Pride and Joy

There can be an immense joy in raising children and that is no different when they have additional needs. The positive effect of a child making you laugh or stop and think are to be relished. When my son told me recently that his aims for life are 'to watch the iPad and walk around 105 times' it made me chuckle and warmed my heart.

Whatever your child's disability, they are still a child to be loved and cherished. It can be all too easy to forget the enjoyable aspects of having a child when we have daily battles and therapeutic programmes to follow. Simple things like taking them to the park, going to a cafe, cuddling up together with a good book are lovely aspects of parenting to soak in and enjoy. It can be all the more poignant for parent carers if there has been a period in your life when you did not think your child would survive or these activities would be possible.

'Celebrate the inchstones'

We experience enormous pride in our child's achievements, however comparatively small, delayed or different they may seem to others. This may be even more pronounced in a disabled child because in the early days we never quite know what our child will manage to master. Expectations may have been lowered by the prognosis given by health professionals, or the diagnosis itself.

> '[I'm] a lot more appreciative of smaller things...
> she learnt recently to put a ball in a hole and it was
> the best thing that I'd ever seen.'

Stopping and recognising how far you and your child have come, even if they don't meet the typical milestones for a child of their age, can be a revelation. Sometimes formal occasions like annual reviews, or a paediatrician's appointment can be useful in reminding us how life has changed over a period of time. It highlights how you and your child's amazing will to live, thrive and survive enables them to achieve things you may not have imagined possible. Even when targets are not achieved they may take on less importance in our overall life context.

Our achievements

Our child's achievements can also affect our own sense of achievement and mastery – that we have been able to support them along the way. This links to other themes in this chapter, such as knowing how to help our child.

> '[At a party] we took some scripts that I gave to people, that people could read the script and talk to her... and we had people talking to her... She hugged one lady and put her head on her shoulder. [I] could weep with joy and just came away feeling wonderful... It's magical actually, it's magical.'

At times when progress can seem slow, it is important to recognise the small steps you have made in endurance, perhaps attending a doctor's appointment without the help of others, getting your point across succinctly in a meeting or having a few hours' break on your own for the first time without feeling guilty. Taking time to stop and recognise these achievements is important as life can move so fast we often miss them. We can be challenged to the cutting edge of our capacity, and to achieve despite this is something to be acknowledged and celebrated.

Re-affirm Beliefs and Values

On a slightly different tangent to gaining a *new* perspective is the re-affirming of beliefs and values that some parent carers experience. At times when our world view or beliefs are shaken by events it can make us reject them, or alternatively make us commit to them with greater vigour.

> 'I've got a great sense of social justice and so on... I guess that runs throughout my life.'

> [The social model of disability knowledge helped] 'because I didn't see her birth and her disability as a disaster.'

Whatever their values are, whether it's 'family', 'helping' or 'being creative', for many parents their commitment to them is strengthened.

Faith

For a number of parent carers their faith had helped them through some difficult times and reduced stress. Their experiences strengthened their belief in, and connection to, the spiritual (whether part of an organised religion or something else).

> *'I have a strong faith and so God gives me daily strength.'*

Sometimes it's the physical presence of community through faith-based provision that helps reduce isolation, for example, groups arranged by local spiritual leaders, as much as faith itself, that is supportive. This was also true for parent carers with no faith who found comfort in the local religious communities such as special needs playgroups and drop-in befriending. This illustrates an important role for local groups in supporting parent carers. However, sadly, many of these groups have struggled through austerity and lockdown.

There are those for whom their belief was shaken, 'who felt let down by God and questioned how God could let bad things happen to children'[89]. However, time may be a relevant factor here and in the long run those who lost their faith may yet return to their beliefs if they are felt to be positive.

There can even be an element of re-affirming who *you* are through your beliefs and values. Reminding ourselves of what is important connects us with something deep inside us.

Skills – transferable across life domains

Many parents use skills from other parts of their life, such as work or hobbies, to help them in their role as a parent carer.

> *'I know how to work the system so that's been a big advantage, so I know if an appointment is cancelled, I know how to go around the system or when to ring the secretary. I know the system...I'm better equipped in that respect.'*

---

[89] Konrad, S. (2006) Posttraumatic growth in mothers of children with acquired disabilities. *Journal of Loss & Trauma*, 11,1, 101-113, p. 108

Although for those who previously worked in the fields of disability they had come to the realisation that theoretical knowledge was not the same as lived experience.

> *'I was a manager in social services and I thought I knew everything about disability and other issues...I thought I knew everything and it was a load of rubbish.'*

Alternatively, new skills gained from the parent carer role, such as problem solving, thinking on your feet and perspective-taking, can also enrich other parts of our life. Our lived experience brings a unique perspective. A father who worked in a predominantly creative work setting reflected how these skills benefited other areas of life.

> *'Generally, the imagination helps with problem solving, because we constantly have to solve problems with him, so every three weeks is a different thing to solve in some respects... it's always lateral thinking.'*

Parent carers become solution focused, using strengths from all aspects of their life, which can create transferable skills. These skills are a positive; yet an interesting area that emerged in my research was how little parent carers were asked to bring their personal experience into their work roles or how rarely parent carers were invited to help develop or deliver services. It was felt that this was a missed opportunity for organisations and services. I'll come back to this in more detail in the chapter on professionals.

Tolerance, Empathy and Patience

> *'She's made me a better person... I think she's the best thing that happened to me. I love her very much.'*

As well as embracing their own child's difference, parents can develop greater tolerance and empathy more generally. In fact, some studies suggest that the more adversity someone has experienced, the more compassion they tend to feel and show to others in their life[90]. In turn,

---

[90] Calhoun, L. & Tedeschi, R. (2010) *Facilitating Posttraumatic Growth: A Clinician's Guide*, Routledge: Oxfordshire

empathy for others can have a positive impact on our own wellbeing, through heightened self-compassion and self-kindness. We can learn to practise what we preach for the benefit of everyone.

'I think I probably have changed in the way that I am very open and aware of difference and disability. You cross paths with people who are just very very different [and] I'd like to think I don't really have a judgement. When my younger kid asks me questions... I'll just try and be inclusive and understanding. He's aware of it more so than other kids because he's got a brother that's disabled.'

Through our own experiences we may advocate for others who find it hard to have a voice. Many parents become campaigners – either locally or more widely – in response to the opening up of their world.

I think parent carers are in a unique position to push the disability rights agenda forward because they straddle both worlds and can help remove the barriers between them.

Patience

A further common development parents express is that of learning patience. On a personal note I was never the most patient of people but I had to learn: patience to see how my child would grow and develop whilst sitting with an excruciating sense of not knowing; patience to wait for numerous appointments and reports from overly busy professionals; patience to know that at times learning a new skill involves multiple repetitions for my son over many months. It's a marathon not a sprint and I have grown in realising this fact. Challenging previously held viewpoints or personality traits is a chance to develop and adapt. This growth can be valuable across all aspects of our life.

Post-traumatic growth

Although many parents of disabled children would not necessarily meet the criteria for post-traumatic stress *disorder*, (although some may) many of them will have experienced an event that 'has a seismic impact on the individual's worldview and emotional functioning'[91].

---

[91] Calhoun, L. & Tedeschi, R. (2010) *Facilitating Posttraumatic Growth: A Clinician's Guide*, Routledge: Oxfordshire, p. 2

Understandably, this can cause high levels of post-traumatic stress. When something shocking happens in life it can shatter our basic, implicit assumptions about life, namely that:

i) 'The world is benevolent' (generally good or kind);

ii) 'The world is meaningful', controllable, predictable and just; and

iii) 'The self is worthy'[92] – we are decent people with the ability to control outcomes.

Our foundations can temporarily disintegrate and require re-adjustment.

There is increasing evidence to show that following a traumatic event, and the associated stress, individuals can also experience post-traumatic growth (PTG). This means that when they reflect on the adverse incident in their life they will report positives (as well as negatives) that have arisen in light of the event. Often it is after some time has passed and once the 'seismic' event has resolved, but it is important personal growth and development nonetheless. In the PTG literature these can include improved and new relationships, greater appreciation of life, better sense of personal strength and spiritual development[93]. These appear relevant to the experiences of many parent carers and to the research I've described throughout this chapter.

Interestingly, those who have experienced the most stress were also more likely to report higher levels of post-traumatic growth[94]. Furthermore, post-traumatic growth can be experienced at the very same time as post-traumatic stress disorder. So it might not always feel like there's been growth at the time but looking back can involve a recognition of how far we have come and all we have learnt.

This does not diminish the difficulties caused by a traumatic or difficult event. Regrettably, PTG is by no means inevitable for everyone. I could find little research looking specifically at the experiences of parents of disabled children in relation to PTG and feel this is an

---

92 Janoff-Bulman, R. (1992) *Shattered Assumptions*, New York: Free Press, p. 6

93 Calhoun, L. & Tedeschi, R. (2010) *Facilitating Posttraumatic Growth: A Clinician's Guide*, Routledge: Oxfordshire

94 Joseph, S. (2013) *What doesn't kill us: a guide to overcoming adversity and moving forward.* London: Piatkus, p. 91

important area for future exploration. In my own research many parents could identify some areas of growth that they accounted directly to the experience of having a disabled child, although not all (at that time).

With regards to parent carers the process is more complex than in other PTG scenarios as there is not always an initial trauma or incident that then resolves itself over time. We may continue to be re-traumatised with new diagnoses, problems and challenges. This is the cumulative or 'small t' trauma which we considered in the previous chapter. Having to re-tell your child's medical story and difficulties numerous times as well as undergoing further interventions can keep the trauma alive and get in the way of any sense of closure or moving forward. One example of how to manage this is a family who typed up the answers to questions asked at every hospital admission and shared this document at Accident and Emergency to avoid having to relive the story.

While some parents may identify growth, for many there were still ongoing worries and concerns, many of which were unlikely to ever resolve. It is not the case that once you identify some aspects of growth everything is fine. As we now know, you may feel positively and negatively about your situation in the very same moment. Even at times of joy a sense of sorrow can be present. Conversely, we may experience pride and sense of purpose at times of great stress. An ability to 'embrace the paradox'[95] that our situation evokes in us reflects a wisdom and growth which can flourish throughout our life. These are also skills we can role model for our children.

Conclusion

What makes us unique and human is often encapsulated by the narrative we tell ourselves. When we face a difficult event our life story can become ruptured, thereby affecting our sense of identity and where we fit in the world. We need to create a new narrative that incorporates these changes in order to re-balance our wellbeing and sense of self. Other people help us to make sense of our life, including recognising that even though life may be different from how we imagined, we are not necessarily worse off.

---

[95] Larson, E. (1998) Reframing the meaning of disability to families: The embrace of paradox, *Social Science and Medicine*, 47, 7, 865-875, p. 865

For individuals and families who can develop new skills, make meaning and identify positives from their experiences, even those events which are traumatic and challenging, post-traumatic growth may be possible. Part of attaining and maintaining emotional wellbeing as a parent carer is reconnecting with who you were before you became the parent of a disabled child. Another part is developing a new sense of self that incorporates your experiences.

Trauma literature often refers to the Japanese tradition of kintsugi where broken pottery is glued together using gold. The vase is not the same as it once was but it is more interesting and unique because of what it has been through. For some parent carers this analogy is powerful and helpful. The idea also connects to the sense of purpose and meaning we bring to our life experiences which will be the focus of our final chapter.

In this chapter we've looked at the positive emotional change that parent carers report. This development often appears to be supported or enhanced by positive other people. The next two chapters will look at how others can help, and hinder, our wellbeing.

Key points

- The majority of families report positives in relation to parenting a disabled child including putting things into perspective and appreciating what is really important in life

- For some, they develop greater acceptance and assertiveness

- Many develop an Enhanced Perspective Taking - seeing your child's viewpoint as well as increased expertise and sense of mastery

- Your child can be a source of huge pride and joy as well as motivation to fight for services and social change

- Parents may recognise an increased inner strength or resilience as well as gaining new skills which they can apply to other areas of their life

- Parenting a disabled child can re-affirm our beliefs and ideals as well as developing greater humanitarian values such as tolerance and empathy

- Some parents may experience post-traumatic growth as well as stress

- It is not the case that once you identify some aspects of growth everything is fine. You may feel positively and negatively about your situation in the very same moment

Part 3

What Helps (and Hinders) Your Emotional Wellbeing

6

Relationships: Child, Partner, Family, Friends, Special Needs Community

'I always think of it as like a triangle in terms of my relationship with my husband, my family and my closest friends and that kind of unit I've always got and nothing shakes any of those things... I can cope with anything else because I know that that solid unit, no matter what happens above it, no matter what happens in the real world and all the things we have to deal with, all the hospital visits, all the practicalities, the logistics, all of that stuff, I can deal with that, as long as I know that this unit at the bottom is solid.'

We are social creatures and as well as time for ourselves we also need others in our life. People who provide understanding, connection and belonging are vital for our emotional wellbeing. This connection and support may come from family, friends or wider community networks. It can also come from professionals and services who support us and we'll reflect more on this (and the qualities required) in the next chapter.

Family emotions are multi-directional, in that if our child is happy then we are more likely to feel that way too. And vice versa. It is helpful to think of it as an inter-connected system reflected in the well-known saying that we are only ever as happy as our unhappiest child.

The network of people around you will also be affected by your experiences – including being a parent of a disabled child. They may respond in different ways – some helpful, some less so. They may share your journey towards acceptance or growth. However, the pace at which people adapt can differ and will not always keep up with your own path. This is the trade-off of connection – relationships can harm as well as heal.

Parents commonly describe how friends and family can respond in strikingly contrasting ways. There are people who 'get it' and know how to offer constructive, compassionate and open support (e.g. asking what you need and giving you space to make sense of what is happening). There are others who withdraw, deny there is a problem and sometimes attach blame. Some people find it difficult to know what to say, in the same way that there is an awkwardness when someone has been bereaved. Sometimes friends do not realise how different life may be for you now and it can be helpful to be explicit about what you need from others. Feeling connected to others banishes loneliness. Without these connections we can become isolated.

It is useful to stop and notice how those around us leave us feeling. Positive others mean surrounding yourself with people who understand you and have your best interest at heart. People who help you when you need it and also turn to you in a reciprocal relationship. Social prescribing is something that the National Health Service (NHS) now offers to patients. And the importance of 'social capital' is increasingly acknowledged – that is the network of relationships you have around you with shared identity and values.

Nurturing our connections, taking part in joint enjoyable activities and providing the chance to talk to someone about aspects of our life, particularly challenges or upsets, can help us regain our balance. A problem shared can often feel like a problem halved. Talking to trusted others can be a more successful treatment of depression than prescription drugs for some. There is something therapeutic about offloading our concerns, as if the other person helps carry the load.

Saying the words often helps us to find a solution or a different way of looking at a difficulty, for example after an upsetting hospital appointment or school meeting about your child.

'It's just getting it out there and just saying, these are
all the things that are happening, because what
I generally find is... you can almost talk yourself into
a solution when you're talking.'

Even writing down your thoughts and feelings or using images can be helpful and we'll look at this in more detail in Chapter 8 and Appendix I.

Belonging to a Group

Belonging to a group or community is consistently shown to improve emotional wellbeing. This has been particularly clear during coronavirus as we have seen the importance of remaining socially connected, despite physical distancing.

Being part of a group can not only provide a sense of identity and belonging, it is also associated with better physical health[96]. It really is a social cure. As Paul Gilbert, the psychologist who developed Compassion Focused Therapy, states:

> 'Our physiological systems, our cardiovascular and immune systems, flourish best when people feel loved, cared for and have a sense of belonging, and when they themselves are being loving and caring to self and others'[97].

Finding your group isn't just about 'showing up' though: it needs to become part of our self-concept – who we are – to gain the full benefits[98]. It is also suggested that being identified with a group 'proves to be protective of health even when the group in question is the target of discrimination and prejudice'[99] as we can use the resources of the group to provide support.

Our sense of self is shaped by the groups to which we belong. Hearing others speak about their experiences, be it successes or failures, including learning and ways of making sense of their life, can impact our own understanding and allow us to create a new narrative about our own experiences. There can be a self-fulfilling

[96] Cantwell, J., Muldoon, O. & Gallagher, S. (2014) Social support and mastery influence the association between stress and poor physical health in parents caring for children with developmental disabilities, *Research and Developmental Disabilities*, 35, 2215-222, p. 2216

[97] Gilbert, P. (2018) Compassion is an antidote to cruelty, *The Psychologist*, February 2018, p. 37

[98] Cruwys, T. (2018) How groups beat depression, *The Psychologist*, May 2018 p. 42

[99] Jetten, J. (2018) Reversing the social curse, *The Psychologist*, May 2018, p. 34

benefit to this, for example, if you identify as a 'carer' it may increase your awareness of what support is out there and your rights within the broader community.

Unfortunately, though, some people withdraw from others at times of need which can worsen the sense of isolation. And loneliness can be deadly.

In this chapter, before I look at the different types of relationships in our lives, I want to dig down a little deeper into some of the psychological aspects of our relationship with others. Highlighting some of the potential pitfalls and unhealthy patterns we can fall into can hopefully make us more aware of what relationships help – and hinder – our wellbeing. In particular, we should be aware of issues of:

- quality not quantity;

- social comparison;

- not everyone goes through the same process or at the same time as you; and,

- coping styles.

Quality not quantity

It is not necessarily the amount of parental support that helps, rather it is the *quality* (e.g. 'someone really understands me and my family situation'). In particular perceiving[100] the support as helpful, reciprocal and consistent can be most beneficial to our wellbeing; suggesting that what we find supportive is personal rather than a one-size-fits-all approach.

We know that parent carers often report friends that don't 'get it' or even break off the friendship after we've had a disabled child. These are not people we want in our lives. It's useful to recognise that things change over time though and previous support may wax and wane as friends experience their own life upheavals such as the death of grandparents, families dealing with their own teenagers and challenges, or moving house. At these times you may need to 'top up' from other sources of support.

---

[100] White, N. & Hastings, R.P. (2004) Social and Professional Support for Parents of Adolescents with Severe Intellectual Disabilities, *Journal of Applied Research in Intellectual Disabilities*, 17,181-190, p. 187

Social comparison[101]

Understanding the dynamics between people can provide a chance to step back a bit and notice interactions and relationships that develop. Psychologists talk about upward and downward social comparison. Upward means comparing to others who have more of something that we deem desirable, sometimes thought to inspire us to achieve great things or aim higher. Downward social comparison is comparing to someone less fortunate than ourselves in order to appreciate what we have.

Although some generic wellbeing studies show that there can be a benefit for both of these types of comparison (at a given time and place), in my own research this did not seem to be helpful for parent carers.

Let's look at upward social comparison first. Obviously there's a personal element to what would be considered desirable but a common example was when parent carers compared to other neurotypical, non-disabled families, which I suspect ties into an idealised image of the perfect family that we are sold via social media, adverts and stories. Participating in this type of comparison did not leave them feeling good.

> *'Social media sometimes as a parent carer is just torture.*
> *All these families doing normal things that just aren't*
> *possible it can drive you insane and isn't really helpful.*
> *Having a bit of a break away from it is really helpful.*
> *I think just seeing other people's lives and you know all*
> *the things that they can do with such ease. I think it's*
> *jealousy more than anything that my life sometimes*
> *isn't so simple and I can't just go and take the kids to*
> *the cinema, because she wouldn't sit through a film*
> *or we can't just go out for dinner because her diet's so*
> *restricted. I think it's comparing isn't it a lot.'*

Seeing what others can manage in their lives doesn't always have an inspirational affect. Similarly, comparing to those less well-off didn't really make parent carers feel good either.

---

[101] Festinger, L. (1954). A Theory of Social Comparison Processes. *Human Relations (New York)*, 7, 2, 117–140

*'I know there are parents who have much harder tougher
life and I have friends who have life-threatening conditions,
their children... then I think well why am I complaining, but
then it... doesn't help me. I just put it in a different kind
of perspective. It doesn't help me, 'oh they are worse off,
that's good for me', it doesn't no. It just makes me more
sad for them that they have to go through that.'*

At times the use of comparison can feel hurtful when used by
professionals to justify why we don't meet the criteria for services.

*'I even said to one of the Social Workers that came [and]
assessed him... I said, you come to my house and trying
to be supportive and tell me there is someone worse, it's
really not helping me... I'm sorry for everyone else, but I
have this situation and it's really difficult for me.'*

There are better ways of getting the message across that does not
dismiss the parents' own needs and difficulties. Attempts to categorise
disabilities by severity are fraught with difficulties. There is only what
is the most challenging to us and society at that given point in time.
This is changeable and malleable.

While it is not always possible to remove our tendency to
compare, it can help to focus on the personal positives that you've
gained and developed over time both in yourself and for the whole
family. Comparing to an earlier version of yourself or your family
rather than being overly concerned with others. People often report
a new perspective on life and the burgeoning mastery and unique
skills that our experience gives us. Often finding our own tribe of
other parents of Special Needs families can be supportive.

Many parents of non-disabled children also feel a sense of
parenthood being different from how they had imagined it because of
the false images that are presented in society[102]. It can help to realise
that no family is perfect; all families have their stresses, challenges
and differences. Despite the image we are presented with from others
and the selective things people share with others (often hiding the
less-than-perfect side of life), family life is full of chaos, uncertainty

---

[102] Arnold-Baker, C. (2019) The Process of Becoming: Maternal Identity in the
Transition to Motherhood, *Existential Analysis*, 30.2, p. 260-274

and unpredictability. In no way am I denying the toll of additional demands of special needs parenting; I merely wish to recognise and remember that we never fully know what others' family life is like when we are only given a snapshot.

If you are finding that comparisons, particularly on social media, are becoming harmful for you, take a few moments to reflect on the following:

> When you're feeling not so good and you look at someone's posts what effect does it have on you?
>
> Are there certain accounts that have a particularly negative effect on how you feel about your life?
>
> How do you usually present yourself or your life on social media?
>
> If you're feeling sensitive what could you do instead of going on social media?

There is another dimension of comparison, what I'm calling sideways comparison as opposed to upward or downward – that is, seeing that others are in the same boat as you (or at least in the same storm). This is shown to be highly helpful for parent carers. We want to connect with others who understand our situation and can provide us with a sense of belonging.

Our situations will never be exactly the same but we may find precious pockets of understanding. It can take time to find exactly where you belong and in what group but it's worth persevering to find them. What this group looks like and how it supports you may change over time rather than staying static. And you may need different things on different days.

Not everyone goes through the same process or at the same time as you

Of course the difficulty is that, while we may go through the process of adapting to our new world, this is not always the case for those around us. This can cause a sense of disconnect and pain.

'One of the hardest things is family support or lack of...
it's quite isolating from that perspective and one side
particularly don't get [our daughter] at all, they seem to
view her like she's a piece of furniture we carry around
with us, they don't engage with her.'

For some this is a cause of difficulty whereas for others there may be a sense of accepting that different people bring different things to our relationships – for example, friends who aren't very good at supporting your child, but still offer you something in your personal life.

'My best friend [is] just really not good and I could take
offence to that and think well you're a useless friend,
but you know what, people have got their own lives and
maybe I would have been just as crap if she'd have had the
disabled child, actually, put us both together, you know,
for a pub lunch, and we're screaming and hooting with
laughter, so I am allowed to be me and I am allowed to
have friends. I think it's better to be more forgiving and
keep some of your past with you.'

People can respond in countless ways. Just because someone doesn't respond in a similar way to you does not necessarily mean they are not affected or that they care any less. And for some it can be so unbearably painful that they take a path of denying or ignoring the situation. It can be helpful to be aware of some of the different styles of coping and see if this makes sense for those around you.

Coping styles

In response to an unexpected event, some people may focus on activities and problem solving. It enables them to take back an element of control and feel like they are doing something useful; it may also lead to a reluctance to talk about what they are going through. For these people thinking is prioritised over feeling whereas, for those who fall into the latter camp, they may need to talk about their emotional responses in depth. These styles have sometimes been referred to as problem-focused coping as opposed to emotion-focused coping[103],

---

[103] Joseph, S. (2011) *What doesn't kill us: A guide to overcoming adversity and moving forward*, Piatkus: London

although it is overly simplistic to state we only access one or the other (or that they are mutually exclusive) – most people use a mix of both. Traditionally assumptions have been made about problem-focused coping being a typically male response, and emotion-focused coping being predominantly female. It's useful to remain open-minded about this generalisation[104] in part because it may be the role that requires a certain type of coping rather than who does it. In fact research is increasingly showing that coping is personal, multidimensional and multifunctional[105]; in other words people use different strategies dependent on the situation (when and where).

There is also the spectrum of introverted people, those who are more private and need quiet time before being ready to talk (or who will only talk to a small group of people), and extroverts, who seek out support and talk to other people in order to identify how they feel. People need time and space to process what at first seems unfathomable. This may mean they need time on their own making or sourcing something practical for their child to use or they may need to discuss the same thing many times before being able to move on. These are both ways of making sense of something that we find confusing or shocking.

It is useful to bear in mind that at times of high stress we often rely on less effective coping strategies – alcohol or drugs (legal and illegal), social withdrawal or neglecting our basic needs such as eating well, exercising and getting enough sleep. These will make us more vulnerable to mental health problems. They're also only a sticking plaster providing a short term answer to a greater obstacle that needs to be faced.

The majority of parents report their relationships changing. Partner, family and friends are affected and it may be that your resources are so taken up with your child that there isn't much left over for anyone else. Friendships may fall away and new ones develop. Relationships can be tested and even split under the pressure, but others may flourish in the joint venture of parenthood. Family may

---

[104] Spendelow, J. (2019) Who says men can't cope with emotions?, *Therapy Today*, 30, 5, pp. 26-29

[105] Skinner, E.A., Edge, K., Altman, J. & Sherwood, H. (2003) Searching for the Structure of Coping: A Review and Critique of Category Systems for Classifying Ways of Coping, *Psychological Bulletin*, American Psychological Association, 129, 2, 216-269, p. 217

be your greatest support or add to your burden. The relationship with your child is also key and can affect your wellbeing on many levels. Take time to reflect on each of these – ensuring there is balance across and within these different relational dimensions.

This chapter therefore looks at the P – 'Positive Others' – in the SPECTRA of parent carer wellbeing as well as the C – 'Child' – to which we will turn first.

Your Child

One of the strongest themes expressed by all the parents I have met is their absolute love for their child. These parents have an unconditional commitment to try their best for their child even when there are challenges. Having a positive view of your child also supports your own wellbeing[106].

> *'My son, I love, I'm always going to love, difficult as it can be sometimes.'*

> *'It was like me and her, versus the world... I talked to her so much... it was like this sort of ridiculous bond.'*

Often parent carers require a safe space to voice their difficulties (particularly a current battle or challenge) before naturally coming round to an expression of love for their child. This beautifully illustrates the arc of the parent carer path – we need to be allowed to process the negatives to get to the positives. If we're not allowed to share our difficult narratives or worries it can hang over us like a toxic fog. If you are finding it hard to relate positively to your child it may be due to stress or overwhelm and it is important to find support enabling you to have a break. Training and gaining information to help understand your child can help you connect. Your relationship is important (for both of you) and worth nurturing. If you feel you need to talk to someone about this, support such as talking therapies may help.

In general, if your child is having a good day, so are you. Yet it is healthy to have other relationships in your life that nourish you as well.

---

[106] Pepperell, T.A., Paynter, J. & Gilmore, L. (2018) Social support and coping strategies of parents raising a child with autism spectrum disorder, *Early Child Development and Care*, 188, 10, 1392-1404, p. 1398

No parent should be totally reliant on their child for their own wellbeing as we are separate beings. In the same way, our child shouldn't be totally reliant on us as they grow into adulthood, as there will come a time when we are no longer around. They need other things in their life, just as we do.

One particular study suggested that how much we personally identify with our child's condition can also influence how much our mental health is affected (negatively). Those who perceived more overlap between their own identity and their child reported more symptoms of depression and higher stress[107]. Maintaining your own sense of self that is separate from your child is key for your emotional wellbeing. The parent carers with the most well-rounded wellbeing are those who, along with a positive relationship with their child, have other important connections in their life, whether it's family, friends, partner or a special needs network.

Time and Reorienting

When your child is first diagnosed it may involve a period of adaptation and learning; I refer to this as reorienting. You may have moments of overwhelm and confusion. I had days when I didn't have a clue what my son needed and it left me feeling useless. I held onto my unrealistic and rather rigid view of what being a mother was for a long time. Gradually I realised it needed a radical overhaul as the things I was doing and the ways I was trying to make sense of my son and my prior beliefs about parenthood were all being overturned whether I liked it or not. It was a revolution in my mental image of motherhood and I know that many parents go through this transformation.

An area of learning for me concerned birthday parties and I wish I had realised earlier on who I was actually arranging his party for. I had some 'model' in my head that children like birthday parties and therefore being a good mother entailed me organising this annual event.

Over a couple of years my son had become quite irritable around the time of his birthday. I had spent a lot of time considering what type of party might be possible for a small group of his classmates, realising that each of them would have particular needs. We settled on bowling

---

[107] O'Brien, M. (2007) Ambiguous Loss in Families of Children With Autism Spectrum Disorders, *Family Relations*, 56, 135-146, p. 143

as I know that his special school had arranged this a few times and I carefully chose the party bag items to include sensory toys and no balloons (as his closest friend disliked them). However, after a couple of years of this it became clear that our son would enjoy the first half of the party and then become increasingly unhappy and on edge. As his communication improved he told us he did not want a party. I thought this might be a throwaway comment but he became adamant in his request. As the day of his latest birthday approached (where we had not arranged a party) he said, 'I'm happy about my birthday because I'm not having a party.' I was quite dumbfounded. Delighted that he'd been able to tell me his wants so clearly, but disappointed in myself that I hadn't realised it until now.

As we've seen in the previous chapter, parents who develop an enhanced perspective taking that allows them to really know, understand and accept their child can better support them.

There is inevitably a mutual influence between parent and child. The quality of this connection, our very precious relationship, is so rich and important. Our child will have to come to terms with their own disability and learn to live in this world exactly as it is – and will look to us for guidance on this. Role modelling standing up for yourself, expecting life to be inclusive, as well as managing our own wellbeing and stress levels will all show our children how to *be*.

Partner or Spouse

Although there is a slight increase in the risk of parents of disabled children splitting up (compared with other parents), this is by no means inevitable. Many report a strengthening of their relationship following a crisis.

Relationships are complex, and added factors, such as exhaustion, lack of support or even coordinating work and numerous medical and therapy appointments can increase stress.

> *'Since his diagnosis his mother and I have divorced,
> but not because of his needs or disability, simply
> because of long term problems in the relationship.
> However, those problems were refracted through the
> difficulties we had in agreeing about the best ways to
> support our son. It's complicated.'*

One of the key strains on relationships and the mental health of parents is a lack of practical support, such as short breaks and benefits. Being aware of 'passporting' benefits, such as if a child receives Disability Living Allowance (DLA) the parents may be entitled to Carer's Allowance, can help with financial pressures. The Disabled Children's Partnership report that 64% of separated parents of disabled children say a lack of support had a major impact on the breakdown of their relationship. Parents need clear, accessible information on what help is available and they need to find support from other people in order to avoid isolation.

There may be a greater number of 'distressed' relationships (34%) compared to other parents (26%)[108] but couples can help by having greater self-disclosure and sharing with one another how they feel. Your relationship can become closer which, in turn, reduces levels of stress.

'I completely understand, and he completely understands, because we're the only ones that do, really. Because they are doing what you're doing, they're the only other person doing that.'

Parenting can be hard (as well as rewarding)

Becoming a parent is always life changing and it has been suggested that parents have lower levels of emotional wellbeing than those without children[109]. If there are additional issues to consider it can reach breaking point if a relationship is already on rocky ground.

All couples have periods of strength and challenge as no relationship stays the same forever. It is the ability to adapt and change to new circumstances that can provide a buffer against adversity. Parents need to work together in terms of how they see, support and understand their child. This includes recognising when each of you brings something different to the relationship.

---

[108] Relate, Relationships Scotland & Mencap (2017) *Under Pressure: The relationships of UK parents who have a child with a learning disability,* https://www.relate.org.uk/policy-campaigns/publications/under-pressure-relationships-uk-parents-who-have-child-learning-disability

[109] Glass, J., Simon, R.W. and Andersson, M.A. (2016) Parenthood and Happiness: Effects of Work-Family Reconciliation Policies in 22 OECD Countries 1, *American Journal of Sociology.* University of Chicago Press, 122, 3, pp. 886–929

*'I think [partner] has a better instinctive grasp of it...
because he's naturally an introvert and I'm naturally
an extrovert, so our thought patterns are quite different
anyway, so he tunes in to how she's feeling when she's
feeling socially overloaded.'*

It may be that you take on a 'tag team' kind of approach and this can work well, or feel unfair, depending on what has been agreed and how far either parent feels understood and their needs recognised. Often there are discrepancies and these can be worked on but at times they become insurmountable.

Affect one another

What is clear is that partners have an impact on one another – in negative and positive ways. For example, if one person is depressed it increases the stress on their partner[110]. Conversely, both parents taking an active role in caregiving can improve mental wellbeing in the whole family unit. It is a dynamic system. There may be times when we don't wish to overload our partner, to protect them, which means it's even more important that we find other people to talk to.

*'I could talk to [partner] about any other problems
[but with daughter with special needs] it's different,
because he worries so much more about her as
well, that I'm just a bit more conscious of what
I bring to him and what I don't in terms of what
I'm worrying about.'*

A partner also brings unique aspects to the relationship (as we all do) – personality, upbringing, beliefs about parenthood, even their own diagnosis, learning or emotional needs. These bring new factors to the relationship that need consideration.

---

[110] Hastings R.P., Kovshoff, H., Ward, N.J., Espinosa, F.D., Brown, T. & Remington, B. (2005) Systems analysis of stress and positive perceptions in mothers and fathers of pre-school children with autism, *Journal of Autism and Developmental Disorders*, 35, 5, 635-644

Traditional roles

There is still a tendency in our society for mothers to take on the traditional caring role and fathers to focus more on 'providing' for the family. Of course this is not the case in all families but remains the dominant dynamic for now. It can be useful to discuss with your partner what you see as your roles, as working together as a team is the best way to assuage the extra pressures.

Particular difficulties may be more associated with the role rather than who does it – including the 'absence of employment and an alternative role to being the parent of a child with autism'[111]. Going to work may provide an outlet and an ability to re-engage with who you are as a person besides being 'a carer' or 'a parent'. Conversely, pressures of work and feeling you need to 'provide' can cause stress in families and the provider may feel unappreciated. There is little research that focuses specifically on fathers and their coping mechanisms[112]. Those that do exist suggest that fathers may find it particularly hard to find support and talk to others, and many have expressed frustration with the lack of father specific services[113].

Other research suggests that having a sense of control was more of a protective factor against depression for mothers than fathers but the authors felt this could be because mothers' 'greater interactions with the health care system may make them more vulnerable to feelings of helplessness and subsequent depressive symptoms'[114].

In my personal situation, reflected in other parents I have spoken to, I found that I was always slightly ahead of my partner in coming to terms with our son's disability or dealing with a current challenge.

[111] Gray (2002) Ten years on: a longitudinal study of families of children with autism, *Journal of Intellectual and Developmental Disability*, 27, 3, 215-222, p. 218

[112] Langley, E., Totsika, V., & Hastings, R.P. (2020) Psychological well-being of fathers with and without a child with intellectual disability: a population-based study, *Journal of Intellectual Disability Research*, 64, 6, 399-413.

[113] Seymour, M., Giallo, R., & Wood, C.E. (2020) Perceptions of social support: comparisons between fathers of children with autism spectrum disorder and fathers of children without developmental disabilities. *Journal of Intellectual Disability Research*, 64, 6, 414-425

[114] Smith, A.M. & Grzywacz, J.G. (2014) Health and Well-being in Midlife Parents of Children with Special Health Needs, *Families, Systems & Health*, Vol. 32, 3, 303-312, p. 308

My husband was busy with a full-time, demanding job and because I was the person attending appointments and dealing with school, the difficulties would hit me quicker and sooner than him. At times I felt he was around one to two years behind my own process. As our son has grown older our stance and acceptance of family life has corresponded more closely and there is something extremely beneficial in a more harmonious viewpoint and approach. For some couples who are in dissimilar places in terms of making sense of their situation, seeing their partner react in different, and sometimes incomprehensible, ways can cause a distance in their relationship. If one parent is in denial and the other has to deal with the appointments and challenges, this inevitably becomes a source of tension. Hopefully by being aware of different coping styles, partners can learn to support each other with more compassion and understanding.

Every relationship is different, every person unique. The important thing is to try to keep lines of communication open between you and make time for your relationship. Sharing your feelings, expectations and struggles can allow a more open conversation to take place. Sometimes this opens up the very different perspectives people bring to relationships as well as to parenting. At least by talking about it you have a chance to make some changes. Talking about how you feel, using 'I feel' rather than 'you make me feel' language may allow a greater understanding without it seeming like a criticism. There may be particular times when support for one another is most crucial, such as around birth, periods of transition or high demands of medical appointments. Certain things can exacerbate our ability to cope and it may be personal to you what is most taxing.

For some families the division of labour can lead to a natural path of spending less time together. It may be even more important in these situations that you get some time with one another, to re-connect as a couple.

> *'And so we started to divide. It was kind of my wife does things for my daughter. I start doing things for my son.'*

Unfortunately, at other times the relationship itself becomes a source of tension, and difficulties may become unresolvable.

Single Parents

Contact found that 32% of families with disabled children were single parent families, compared with 25% of families with non-disabled children. Parenting predominantly on your own brings up unique challenges.

For single parents it is vital to find support from others, be it family members or friends. Often other significant relationships become more important in coping with family life and finding other people in a similar situation can be really valuable. Recognise the greater strain you are bearing and make sure you give yourself the time off that you need to re-charge your batteries. Some demands on your time will have to be prioritised and other things left undone or unfinished.

It is not always negative: some single parents report feeling happier on their own as they have more control over what happens with their child; how to support and care for them; as well as being clearer about their own needs and how to meet these. It all depends on the level of support from your social network and statutory services.

In recognising this I'm not undermining the enormous pressure parents are under. Being the sole person responsible for all aspects of your child's care is tough. Having fewer opportunities to hand over caring duties, change a nappy, or put a child to bed, can be draining and exhausting. Even missing out on the chance to talk through difficult decisions or events throughout the day can be hard.

Finding groups or other single parents can help. Even a professional in a key worker role may be able to take on some responsibilities. It may be that bit harder work to find the positive others (professional or friend) but if you manage it (and most do), it can be a lot less stressful than sharing your life with someone who is not compatible with you. A negative relationship can be very detrimental to your wellbeing and the family as a whole.

There are organisations that provide support for single parents, including those with disabled children. *Gingerbread* provides information and advice as well as local support groups (details in Appendix III).

Step-parents

If you embark on a new relationship this can also bring up unique issues. It may be difficult to meet a new partner; there can be discrepancies over understanding the child and their additional needs as well as different views on bringing up children. It can take time for the bond to develop between child and step-parent. This is the case in any relationship but can be exacerbated for those with additional needs, particularly if there are issues with communication or social understanding.

'It's caused so much heartbreak... this continuous miscommunication.'

If there are difficulties with the step-parent and child relationship then the parent carer will take on more to avoid overloading the step-parent. It can be hard if your partner does not fully 'get' the child's needs, particularly if the relationship is fairly new. Likewise, it can be hard for the new step-parent to be fully included in a close bond between biological parent and child. This can feel de-skilling and like you're playing catch-up. The whole bonding process for the new blended family can be up and down and take time and effort. It is possible, though, to work through and create a wonderful new unit full of love and strength.

Same Sex Partners

Different variables will also potentially create additional tensions. For same sex partners there are very specific challenges – for example, external stigma, judgement and misunderstanding – that already require careful management. As one parent said to me, *'there is no guidebook for same sex partners and having a disabled child'.* Particularly when the child is an infant, same sex couples often seem to experience similar splits as heterosexual ones where one parent takes more of a carer role and the other more of a provider role. The process of becoming parents can be more emotionally taxing, for example, adoption, in vitro fertilisation (IVF), choosing a donor or a surrogate, and if roles don't play out as envisaged this can exacerbate tensions around who carries the greatest emotional and practical burden of caring and requires communication to support one another. One parent carer shared her views.

'The lack of a "guidebook" may enable these families to construct strategies free of typical societal gender expectations that better suit individual strengths, however, same-sex families may feel additional scrutiny from their communities and the media which can hold negative assumptions and portray "rainbow families" as somehow dangerous for children both morally and physically. This pressure leads to these families feeling as though they have to work harder to prove that their children are capable of being just as safe, happy and loved as children raised in heterosexual families. Often these families may be the only example of such a family in their neighbourhood and this adds a pressure to be a "good example" to help challenge those negative assumptions. If the child is disabled, depending on where they live they may need to cope with additional overt comments that somehow the parents have caused the disability "Is it because they don't have a mother or a father?" "Is it a punishment from a God?" The suggestion being that they did the conception process 'wrong' somehow. This is difficult to write but these views exist. For same sex couples this constant scrutiny adds to the existing mountain of self-doubt that first-time parents often experience, but sadly can be another barrier in seeking support "Will the doctor make these assumptions about my family?".'

Conversely if parents have already had to find ways to live 'openly' despite discrimination and bigotry, it may be that they are better equipped to then also challenge ableist narratives. As with all forms of discrimination, these issues may be compounded if the parents are disabled themselves, experience pay inequality or are from Black, Asian or minority ethnic groups.

Siblings

Often, the impact on siblings is of great concern to parents. This is an understandable reaction. When a new child comes along there is always some adjustment within the family. It may be more so when a child has additional needs, but not always as much as parents worry or in the way that we think. There are also things we can do to mitigate additional stress. For so many special needs families, though, siblings just muddle along, as in any family, and it 'just works'.

The charity Sibs, which supports brothers and sisters of disabled children and adults (link in Appendix III), state that there are an estimated 1.7 million adult siblings in the UK who have grown up with a disabled brother or sister. The ways in which siblings can both be affected by *and* affect the family vary enormously. Acknowledging the overly simplistic terminology of positives and negatives (as already highlighted in relation to parents), many parents I spoke to recognised that siblings developed a unique understanding of their disabled brother or sister and greater awareness of difference and disability issues than in other families.

> *'Sometimes my [disabled daughter's] needs have to be responded to immediately and she's not capable of waiting in the same way as I will make [sibling] wait, I'll be like, no, you have to wait for a minute and then I will deal with your Lego crisis because the crisis is... she's pulling her feeding tube out.'*

However, there can be difficulties when siblings' needs consistently come second to that of another person: Sibs state, 'They are vulnerable to isolation and are at risk of anxiety and depression.'

Siblings may feel angry or embarrassed about their brother or sister and it can restrict family activities. They may also witness bullying and judgement towards their disabled sibling and this can be very confusing and distressing. It requires an adult to explain the scenario (however upsetting we may find this) and acknowledge that discrimination and prejudice does exist in this world.

Some siblings also experience guilt over what is happening to their disabled brother or sister and may be concerned the same things can happen to them. Sleep, space or peace and quiet (e.g. to do homework) may all be impacted and, if these problems can't all be solved, they must at least be acknowledged and validated.

From conversations I've had with many parent carers, though, it doesn't seem inevitable that the impact on siblings is always negative.

> *'His siblings have learnt so much and become such tolerant and accepting individuals.'*

The Sibs e-book 'Self-care for siblings' highlights the many positives that adult siblings also report (if they were given enough support):

> 'I thought, there were absolutely no positives to being a sibling, it's all been an overwhelmingly negative experience.

But when I thought about it a bit more, I had to admit that it has probably made me a "better"'' person in some ways; I am more empathic, more open minded and accepting, and more aware that other people have hidden problems too, than I would have been otherwise.' – Sibling

Other examples included:

- Having a strong and meaningful bond with your brother or sister that others can't relate to

- Being the one who 'just knows' your brother or sister best, and who is able to communicate with them like no one else can

- Becoming closer with other family members as a result of the challenges you've faced and how you've overcome them together

- Sharing humour with your family about some of your unusual experiences together

- Having a deep insight into the lives of disabled people and using this to campaign for, and influence, service provision

- Having a deep insight into the human condition and empathy with others[115]

Acknowledging that there are positives does not remove the possibility that there have been times of difficulty.

> *'My wife spent quite a long time making a chocolate cake with my daughter, came in to let the icing set, and by that time he'd got in the kitchen, got hold of the chocolate cake and thrown most of it at the ceiling, the rest of it on the walls, the rest of it all over him. Destroy, destroy, destroy, any time my daughter did a really nice drawing, she'd turn around 'look at my drawing', you'd turn around and it had gone.'*

---

[115] Sibs, (2020) Self-care for siblings. An e-book for adult siblings in the UK who have grown up with a disabled brother or sister, p. 8

There is a potentially greater risk of family conflict and parents being on the brink of exhaustion. The risk of trauma – when you've be in direct contact with something threatening, such as being hit or punched by your sibling – may also be elevated. It can be traumatic to witness distressing things, such as seeing your sibling hurt themselves, and siblings may also experience secondary trauma when their disabled brother or sister goes through something upsetting, such as abuse in care. All of this can have a traumatic impact on the family's mental health.

Talk about it

The key, as Frances Danylec, Sibs Development Officer for Adult Siblings, states, is to talk about it with your children:

'The absolute best thing parents can do for their sibling son or daughter, is to talk about things. Just to involve the sibling in the conversation. Ask them how they're feeling, ask them what it's like for them, acknowledge it, and keep acknowledging it throughout the life span. And don't take it personally. Don't take their feelings as a reflection on your parenting – it's rarely about that, and more largely about their sibling experiences and the situation generally.

Acknowledge what has been hard, the regrets they have as a family, their fears for the future. It makes a world of difference to adult siblings when someone says "I see you". It makes a whole universe of difference, when that person is their parent. "I'm sorry I couldn't spend more time with you when you were younger"; "I'm worried about X's future too, let's look at this together"; "I wish that your sister could understand your graduation and be as proud of you as I am". Also adult siblings still need time with their parents into adulthood – they still need that acknowledgement. Small amounts of undivided attention really add up. And if a parent hasn't done this before – it's never too late to. It's never too late to turn around to a sibling son or daughter and say "I'm sorry we've never talked about this, but let's start".'

No one wants to feel that their experiences are belittled or ignored. In the same way that parents do not like unhelpful comments, such as a dismissal of their experiences, siblings also want to know their responses are heard. Talk to them and listen to them. It's ok for them to express negative as well as positive emotions. Give them information about disability as we never know what worries they may have (some siblings report worrying they may 'catch' autism).

Looking back on my own experience I used to feel sorry for my disabled son because of the procession of professionals coming through our door or the number of appointments we had to attend. I used to try to shield my middle son from this by getting someone else to look after him while we were attending them. One day, though, he told me that he liked going to the hospital because of the toys and enjoyed joining in with his brother's physiotherapy. It surprised me that my child's experience of these events was so different from my own. It really helped to have had that conversation and hear his perspective.

In my discussions with parents it became clear that siblings can affect our wellbeing in different ways.

Siblings offer time in a different world

Siblings could offer a chance to live a slightly different life.

> 'You know the best thing that we ever did was to have another child, because I can talk to [him] I help him with his homework, I've taken him to school this morning.'

> 'I think when things are really hard with his sister, he's always there to cheer me up and brighten the day. He is very funny and very kind and very loving. Seeing all that he can do is very alleviating.'

> 'It does feel like I have a foot in two worlds especially if I bounce from one to the other really quickly. I remember once I went for coffee with a friend whose daughter had just died and then I did the school run and I found it quite hard to switch between the two worlds. So coffee shop, going straight to the school run, but I do feel I've got a foot in two separate worlds, but sometimes it's quite nice to go and hide in the other one, the normal one. And pretend.'

Overcompensation

A number of parents felt that because they were so caught up in 'protecting' the sibling from the disabled child (maybe their behaviour or even the extra emotional load) they overcompensated by never wanting the sibling to feel anything negative. Guilt can have a detrimental impact on the parent and family as a whole.

'I think the other thing is we also put a lot of pressure on ourselves to make [sibling]'s life as normal as possible, to make everything that happens as least disruptive for her and I know we put a lot of pressure on ourselves to do that and like we don't want her to miss out on things.'

On reflection parents realised that life can't always be perfect, and experiencing some negativity, such as not always getting your way, was part of growing up.

Although special time with siblings is beneficial, ensure it is built into your life in a way that is manageable rather than increasing your emotional burden at times when you're already overloaded. It's crucial that parents don't burn themselves out trying to meet everyone's needs over and above their own. One study queried whether a negative impact on siblings was due to the disabled child or related to when the parents were 'under significant stress or are suffering with mental health problems'[116]. This illustrates the interdependence of family members' wellbeing; it is no good if you become so overwhelmed that you can no longer support your children. Looking after yourself is crucial.

What can help

There are some useful basics to consider. A primary consideration is to keep children safe from harm – so sometimes a lock on their bedroom door will enable a sibling to keep themselves, and their possessions, protected. You know your family best and what will work, and what won't, so below are guidelines to consider rather than absolutes.

Fairness

Commonly siblings say that they do not like the lack of fairness in discipline. For example, I would often say to my other children that my son couldn't understand the rules in a game, or help it when he broke something of theirs, because of his disability. I thought I was being open and transparent and encouraging a sense of nurturing and understanding in them.

---

[116] Hastings R.P., Kovshoff, H., Ward, N.J., Espinosa, F.D., Brown, T., & Remington, B. (2005) Systems analysis of stress and positive perceptions in mothers and fathers of pre-school children with autism. *Journal of Autism and Developmental Disorders*, 35, 635-644, p. 642

I then attended a training by Sibs for counsellors working with adult siblings and it was clear that a comment siblings hated was being told 'he can't help it because of ... X'. Although children in any family sometimes require different parenting styles, one of the things all children want is a sense of fairness and justice in the world, as far as this can be controlled. Finding activities that siblings can do together that recognise each of their strengths may help as well as ensuring that some form of rules and rewards apply to everyone.

Another tip is to let your sibling child go first sometimes. So often sibling children are the ones that miss their activities if things go wrong, have to sit in the uncomfortable seat or watch the movie their brother loves. We all need to feel that we matter and that sometimes our choices come first.

Don't expect them to be carers long term

Many siblings are carers by default and for some families this is unavoidable. All members of the family have to chip in and contribute and families will have different rules and expectations in this area.

One area I do feel strongly about though is that a child shouldn't be *expected* to be a carer for their adult sibling. Hopefully there will an interest in their disabled sibling's welfare but they should not take on the role of full time carer without being given other options. Of course some siblings want to do this. But it needs to be freely chosen, not decided by the parents – so avoid making assumptions.

Let them be a child and encourage them to develop their own social life away from the family home. Some siblings overcompensate for their disabled brother or sister or, as Sibs' Chief Executive Clare Kassa calls it 'running for two'; feeling pressure to achieve things or be the 'good' child. Above all else, children want to be loved and valued for who they are, not what they bring to others.

Remember the family dynamic

As we've already noted, emotions within family systems are multi-directional. This means that if someone in the system is experiencing negative feelings, this can affect the whole unit. Siblings will pick up on your mood and you theirs. You all need space to look after yourselves and have a break if necessary.

Siblings do better 'where communication is encouraged and they experience warm and cohesive relationships, providing them with skills to deal with both positive and negative feelings'[117]. This may include having to accept that they can't always have everything they want. It is also about being heard and getting the right support when things become too much.

Despite fears, for many families the pressures of family life, including meeting sibling needs and issues such as conflict or jealousy, works out ok in the end. Hold onto this hope. Families change and develop anyway as children grow and relationships change. You never know what is around the corner – this is true for all families.

Remember that there is also a dynamic you bring from your own family and upbringing. We all adopt roles in families – such as the rescuer, the clever one or the rebel – and these follow us unconsciously if they are not looked at and acknowledged. This can then impact the next generation. These can change with awareness and understanding so if it's something you feel you need to reflect upon it might help to explore it further with some therapeutic support.

There is more information on supporting young siblings here: www.youngsibs.org.uk

Wider Family

Parents commonly report wider family (grandparents, aunts, uncles, cousins and others) being affected by their child's diagnosis. Sometimes they are helpful and other times not so much. When family are on your side it creates a resilience where the family can not only withstand stressful life events, but also become stronger and more resourceful.

'They just look at him in a very positive way.'

The strength and nature of your relationship before having children will of course be a factor in how much support you get from family members. Although the relationship may change, you hope that bond will continue. I know that I have been very lucky to have a supportive wider family, who not only provide practical help but also give an emotional, shared

---

[117] Gressman, M (2014) Changing role of family carers in *Learning Disability Practice*, 17, 4, 34-39

'holding' of my son. All my children know they are loved by the family, including his special aunties and uncles and doting grandparents. And we also see that bond, which is a great comfort. I know other parents really appreciate their family being there for them as well.

> *'Knowing that I can just go round to my parents' house and have a coffee whilst my Mum plays with her, for example, is really helpful.'*

Family members processing the news at different rates from you can be problematic, though. For example, if parents are fighting the Local Authority for educational support and the grandparent denies their grandchild has a disability and thinks the parents are making a fuss, this input won't be helpful. At times like this another family who are at the same stage, or even professionals, may be more help to the parents.

There is no doubt that the wider family often feels upset or helpless on hearing about a disability diagnosis. Unexpected news is something to come to terms with, adapt and accept. As with all emotions, sometimes pain or difficulty may come out in other ways, such as in criticism or denial. The parent may be blamed for over-indulging the child, or accused of bad parenting rather than acknowledging the diagnosis or difference. It may be that hearing the diagnosis from a professional can help wider family members accept things rather than the parent having to relay the news.

Often it's a simple case of education and awareness. If people have had no previous contact or experience of disability before it can appear scary and unknown. They may not know how to help. People make assumptions not necessarily due to malice but rather from uncertainty, confusion and needing some direction. Signposting to information for the whole family may help. Role modelling talking to, and being with, your child can show others how to interact with them.

Sadly there are times when other people let you down.

> *'Neither side of our families are amazingly supportive.'*

There may be a whole ream of reasons why, that are too personal and complex to examine here. If, despite your best efforts, your family can't properly be on your side then there are some hard decisions you have to make. As some parents report, you may accept that others are limited in their understanding and decide to set some boundaries and hold your tongue. Alternately, you may feel you have to disengage. Neither option is easy and it may help you to talk them through with someone who can provide an objective ear, such as a counsellor or therapist.

Grandparents

The relationship with grandparents can be a special one. Grandchildren are longed for and offer a chance for grandparents to enjoy the child without having the responsibilities of being a parent (although sometimes grandparents do take on this role – see below). Parents report that support from extended family members, especially grandparents, helps them cope with the demands of a child with special needs. This involves emotional as well as practical support – such as childcare, babysitting or accompanying parents to appointments. Support can form a solid bond and community around the child. Being able to talk and share your experience can make all the difference to a parent and the family as a whole.

> *'I think sometimes the most helpful thing was the practical support that we received, so for example, my parents were absolutely wonderful and when the boys were young and they didn't sleep at all, they used to take them on a Friday night for us and just have them for overnight and it became a regular thing on Friday night, that my sons would go to my parents, and when we were really struggling and I was so tired, that was just such a wonderful gift.'*

Grandparents can often be as affected as the parents in coming to terms with their grandchild's disability but this struggle is rarely acknowledged or support provided [118]. While this means they can really understand the adjustment involved, it can also lead to a 'double grief'[119], watching their own child's pain and struggles over the grandchild's condition.

---

[118] Hastings, R. (1997) Grandparents of Children with Disabilities: a review, *International Journal of Disability, Development and Education*, 44, 4, 329-340

[119] Langridge, P. (2002) Reduction of chronic sorrow: a health promotion role for children's community nurses? *Journal of Child Health Care*, Vol 6(3), 157-170, p. 163

Conversely, for some parents, there can also be an additional sadness at seeing your family struggle to accept the situation. Their distress can compound your own and add an extra emotional layer to be worked through.

> *'Mum's a bit old-fashioned and if [son] doesn't say hello she gets upset... so sometimes I feel a secondary sadness.'*

Learning that your grandchild is disabled may feel shocking and confusing. Terminology may be unfamiliar and require a huge learning curve to challenge preconceived ideas. Time can help. A study found that initially 'many grandparents were highly critical of the parents' child raising skills and frequently denied that their grandchild had a disability'. However, ten years on this was less of a problem as 'the reality of the child's disability was confirmed over time and the grandparents grew more accepting of the situation'[120].

In my experience seeing my own parents' sadness over my son's diagnosis was upsetting. However, their constant care and concern for him was hugely supportive and made me feel like I was not alone. I wonder if the world of disability was even more alien to them as, in their generation, those with disabilities were less likely to have survived or would have been placed outside mainstream society. Their compass for making sense of the situation was even shakier than my own but their love for him helped them through.

Grandparents may need to seek support for themselves. They may feel sad at the difficulties their child and grandchild are going through and feel unsure how to help.

One Granny's Experience:

We were very delighted about becoming a grandparent in our 70s and longed for grandchildren. When our daughter was pregnant we were overjoyed. Our daughter had a very healthy pregnancy, everything was going well and we told everyone we ever spoke to!

As the day dawned our daughter phoned to say she was going into labour and into hospital. When we didn't hear anything in the night as the hours went by we began to wonder what had happened although we realised first babies can take some time.

---

[120] Gray (2002) Ten years on: a longitudinal study of families of children with autism, *Journal of Intellectual and Developmental Disability*, 27, 3, 215-222, p. 219

My husband was desperate to find out and then telephoned the hospital. He was told our grandson had been born but was very poorly. They said the next twenty-four hours was crucial for his survival. We were stunned. It was very upsetting news and we felt so sorry for our daughter and son-in-law. What had started out as such a hopeful and joyous event was tempered with the knowledge that the baby would have significant problems. They mentioned brain damage but gave us little further knowledge. We were left hanging.

The following morning, because we didn't live nearby, we travelled to visit in the hospital to intensive care. We really didn't know what to expect and had received so little information. It was such a blow. Seeing our daughter in such distress and our son-in-law so upset. We felt absolutely helpless and upset. We really didn't know what we could do to help.

Our daughter was still a bit drugged up so not fully registering the enormity of the situation. We tried to support her the best we could but it felt like the worst thing out. We were very upset ourselves.

When we went to see our grandson in the Intensive Care Unit (ICU) he was so perfect. He was full size compared to the other premature babies, I remember he filled his cot. It felt like he was in the wrong place. We asked ourselves - how did it go so wrong? I remember the notices on the premature babies – 'please do not look at the babies'.

We didn't know what he'd be like or what he'd manage. We wondered whether he'd be so disabled he wouldn't be able to do anything for himself. And more immediately - is he going to survive?

And I thought he should never have been like that – when he was full term, healthy and our daughter's healthy pregnancy. Why hadn't they done something earlier in the labour when they saw that he was in distress? I felt resentful and was left with lots of questions. Why it should have happened? No one talked it through with us.

Later when I went to stay in my daughter's house as she and the baby were still in hospital we saw how everything was laid out (nappies, changing mat) ready for the baby's homecoming... which hadn't happened yet.

But we recognise we are lucky that he survived and it's been wonderful watching him grow and as he started to respond to us more and more. It could have been worse but it shouldn't have been like this at all, is how I feel. Happy to have him and see him make progress, grow and develop. But there's still a sadness about what happened.

Knowing it was avoidable is very hard. It wasn't nature or in his genes, it was human error. It takes a long time to trust people again when this has happened.

How grandparents can help

If grandparents are not sure how to support the family, they can ask. It might help to start with the small things; making a meal, doing shopping or babysitting so the parents can take a break. Some simple words of advice for grandparents on the *Contact* website are worth reiterating here:

- Be led by the parents, they will tell you what they need

- Appreciate that there will be times when your advice won't be listened to – it's nothing personal

- Try not to give your opinions when the parents are upset

- Sometimes parents need someone to let off steam to – be patient and listen

- Spend time with the other grandchildren in the family

- Acceptance of your grandchild's disability may take a while for you and their parents, so be understanding

- When the parents are involved in the practical matters it's best for you to focus on the child and not their diagnosis[121]

For many families, having a child with additional needs is a positive. It brings the family together and the child is loved for who they are and not viewed in a different light. It's important though to recognise that any unexpected news can take time to filter through and it may involve different people adapting at different speeds.

Kinship carers

Kinship care is when a child is looked after by a family member who is not their parent. Around half of kinship carers are grandparents. This can bring unique issues if the child is disabled, including a greater

---

[121] https://contact.org.uk/advice-and-support/your-child-your-family/advice-for-grandparents/ [accessed 3/9/20]

physical or financial strain. Much of the advice in this book will also be of relevance to grandparents. For specific support it is worth visiting https://www.grandparentsplus.org.uk/.

Friends

When friends understand our situation as parents of a disabled child and all that entails, it can enrich our life. People don't necessarily have to be a special needs parent to be a good friend. Someone who is empathic, compassionate and understanding can provide us with the connection we need. Although there do seem to be times when another special needs parent provides particular support, which I discuss below.

Some parents I spoke to, as mentioned already in this chapter, made the important point that by keeping hold of old friends it allowed them to retain a part of themselves that existed prior to having children. A chance to connect, talk and switch off. For some, their friends offered time away from anything special needs-related.

> *'At some point I just realised I don't want to go [to special needs support group] anymore, just because all that they were talking was autistic kids and autism and autistic kids and autism and then I just thought it's not a break for me. I need to go out, it takes me lots of arrangement to be able to go out for a couple of hours, but when I go there the only thing I don't want to talk about is the same problem.'*

Some friends come and some friends go, never more so than in the lives of parent carers. Unfortunately, lack of awareness and education can lead to prejudice and some friends cannot or will not envisage how much life has changed and disengage. This can be shocking and leave a massive feeling of disappointment.

> *'It's just bizarre and people think that you're milking it and I had a friend tell me that I enjoyed her because she got me attention... Not a friend now... I have the core group of friends that I've always had that aren't judgemental but I have lost a lot of friends.'*

Special Needs Community

Becoming part of a disability or special needs community can have a hugely beneficial impact on our wellbeing. Although it can be a 'bittersweet experience... being involuntarily initiated as a member into the disability culture'[122], finding your tribe can be comforting and provide a sense of belonging. Friends who really understand your situation can enable a social life that fits around your child.

As we've already seen, strongly connecting with your community – face to face or online – can create better wellbeing. It provides somewhere you can be confident and safe in being who you are. Some people find it hard to join new groups so a good way is to go along with a friend or someone you already know. If a professional suggests a group ask if they can come with you or introduce you to the group leader.

Having a disabled child may even be a way of becoming part of a group and thereby increasing self-esteem.

'For many years I was a passionate advocate for disability but I wasn't a disabled person. And then suddenly [daughter] has come... I've suddenly got a valid platform for my political views... So she's kind of completed my circle of my journey and it's almost like you know I feel on some level I feel I had to have a disabled child, it's so right that I've got a child with disabilities.'

People may come together for different reasons – same diagnosis, location or school. Many parents also report appreciating groups, teaching staff and support workers with immense positivity and compassion towards their child which builds a cohesive sense of community around the child and family. At times this can help us to know how to be with our child, especially when we may feel lost or uncertain.

It can be a particularly unique type of support provided by other special needs parents. There are two key areas of support: one aspect is the **emotional** support – feeling like you're not alone, being able to have open conversations with people that understand.

---

[122] Konrad, S. (2006) Posttraumatic growth in mothers of children with acquired disabilities. *Journal of Loss & Trauma*, 11, 1, 101-113, p. 106

'Well they know don't they, I mean, they know on a different level.'

The other aspect is the **practical** – seeking advice and chances to problem-solve with others who are in the same boat. Some groups offer both and others focus more on one area. This is alongside the fact that there are certain people we are drawn to more than others – due to personality or shared values and interests. We cannot assume that we will get on with all special needs parents just by virtue of being a member of that group.

A challenge or search for practical solutions can bring people close for a time, particularly online where there may be a problem that needs solving and, by exploring solutions that can be found. And then this may change as we move forward.

Some particular themes came out of my research about what parents found helpful:

- 'venting'

- a safe and trustworthy space

- not trying to fix things or make you feel better

- talk about difficult things

- no pity

- unique situations.

'Venting'

Parents commonly referred to the usefulness of being able to 'vent'. It's interesting, as this term has a negative connotation when really parents are referring to an understandable need to have a conversation around difficulties experienced (i.e. frustrations with services) and a chance to offload.

'Being in a room of people that have the time to sort of get some practical ideas on what to do, but also vent (laughs)... And it was really the venting that helped... with other people that get it, yes. They were all parents of children with autism.'

In the academic literature on coping, venting is often portrayed as unhelpful to emotional wellbeing. But this was not the case with the parent carers I spoke to. In fact having the chance to do this with others who truly understood and would not judge, was seen as massively beneficial to wellbeing. It helped parents know that they were not alone and it got the weight of the problems off their chest.

Generally, if expressing emotions lets someone return to a 'baseline'[123] mood then it is helpful. If, however, it means the feelings become more intense or go on for longer than would be expected it may be that expressing the emotions are becoming unhelpful and verging on brooding rumination (with a downward spiral or repetition). Constantly repeating 'I'm miserable' doesn't help. But venting about a frustrating experience and then being able to move on does.

A safe and trustworthy space

Before being able to offload, parents need to know that they are in a safe place. This might mean that they will not share their feelings with a professional, but would with a fellow parent carer.

> *'What you say is safe because the person...understands just how difficult it is.'*

In certain situations there seemed to be a risk associated with sharing how you were feeling in case you were judged or not understood.

Not trying to fix things or make you feel better

Although at times parents want to problem-solve or find practical solutions, much of the time when talking to others they want active, supportive listening rather than someone trying to fix things.

> *'I don't need it escalating [or fixed], I just need to say it out loud.'*

Parents know that there is not always an easy answer but still want to voice their concerns and have them heard rather than dismissed.

---

[123] Roos, S. (2002) *Chronic Sorrow: A Living Loss*, New York: Routledge, p. 191

Talk about difficult things

One parent beautifully encapsulated a unique aspect that special needs parents can provide, that is 'the ability to have honest conversations'. These may be difficult conversations about painful things yet parent carers may be more willing, and able, to go there and say the unsayable. They have gathered the necessary skills to cope with the complex side of life.

There can be a sense of camaraderie between parent carers which sometimes includes a 'gallows humour' about the absurdities of life. Laughing about some inappropriate behaviour, bodily fluids or catch-22 style frustrations in the system can be a great coping mechanism and bring us closer to others.

> *'Finding your own humour, laugh, two weeks later, we've had the poo murals all over the wall upstairs when he was young. You can laugh about it now.'*

Sharing our vulnerabilities can provide a shortcut to greater intimacy. Despite this connection many things may still go unsaid between families and if you need support, tell others and reach out for help.

No pity

Parent carers also don't want pity from others. Non-special needs parents may inadvertently provide unhelpful comments such as 'poor you', or 'I don't know how you do it', which can make parent carers feel like that is what they're suggesting they want from others. But this is not what they want. They want to be able to have open conversations, as part of a 'normal' discussion about the inevitable trials and tribulations that arise in a parent's life.

> *'you don't really want sympathy, you just want someone to go, 'oh God, that sucks, here, have this coffee'... it's more just a typical parent interaction, just an ordinary parent interaction'*

Unique situations

For some parents there were times when it was useful to connect with other people with the specific condition e.g. online for advice or attending conferences or events. This may be particularly the case when your child has a rare condition or not the predominant disability in local special needs groups.

> *'Well it was just fascinating because you knew that you were there because everybody has a child like your child and they have exactly what your child has. It was interesting and some spoke a few words, a few more words than [son] does, there was older kids, there was nineteen, twenty year olds, it was a real insight.'*

It can also be informative to see others with older children in terms of gaining an insight into the future, although this does always have to include a word of caution. No one fully knows what our child will be like, how their destiny will play out. This is often an issue that parents fear and remains in the back of their mind for a long time.

Connection and Empowerment for Social Change

Connections made through a shared endeavour to create social change and improve conditions for families with a disabled child can also build our community. There is an empowering strength and comfort in knowing that others are out there and you have the 'whole legal rights behind you'. In fact the personal becomes political as we take up our position on the advocacy to activism continuum[124].

As well as legal rights, knowing that there are movements for social change can help illustrate a different way of viewing the world which can then be internalised to make sense of your child's disability.

> *'The whole [neurodiversity] movement has been so powerful and positive.'*

When I reflect on finding truly inclusive and accessible places, such as the Chicken Shed theatre in North London, I realise that seeing the acceptance of my son, exactly as he is, from others provided an unconscious role modelling. They showed me how to be a disability advocate, how the world could be and how little effort it really takes to make the reasonable adjustments he needs to contribute to the community. This mentoring,

---

[124] Ryan, S. & Runswick-Cole (2009) From Advocate to Activist? Mapping the Experiences of Mothers of Children on the Autism Spectrum, *Journal of Applied Research in Intellectual Disabilities*, 22, 43-53

unspoken and often not consciously acknowledged, is a precious antidote to some reactions from other groups in society.

It has been suggested that there is a stage of adaptation beyond acceptance called 'appreciation' stage. Parents at this stage can help others: 'Several parents reported that contact with individuals who have a positive attitude helped them to make their own positive attitude shift and therefore to cope more effectively.'[125] Having positive others in our life can help to re-frame our experiences.

Further, knowing that you are working together with other people to make social change can create a sense of connection and improve our self-esteem. It taps into the trait many parent carers exhibit in wanting to help others – this may form part of our sense of purpose or meaning-making that is crucial to emotional wellbeing.

Potential Pitfalls of Special Needs Networks

There are some potential difficulties to be aware of in relation to special needs networks.

Same but different

Parents helping parents can be useful as there is a general under-standing that is sometimes lacking from non-parent-carers. However, sometimes people can extrapolate, incorrectly, their own experience onto others. For example, they may say my son had such-and-such therapy and it worked amazingly, but it would not work or be appropriate for your child. What one parent experiences as devastating, another parent may take in their stride. People are different and how they make sense of things they encounter will vary enormously.

Many helplines use other parents of disabled children to support those needing help, advice and signposting. Whilst there can be a helpful general understanding of what the parents are going through (and the majority are appropriately supportive), you can sometimes also find yourself caught up in an extra layer of the helpers' own concerns (which may be different from your own). For example, a parent had spoken to a helpliner who had taken up space talking

[125] Hastings, R.P. & Taunt, H. (2002) Positive perceptions in families of children with developmental disabilities, *American Journal on Mental Retardation*, 107, 2, 116-127, p. 123

about their own difficulties. While a short acknowledgement of commonalities may be helpful, if this takes up too much time it suggests these parents aren't quite ready to take on this role.

Social media groups

I want to add a note about social media and online groups, as, for many parents, online support is a lifeline to other families in a similar situation. The understanding that one gets from a family with a shared experience can be wonderful and being online obviously widens our net for potential connection. Particularly if your child has a rare condition it may be the only way to connect with others in a similar situation.

As we've seen, comparing our own lives with the 'perfect' lives people sometimes present can be difficult and this is probably more apparent online. Even within special needs forums it can be wonderfully uplifting to connect with others but it can also expose you to different viewpoints, judgement or difficulties.

People sometimes post things without thinking and use this medium to express anger or negative feelings that they can't process themselves. Venting can be useful, but only in a safe space, and at times people are criticised. If you are on the receiving end of this, or even witness it, it can be upsetting and at times traumatic. Make sure that you are able to leave a group, turn off your phone, or avoid certain communities or times in a group. Gaining a balance of face to face and online connection with others is important to stop us falling down a social media rabbit hole. It may be you need to put in boundaries to keep you safe and healthy from negative input or people that you find draining or worrying. Something that has appeared to be overwhelming online suddenly becomes manageable when you've had the rest of the day doing other things in the physical world.

Exposure to difficult material

There is a risk that through connecting with other special needs groups you are more likely to be exposed to upsetting stories. It may be news of behaviours that challenge, parental and child struggles, school exclusion, burnout or even premature death.

'Having a child like this and all of a sudden you're surrounded by death.'

Some children with particular diagnoses are at greater risk of dying young, due to their diagnosis or reasons connected to their difficulties. Unfortunately, mainstream health and social care for many with additional needs still falls way short of what is required, so that may mean other unrelated illnesses are missed or diagnosed too late. I reflect on this further in the final chapter.

Being part of a special needs group can therefore bring up issues that you may need to be aware of, although not necessarily at this time in your life.

> *'And I'm thinking these kids are dying all over the place. Is [my daughter] going to be next? And then I [get] absolutely paranoid she's going to die.'*

There may be a time when you need to protect yourself from such news and remove yourself (or at least have a break) from these groups. Even a simple strategy like turning off your notifications from an online group may help so that you can re-connect with the discussion at a time when you are ready rather than feel overwhelmed. Or at other times you might need to have a digital detox over the weekend by turning your phone onto airplane mode except at specific pre-agreed times. Take time out in nature to have a break from all technology. Be present with your child(ren) or friends. Make a mindful conscious decision when you will be on your phone, and when you will put it away.

Unhelpful Comments

In direct contrast to those who offer understanding and connection are those who don't get it and also don't make any genuine attempt to understand. Parent carers sometimes find comments they receive from others really unhelpful. At times they could be hurtful and leave parents angry or withdrawn. These comments had different commonalities to them which we'll look at next.

> *'[People say] "You know it's such a blessing" and you think, for who? Why are you telling me it's a blessing that my child's disabled, no, it's not...I'm quite blunt and I will say, are you joking, how is it a blessing that she has seizures, or that she can't talk, or she can't communicate, what are you talking about?'*

Lack of true understanding and humility

A commonly heard comment was when people said that an aspect of their neurotypical child's life was similar to the parent carers'. I have experienced this when talking about the difficulties of not knowing what has happened to my son at school because, although he is verbal, his recall and memory are unreliable. Occasionally other parents (of typically developing children) have said 'oh my child doesn't tell me anything about school either'. I understand that they are trying to relate on some level but they are missing a concern that is particular to our situation.

> *'I think what used to annoy me more was other people would say "oh it's just the same for us", and I would think, really? That annoys me. That annoys me more than anything actually. That lack of humility of people of privilege have because... if you have a child who is typical, life is easier, generally. Because the world is designed around you.'*

Further, some people may think they're helping by making comments based on limited information, such as a film about autism. A little bit of non-direct knowledge is often worse than total lack of familiarity, if that latter person asks 'how is it for you?' or 'what is your situation like?' rather than jumping to (wrong) conclusions. I think it's best if people are honest about their knowledge and really try to engage in a conversation in the spirit of interest and learning.

Poor you

Many parents reflected on the 'poor you' narrative that they had experienced from others – predominantly from other people who did not have children with special needs. This response was seen as patronising and unhelpful; one parent referred to it as the 'killing kind. They think they're being kind but actually they are killing one little piece of your soul at a time.'

> *'It's just not helpful. It's not going to change anything or make me feel any better... it's just kind of highlighting all the burden and the negativity around it.'*

While there may be additional challenges parent carers are experiencing, it's not pity they want, rather it's compassionate active listening or some real offer of practical help – like providing childcare or lobbying for better services.

Linked to the 'poor you' narrative was faux-admiration – also a source of anger for some parents.

> *'When they say, "oh I don't know how you do it",*
> *because I have to. I can't just leave her in a ditch.*
> *You'd do it too if she was yours.'*

Lack of adjustment by others

Being rejected because of your child's needs or the new requirements your life demands is deeply painful. Parents spoke of being left out of events or encountering rigid adherence to rules meaning they were unable to attend. They even experienced direct judgement to their faces about their child or parenting skills.

The sad thing about this is that often the adaptations necessary are small. A little bit of thought can make a significant difference in our lives.

> *'I couldn't always get her wheelchair in to one of the*
> *houses, so it was like, well let's go to someone else's*
> *house [and] people would talk to my daughter and*
> *include her and make sure that she was included*
> *with the other kids... simple.'*

You will find your community

If you have not found your community please don't give up. Join groups, online or face to face. Talk to people and see how things go. If your child is at school, see if they can help you meet other parents. It can make the world of difference.

> *'When people who are outside of our world get her, it's*
> *really special, because it doesn't happen that often.'*

As in all human interactions there are some people you get on better with than others, maybe due to shared perspective on life, sense of humour, background or personality. This may mean that you need to try out a number of different groups before you find the right one for you.

You may be able to find local community support groups by asking your GP, local authority or other special needs parents. On a national level there are also online and face to face groups via charities, such as Contact, Scope, *Mencap, National Autistic Society* and the *Challenging Behaviour Foundation.*

Conclusion

Finding the right relationships with people who understand you, your child and your situation can maintain your wellbeing through thick and thin. It is worth nurturing this and shopping around for positive others in your life – providing a balanced and nurturing connection.

This is particularly important when your child grows and other support networks change. For example, when there are fewer opportunities to socialise at the school gates or teenage behaviours emerge that make socialising more difficult. Having a wide community of support (whether that's family, friends or network) that truly know and accept you and your family can help protect against isolation.

Sometimes having a neutral person to talk to can really help, particularly at times of isolation or acute stress. They can also provide expertise or practical support, and I discuss professional support in more detail in the next chapter.

Key points

- We are social creatures and as well as time for ourselves we also need others in our life
- People who provide understanding, connection and belonging are vital for our emotional wellbeing
- This connection and support may come from family, friends or wider community networks
- It can also come from professionals and services who support us
- It can help to think of family (including partner, siblings and wider family) and community as an inter-connected system that affects one another
- We come with our own social, political and cultural identities which will shape how we view our current situation

---

- Other variables may create additional considerations, such as being a single parent, step parent and same sex parent
- Social comparison doesn't always help
- Take time away from social media if you need to
- Friends and special needs networks who 'get it' and provide compassionate, constructive support can be helpful
- Sometimes others are not supportive and this can be difficult, disappointing and at times hurtful

7

Professionals, Services and Support

'This is your job but this is our life.'

As we have seen in the previous chapter, having supportive people in our life is key to our wellbeing. As well as personal or informal relationships, positive others can also include professionals and services.

Introduction

It is possible to get good quality support that transforms the lives of families with a disabled child. However, sometimes the support (or lack thereof) adds to the burden and emotional load rather than being helpful.

> *'[My daughter's] diagnosis isn't what stresses me out. It's everything else that's attached to it.'*

Services can be a mixed bag. Some parents experience them as limited and not person- or family-centred. There are issues with services being erratic and different levels of care being provided across the country. Criteria can be applied so strictly that many who need the support do not get it. Parents do not always know what is available to them and it can become a closely guarded secret.

The focus for many professionals is solely on the child, whereas, by developing a more family-centred service, it can support emotional wellbeing for the whole family. Families benefit from services that are responsive and flexible to their individual needs, including their culture, background and resources. It also means responding in a timely fashion rather than waiting for a crisis to occur.

> *[On services] 'You've got to spend six months*
> *in absolute torment, and then we'll bring you*
> *something which doesn't fit.'*

Support can entail empowering the parent to gain knowledge and find answers for themselves and, at other times, particularly when stressors become too much, they may need services to help share the care.

Although there are inevitable pressures on resources, some elements of support cost nothing. It may be an understanding look, a compassionate comment and a recognition that life is hard and there isn't enough support. It may be a meaningful moment of connection that transcends power and control. Services and professionals often have the control and this can mean we are starting from a disempowered place.

> *'You have this group of people with all the power.*
> *Gate-keeping everything we need and you have a group*
> *of people who need something from that group of people.*
> *And the two never mix.'*

Families will generally have more services and professionals in their lives with the aim of bringing extra support and expertise. At times, though, this also has the potential to create more conflict, invasion of privacy, feelings of vulnerability and judgement. This may be why in some studies 'parents who accessed more professional and service supports reported higher levels of... stress'[126] as well as helplessness and in some cases depression.

> *'The thing about parents of disabled children is that*
> *we can't hide our vulnerability, we're so vulnerable,*
> *because professionals are constantly wanting to know*
> *what our child had for breakfast and wanting to*
> *know how they are going to the toilet.'*

---

[126] White, N. & Hastings, R.P. (2004) Social and Professional Support for Parents of Adolescents with Severe Intellectual Disabilities, *Journal of Applied Research in Intellectual Disabilities*, 17, 181-190, p. 186

Intersections

Professionals benefit from considering how aspects of our social or political identity affect the lives of families with a disabled child. People bring their own interpretations and perspectives based on different factors. Awareness is needed as to how this affects the family – such as accessing and making sense of a diagnosis, isolation and discrimination as well as language barriers.[127]

> *'I felt that we were being judged and I felt that if you don't know my culture you don't know the things that are important to us. You haven't been in my shoes...*
> *I think that is down also to under-representation of certain people within that kind of field as well. So the lack of understanding of what might motivate me to engage... and in the end I just felt it was a waste of my time. And I stopped attending quite abruptly.'*

Timing and Sensitivity

It is helpful if professionals and services have some awareness of the parent carer landscape we've outlined throughout this book. Feelings change and adapt, though not necessarily in a neat linear order. Seeing the parent's context can prevent advice or comments being given at the wrong time.

To suggest someone should 'be grateful their child is alive' when they are in the depths of despair and fighting on all fronts is not only unhelpful but also deeply shaming. Comments such as 'he doesn't act like that at school' regarding a child's behaviour may be true (it's very common for a child to hold everything together at school and let it all out when they get home) but think how that can be received by an exhausted parent at their wits' end. On some level it can be seen as a judgement, however innocuously the words are spoken.

One excellent physiotherapist we had in the early days said to me 'you have to let go of the child you thought you were going to have

---

[127] National Autistic Society, *Diverse perspectives: the challenges for families affected by autism from Black, Asian and Minority ethnic communities* https://www.scie-socialcareonline.org.uk/diverse-perspectives-the-challenges-for-families-affected-by-autism-from-black-asian-and-minority-ethnic-communities/r/a11G0000005lcmwIAC

and accept this is your child now'. I knew, on some level, it was true. But it was too early for me to hear this.

I know it is not always easy to tell where parents are emotionally and I acknowledge that professionals are busy people. Yet honing empathy skills to pick up on the signs will improve their capacity to connect to families – one of the important aspects of being a professional in this field. Sometimes a family just wants a service to 'be' with them rather than 'doing to' them.

> *'Our local consultant... is brilliant, I mean she would say [daughter] is very complicated, and it's been a learning curve... for everyone involved.'*

Some professionals manage this automatically. They are confident in their ability and knowledge of the field but not arrogant or ignorant of the family's life experience. They are compassionate and non-judgemental if the family needs a kind word, encouragement that they are doing a good job or referral for more support, including respite. There can be a lot of guilt in asking for support and professionals who show understanding and sensitivity are to be lauded.

Support involves teaching or sharing the skills the parent needs to know without being patronising. It's ok to not have the answers. It's not ok, however, to lack compassion.

Although the early years are often the most challenging, that is not always the case for all families. It's helpful if professionals are aware of the ebb and flow of parental responses, dependent on what else is happening in their life. There may be particular points or milestones in their child's development, battles with services, or changes in other areas of the parents' life – relationships, work or health, that create difficulties. The teenage years or transition to adult services can also be tumultuous especially when previous support changes or disappears. It is crucial parents are able to receive the support they need when they need it, rather than when it suits the system.

Many professionals are so focused on the child that we as parents are sometimes forgotten. This failure to see the family as a system means only one part of the whole is supported. Professionals can play a vital role in helping parents recognise the complex emotions triggered in daily struggles as normal and understandable. People need not feel alone or ashamed of their emotional responses, instead they can be supported to process these with compassionate understanding.

I suspect that some professionals working in the special needs world have become so used to that world that they forget it may be confusing or overwhelming for those who have recently joined it (not out of choice) through their child's disability. With time and support we can gain the knowledge and perspective that can transform our lives but we may need help along the way to navigate the new terrain.

The rest of this chapter summarises what parents have found helpful, and unhelpful, for their wellbeing.

What Parent Carers Need

What parents consider helpful, rather than harmful, is quite simple. Services need to demonstrate the following attributes:

- Compassionate, human relationships

- Empowerment and collaboration

- Holistic – practical and emotional support

- Co-ordinated, consistent and transparent

- Sharing the care

Compassionate, human relationships

'I felt very frustrated at one particular appointment with a professional. I felt it was obvious I was falling apart and I did not know what to do with regards to my son's behaviour. There seemed to be a block in the connection with the practitioner rather than relating to me as a human being. I was frustrated that she was able to keep a professional's distance and shut the door on us when this was my life, day in day out, that often felt unbearable.

After many different requests to get my son to do X and Y or play with this toy or another and my futile attempts to stop him hitting the radiator (the one thing he was interested in doing) my son grabbed a ball and promptly threw it out of the window. The doctor did not notice this. I watched it roll away down the road and silently smiled to myself, congratulating my son's communication that he did not want to be here and neither did I.

I wondered what we were doing there when there seemed so little the doctor could do to help us, with limited resources, as well as such a restricted ability to relate to me and my son in our hour of need.'

Parents want contact with services and professionals that are compassionate, trustworthy and understanding. They need to connect with services that offer good communication – listening as well as talking. Talking to us *and* our child. A simple question of 'how are you?' can be a moment parents remember.

It can help professionals to understand the emotional context in which parent carers find themselves. There may also be other pressures on a family at any given time – looking after siblings or financial difficulties – which can overload a carer's resources. They don't want pity, but they do need care and understanding.

Although at times parents need practical advice, this always needs to be given using a caring, empathic, human approach.

Positive approach to our child

Parents understandably want to feel that any professional in their life feels positively towards their child and is able to develop a rapport. I remember one professional who visited us in the early days made some comment like 'I can't work with this' gesturing towards my son who was not doing what he was asked. I was horrified. As it was early on I felt some guilt myself that I hadn't managed to make my son comply and that we had in some way failed as a family. Now I would see that the responsibility lay in her inability to connect with him or make allowances for his own needs, and I would probably ask her to leave. I suspect she was in the wrong job. Again an element of empathy and compassion in this situation would have gone a long way to restore a difficult appointment.

This point connects to another requirement of professionals – that they have a strength and resilience to manage some of the difficulties that will come their way. I recognise the ones who need something from my son in order to feel confident, who then seem embarrassed when he doesn't reciprocate in social communication. This response doesn't help my son or me.

Those who aren't offended if my child doesn't say 'hello' or respond in the way they wanted seem the most competent and resilient. If a professional is overly sensitive and feels embarrassed or awkward, for example if a child doesn't return a high-five, then perhaps this isn't the right vocation for them or further training is required. I appreciate the teachers and other staff who have really 'got', and liked, my son, often understanding his manner and capabilities more than I have always recognised. They connect to him on his terms and it is beautiful to see.

Lived experience of professionals

'I find it very hard to take advice from someone that's not in my shoes.'

A number of parents reflected that using their own personal experience made them a better professional; therefore if services or professionals have the lived experience then it makes sense to use it. It helps form connections with other families and normally means there is already a level of understanding of the family's situation. It is not something that needs to be hidden – rather the personal can inform the professional in the support and understanding they provide.

Yet parent-professionals felt that they were very rarely consulted in their roles, and this was a missed opportunity for organisations and services.

'I think we are the solution really. We need more family carers in professional teams, giving their perspective, and taking away the idea that families are difficult and then able to go to the families with that different approach that I really think we have, to say, actually, we will help you.'

Valuing, and remunerating, this input will help ensure services provide meaningful outcomes for families.

One thing to note though is that if the parent-carer-professional has not been able to make sense of their own emotional journey, or is not supported enough, there can be times when their own experiences may be overwhelming. Ensuring that parents don't project their own experience, say on a helpline, onto an over-burdened parent calling for help requires adequate supervision and training. Charities or services that use parent carers' expertise should ensure they have enough support to be able to manage their role.

Empowerment and Collaboration

'You need to feel like you're somewhere near the top of that decision making tree.'

Parents are experts by experience on their child and therefore want to work in partnership with professionals. This involves consultation and collaboration to ensure both parent and professional have the information they need.

'What helps is when services work with me. I think when I have really good communication with people that are supporting my daughter.'

Valuing the role carers play and building on their strengths can help improve the well-being of the whole family. A lack of value of parental viewpoint can be experienced in certain behaviours such as referring to 'Mum' in meetings rather than using the person's name. Services that seek, and use, parent involvement on all aspects of service delivery will benefit from true co-production.

Having a plan

As we've already discussed in previous chapters, having a sense of agency or control can positively affect our wellbeing. With the right skills we can re-gain a sense of mastery in life which protects against depressive symptoms; professionals and services can support us in this. Identifying what you're going to do, what the next target is, or realising that you *can* support your child, can counter helplessness. 'Having a plan' can be helpful while recognising we can't always control everything in life.

'I guess... most of the time if it's logical or there is a way through things, I'm fine, you know, if I know that I've got to press this button and then it will happen, or I've got to write that report and it will happen, or go to this meeting and it will happen, that's fine. What I struggle with is the irrational bits.'

Information and knowledge

Parents require access to good quality information and training to help with the upskilling process. This supports us in finding solutions to problems and feeling more in control.

> *'I think it's given me the vocabulary... so I've got an internal dialogue... that makes sense now, so when something does happen for [daughter]... I now have a clear thought process, so we have a behaviour, and my first thought is, "okay, what is she trying to tell me?" whereas years ago, it would be, "how do I stop this, how do I stop her doing that?"...It's transformational.'*

Training can also be a great opportunity to meet other special needs parents, thereby reducing isolation. However, the quality and relevance of the training is key and some courses may not always address the very specific needs of parenting a disabled child. Suggesting that parents attend a generic parent training course can be shaming – as if any difficulties they are experiencing are down to bad parenting. This fails to acknowledge the additional challenges a disabled child brings. Unless the training is specific to disability then it is not always beneficial for the parent, as many standard behavioural practices do not always work for all children. I lost count of the number of times people recommended I use a sticker chart for my son. This was not only totally unappealing to my son on so many levels, it was also deeply insulting in the assumption that I hadn't already tried it. His needs and the ways to motivate him were far more complex than that a one-size-fits-all approach. The strategies I successfully used with my non-disabled children did not work for my disabled son.

If the reality is that there are no appropriate services to which parents can be referred they will generally prefer this to be explained honestly rather than being shoehorned into training that is not appropriate.

Other parents will seek information and guidance from those within the special needs community – such as online or reading books.

*'That helped me when I went online – a video series called
Ask An Autistic and she was brilliant at explaining stimming.
Once I looked at other advocates basically and they explained
some of these things, and how important they were, and it
chimed with my instinct ... He was a little bit dysregulated and
stressed and then he'd do that and he'd be nice and calm.'*

Part of the empowerment parents need is understanding the law,
system and terminology of the special needs world. This includes
learning new acronyms (e.g. EHCP, LA, DLA, SLT) (See Glossary)
and how to use the jargon. Sometimes parents need help with this.
An example one parent gave was talking about 'my child's unmet
need' rather than 'I want X for her' and I found it useful to talk about
'differentiating the curriculum' in terms of what school needed to do
to help my son access learning in the classroom.

*'Knowledge is power. So you skill-up and if you can
produce evidence and build your own confidence to
provide that evidence then people have to listen.'*

Valuing our role as parents and building on our strengths can help
empower us not only in family life but also in transferring out to other
areas of life (e.g. work).

*'It's given me a different career... I've worked in social care
for most of my life, but it's focused down on challenging
behaviour, learning disability, autism.'*

Out of the knowledge and information there is growth – the wisdom
and enhanced perspective taking to understand your child, meet
their needs and gain a broader perspective on life. It is an ongoing
'continuing professional development' of the parent that can work in
tandem with professionals.

Holistic: Practical and Emotional Support

The most holistic services offer both practical and emotional support
for example being solution focused and empathic. Even if the level of
practical support is minimal, due to lack of resources, the emotional
support can still be meaningful for parents.

'[The professional] got the Autism but she also got the
parental exhaustion, so you've got the double-whammy.'

Good practitioners know their field but are also open about when they don't have all the answers; furthermore, they reassure parents that if we struggle it is not that we have failed in some way. Parents welcome signposting to charities and online groups that can provide a level of support that statutory services may be unable to provide, in particular linking up with other special needs parents. At times it can be hard to join new groups and professionals may be able to help by providing a 'social scaffold'[128] to help access communities. At times just knowing that the group is there can be useful.

Professionals can role model how to play and interact with your child. This helps provide practical solutions as well as developing parental understanding of their child's perspective. This can take time. Once you know it it's hard to remember what it was like when you didn't know it. The most supportive professionals avoid making assumptions and allow time and practice for our perceptions to change.

'She was very knowledgeable about kids and behaviour
and stuff and I remember once I was telling her [my
son] is very confident and he goes to other people and
he says hello to them... and then she explained to me
it's not about him being confident, it's about he's not
aware of a stranger and the people he knows. That's
why he goes to everyone and says hello. And she
opened it up and she explained to me and I really liked
that... it helped me to understand that it's not about
him being confident and greeting people, it's about he
doesn't understand the concept of you greet people that
you know. And you keep the space between the people
you know and the people you don't know.'

The emotional recognition professionals can bring is also useful – ensuring parents realise that they are not alone in their feelings of worry or overwhelm. Parents can find it helpful to have a safe space to share their frustrations, to vent or offload, before being able to look more rationally at finding solutions for specific problems. At other

---

[128] Haslam, C. (2018) Scaffolding a stronger society, *The Psychologist*, May 2018, p. 44

times, particularly when experiencing high levels of stress, emotional support may not be enough[129] and practical support such as respite may be necessary (acknowledging that the strict criteria for this support makes it difficult to obtain).

Although many parent carers fully immerse themselves in the disability world, at times, some want a break from special needs. Services or professionals can offer a variety of things to encourage different families to take part and connect. This could include ensuring parents take some time for themselves. One parent told me of a group that provided tea and coffee for parents and, while the children played, the parents could access a masseuse. She talked of the importance of feeling welcomed by someone friendly and smiling to form a sense of community and acceptance. Other services could include one-to-one support – either face-to-face or by telephone, as not everyone feels comfortable attending a group.

Sadly many of the parents I spoke to had to pay privately to access much of the appropriate support, including behavioural advice, diagnostic services, talking therapies or going to the local SEND tribunal.

Co-ordinated, Consistent and Transparent
Co-ordinated

Services that fail to work together can add to the emotional load for parent carers. Parents find it supportive when services take on some of the burden of coordinating appointments or chasing up reports. This allows the family to focus their attention elsewhere.

> *'I don't think anyone ever went into social work thinking I'm going to make a massive difference by coordinating the departments to communicate together, but that is what I have found to be the most beneficial part of having a named social worker, is actually just someone that can coordinate different departments.'*

---

[129] Cantwell, J., Muldoon, O.T. & Gallagher, S. (2014) Social support and mastery influence the association between stress and poor physical health in parents caring for children with developmental disabilities, *Research and Developmental Disabilities*, 35, 2215-2223, p. 2221

Parents find it challenging when clinics clash or only run on certain days. This partly explains why working as a parent carer is so difficult and why so many give up work – which of course can have a knock-on effect on their wellbeing, sense of meaning or time away from the caring role.

Having a one-stop service that can meet all of the family's needs in one place helps lighten the load of navigating different systems and appointments.

> *'They get a lot of advice from the [charity] in terms of benefits, they will advocate for them, so they will go to tribunals with them, they'll write letters to schools, they will help them get adaptations to their houses, so they have a whole department who will help you with all of that, and they will signpost you so they have a link with a bereavement charity so they will signpost you to that.'*

Consistent and Transparent

Parents want accessible and transparent signposting to consistent support – with the same professionals and services[130]. This can help build a relationship not only with the parent but the child as well which in turn helps reduce anxiety and stress in parents.

> *'She's been a real consistency throughout his life... it's great.'*

Where there was felt to be little transparency, such as in a battle with the local Clinical Commissioning Group (CCG), it was very hard and disempowering. This partly comes down to trust. A 'loss of trust', even from one event many years previously (e.g. lack of local expertise, inaccurate information or a lack of preparation by a doctor), can have long-lasting ramifications for parents[131].

---

[130] Stanford, C., Totsika, V. & Hastings, R.P. (2020) 'Above and beyond': The perceptions of mothers of children with autism about 'good practice' by professionals and services, *Research in Autism Spectrum Disorders*, 77, p. 6

[131] Whiting, M. (2012) Impact, meaning and need for help and support: The experience of parents caring for children with disabilities, life-limiting/life-threatening illness or technology dependence, *Journal of Child Health Care*, 17, 1, 92-108

Crisis

Some parents had received good services but only once they'd reached crisis point. For example, it was by 'accident' that they ended up with the psychological support they required – either through going to Accident and Emergency or being referred to a paediatrician under the cancer 2 week rule; only then were they able to speak to a psychiatrist. It felt like they'd had to get to rock bottom to then access services through a back route, rather than there having been a clear pathway for them to receive the services prior to breakdown.

> *'The mental health crisis team... probably offered me the best support, but it's just a shame that you have to fall so low to be able to get a service. I just think that maybe if there had been a better service in place that I would probably never have needed them.'*

Sharing the care

As we've already seen there can be an increase in feeling 'on edge' and overwhelmed for parent carers. At times this may mean that services can provide support by sharing the caring load while a parent takes time to re-charge their batteries.

> *'I was having problems with her equipment, so they said just bring her down and while she was there they contacted wheelchair services, got that sorted out, like they stepped in. They took over. They took the problem, they tried to sort that out and the wheelchair was ready by the time she come back again, they put a blanket around you and they just do it for you.'*

It is important this is not pathologised (treated as abnormal) or seen as a deficiency or failure on the part of the family, rather that there is a recognition of the overwhelming situation. There may be an ebb and flow in when families need to be empowered and can manage on their own and when they need some extra support. This does not mean the family has taken a step backwards; it may be that the demands on their resources have increased and they require help to get through the next stage. Resilience is a dynamic, rather than static, process.

Examples of Good Practice

I include a few examples of services that parents found helpful. Some of the conversations were based on current services that do exist and others imagining what would be useful.

A number of parents wanted access to a place to offload (be it online, telephone or face-to-face), available throughout the day. This would involve active listening skills, not necessarily counselling per se, and require an understanding of the context for parent carers.

Services that provided a space for parents to meet up and combine practical (e.g. advice on benefits or the law) as well as social-emotional support were felt to be beneficial. Examples of this multi-dimensional support took place in some schools (special school outreach service which arranged for parents to meet up), local and national charities and Emotional Wellbeing Mental Health Services. As well as accessing some statutory services (such as physiotherapy and occupational therapy) all in one location in a combined clinic. Specific services that were found to be helpful included portage and family links.

Diagnosis – Support at Diagnosis or on Path to Diagnosis

The process of diagnosis is emotionally complex and often exhausting for parents. Scope states that 41% of parents of disabled children aged 0 to five weren't offered any emotional support during their child's diagnosis[132]. Sometimes the process of accessing, understanding and accepting a diagnosis can be a long pathway rather than a one-off event. And for some families there is no diagnosis.

As we've already seen in Chapter 3 there can be positives and negatives associated with a diagnosis. Sometimes we don't understand the diagnosis and when professionals take the time to fully explain what it means – in neutral and appropriate ways – and allow the parents to ask questions this can help. Sadly parents still report being left high and dry after a diagnostic appointment.

'The referral we had from his diagnosis was 'here's a leaflet' and that was it.'

---

[132] Scope, (2018) Now is the time: *Supporting disabled children and their families*, November 2018

In one study parents described their diagnosis delivery as 'catastrophic' and recommended that medical staff should i) establish what the parent already knows, ii) provide time to digest the information and ask questions (without interruption), iii) provide information to take away and iv) show empathy[133].

A follow-up appointment, telephone call or personalised letter would be the bare minimum to support families as well as clear, useful signposting to other sources of support – especially other special needs parents. It is human nature to seek out understanding and meaning for our child and the family as a whole. This may take time and a lot of searching.

> *'I was in total denial and I was depressed and I was crying a lot and I think that's why then someone from CAMHS came in... that's how everything started and I think, when she was explaining, at the time, I didn't understand what autism is and then after that I start reading and buying books.'*

Other issues to consider around diagnosis

Learning about a diagnosis can lead parents to question whether they or other family members might have the same condition. In some cases this may lead to the parent getting diagnosed which can lead to greater understanding and support. But it may also add to the level of adjustment required by the family.

For some parents a form of emotional support – including counselling or post-diagnostic provision may be useful and we'll consider this next.

Counselling & Therapeutic Support

There may be different points in a parent journey when counselling can be helpful, not only at the point of diagnosis. There may be triggers or difficult points along the path, even for the rest of their life, when counselling may be beneficial.

---

[133] Emerson, A. (2020) 'Room of Gloom': Reconceptualising Mothers of Children with Disabilities as Experiencing Trauma, *Journal of Loss and Trauma*, 25, 2, 124-140

*'I needed counselling at the very beginning. To get me
past the shock. And then I think I needed it again.
Because after you come to terms, with what's happened,
there's other feelings that you need to make sense of...
because you're almost grieving.'*

Being able to go over your story, sometimes many times, can be useful in processing difficult or unexpected news. You may get this support from a family member or friend, or at times you may need a professional – someone objective – to help. This can provide a different perspective, creating a new life narrative, and help you take stock of things in your life.

An important aspect of counselling for some parents was to assuage feelings of guilt. Whether this was related to genetic guilt, difficult feelings or recognising the need for time off from their caring role.

*'When the GP referred me to talking therapy I did a few
sessions... with the therapist, she really opened my mind.
I just thought it's normal, it's life, she said, no, it's not,
it shouldn't be like that... the over-worrying, the stress...
you are putting too much pressure on yourself in a lot of
areas in your life... because of her, I just stopped going
to work. I've realised I need time for myself, it's not just
him, him, him. So, yes, I just want to do little things like
that, like, go and not feel guilty about it.'*

Specialist Counselling Support

Although it wasn't always felt to be necessary that the counsellor had personal experience of being a parent carer (though some parents did want this) it was helpful if there were certain qualities the counselling support provided, including:

- understanding the context
- flexibility
- being trauma informed

Understanding the context

As the practical and emotional aspects of wellbeing are often deeply intertwined for parent carers, having someone who understands the context is important. Otherwise, parents felt they spent time explaining about the condition, or the battle for services.

> *'[The general counselling] was quite helpful, but then in the same breath, it wasn't, because the counsellor didn't clearly understand what it's like to have a child with a disability and you can talk about it until you're blue in the face but it doesn't change it, it's still the situation, it's still there... and support is less and less and less.'*

Many parents welcomed advice or strategies alongside the counselling role. This is not always how counsellors work and requires a certain level of expertise (i.e. around behavioural strategies or an understanding of sensory overload). At times it can be useful to refer parents onto other services to gain the appropriate advice.

Flexibility

Sometimes the system for referrals is inflexible and unhelpful. For example, in Improving Access to Psychological Therapies (IAPT) services some parents were discharged part way through their allotted number of sessions because they missed a session when their child was in hospital due to illness or for major surgery. Rigid adherence to protocol and policy can end up causing more harm than good. Parents also need support in a timely manner, which is at the point that they need it rather than staying on a long waiting list or having to be re-referred from scratch each time they seek help.

To meet the needs of parent carers, an emotional support service requires flexibility in a number of ways. Parent carers may have many appointments and different services they will be juggling so counselling sessions need to be adaptable to changes and cancellations.

> *'[Counselling] was once a week but I had to cancel too many appointments because we were in hospital so much. So we've made it once a month now which is a bit more sustainable.'*

Offering sessions online may be a useful way to accommodate these changes as well as being able to adapt to the parent's requirements, such as bringing the child along to the session (when young or if childcare has been difficult to arrange). (Although this needs careful consideration).

It may also be that different members of the family need support at different times so being able to offer this could help the whole family system. Because of the potential strain on the relationship between parents, accessing couples counselling can be useful at certain times. Group therapy may also be helpful for some as the other parent carers can support one another and provide the helping/helped dynamic that is beneficial for wellbeing.

Being Trauma informed

Many parents will have experienced trauma and may show evidence of post-traumatic stress (see Chapter 4). Feeling like you are battling on a daily basis – with your child, services or society – can take its toll and lead to a cumulative trauma. Services need to work in a trauma-informed way recognising that traumatised individuals have two main requirements:

- the need for physical, psychological and emotional safety through trustworthiness and transparency and

- opportunities to build a sense of control and empowerment through choice, collaboration and equality

What can Professionals do to Help Parent Carers' Emotional Wellbeing?

I give a brief overview of how professionals can support parent carer wellbeing. I address this directly to professionals so that you can share it with them if necessary. They can also access full guidance on the website www.affinityhub.uk

- **Recognise the emotions parents may be experiencing**
- **Consider your interaction style**
- **Comparison to other families is not helpful**
- **If a service isn't available, fight for it**
- **Raise awareness and fight stigma**
- **Look after your own emotional needs as a professional**

Recognise the emotions parents may be experiencing

Acknowledging the potential extra demands on a parent carer's personal resources is a necessary first step. Parents sometimes worry they are the only ones to feel this which can exacerbate a sense of isolation. They are not alone. Meeting other parent carers can help build a sense of community.

The emotional responses to being a parent carer are complex and varying. With this in mind, professionals need to avoid making assumptions and remain open to the individual's experience.

Being aware of what the parent might be going through enables staff to better support the parent – even by preparing them for changes in routines or systems that can be very unsettling. I remember while my son was in Intensive Care, we returned the next day to visit only to see his bed empty. As it turned out they'd just moved him to another ward but the heart-lurch I felt on seeing that almost floored me.

Often the focus may be on the medical side, which is of course important, but often a 'how are you?' or 'how are you feeling about this diagnosis?' goes a long way. Professionals can create a safe and much needed space for parents, acknowledging that intense challenging emotions may be experienced but also providing hope that these are normally transient[134].

Consider your interaction style

Parents report that the way some professionals and services interact with them can be problematic and damaging. This includes experiences of:

1. Being undervalued and excluded from discussions and activities central to their child's life

2. Feeling judged, criticised, mistrusted or patronised

3. Being perceived as difficult or challenging

Be mindful of the language you use and how this can come across. Parents digest information in different ways and being flexible to

---

[134] Sheehan, P. & Guerin, S. (2017) Exploring the range of emotional response experienced when parenting a child with an intellectual disability: The role of dual process, *British Journal of Learning Disabilities*, 46, 109-117

individual needs will help provide the support they need at the right time.

Comparison to other families is not helpful

Parents do not generally find it helpful to be compared to other families. For example, being told that they will not be able to access a service because there are 'people worse off' really doesn't help.

Having a professional who understands the situation and worries, yet remains objective, can allow parents to say what they are feeling without the worry of the impact on the other person. This is something unique a professional can offer that is sometimes lacking from other networks. Your objectivity doesn't equate to a lack of compassion though: rather it can give you insight and perspective.

If a service isn't available, fight for it

Parents won't always know what is available to them. For example, I did not know for some time that we were eligible for continence pads and use of a wheelchair. Professionals can make it easier for parents by signposting to these services. Being told there are no occupational therapists at the moment shouldn't be the end of the conversation. What is being done about it? To whom do we raise our concerns? Parents can be a powerful advocate and may help you in your work.

Raise awareness and fight stigma

Sometimes the more generic services – for health or education, say – do not have enough knowledge about helping people with disabilities. Discrimination and prejudice are still widespread in society. Raising awareness and education across different communities can be an important public health role for professionals as it is clear that stigma and discrimination have a negative impact on the wellbeing of families with a disabled child[135].

---

[135] Song, J., Mailick, M.R. & Greenberg, J.S. (2018) Health of parents of individuals with developmental disorders or mental health problems: Impacts of stigma, *Social Science and Medicine*, 217, 152-158

Look after you own emotional needs as a professional

Utilising your own emotional intelligence and skills such as active listening may help to create a connection with a parent. At times it may be upsetting or even traumatising to be in contact with families in distress. Ensuring that your own supervision, peer support and continuing professional development requirements are in place will enable you to better support the families with whom you work. This will prevent compassion fatigue.

Sometimes the nature of the institution in which you work may make it harder to emotionally support parents. The recognition of self-care as an important part of your role needs to be embedded in the structure of the system. That means that quality of care is just as important as quantity of care and can have longer term benefits.

Conclusion – avoid the fight in perpetuity

A common frustration for parents is that the fight continues, in perpetuity. When your child has a lifelong condition services have a chance to prepare, plan and prevent families falling off a cliff-edge, or at least having to repeat the same processes unnecessarily – such as constantly having to re-apply for support.

Unfortunately, it often seems that although parents get support initially it can tailor off, or has to be fought for again the following year.

> *'Some people become more complacent the older your child gets almost. It's like people work really hard to get things in place and then they think, oh well, we can just relax and let the system take care of it, but the system is made up of human beings.'*

Where possible, if professionals can work together with parents to recognise, and plan for, the long term needs of disabled children (and the personal toll it takes on families to continue to fight), this can help reduce the burden on families.

It can feel like we are in this together.

Useful resource for professionals:

'Guidance for Education, Health and Social Care Professionals on Supporting Parent Carer Wellbeing' – I have written, along with colleagues, an information sheet for professionals that is available on www.affinityhub.uk. Parents can share this with professionals and services.

Key points

- It is possible to get good quality support that transforms the lives of families with a disabled child

- At times though services or professionals add to the burden and emotional load for families rather than being helpful

- It is useful when services are family-centred and therefore work towards meaningful outcomes

- Awareness of the context in which families find themselves can help professionals have greater sensitivity to their needs

- What parents consider helpful, rather than harmful, is quite simple. Services need to demonstrate the following attributes:
  - Compassionate, human relationships
  - Empowerment and collaboration
  - Holistic – practical and emotional support
  - Co-ordinated, consistent and transparent
  - Sharing the care

- Sometimes parents need empowering and other times 'holding' by services. This is not a deficiency on behalf of the family, rather it represents the dynamic state of balancing stressors and resources

- Counselling for parent carers benefits from certain attributes: understanding the context, flexibility and trauma awareness

8

Replenish and Recalibrate: A Swiss Army Knife of Self-care

'It could be all manner of things, bath, yoga or getting out of the house and whatever, just a change of environment & situation.'

As we've seen over the previous two chapters our wellbeing is inextricably linked to relationships (in their widest sense), society, community and the services we receive. Connection, understanding and belonging are vitally important. Being supported and empowered to take control of our own lives and to access the information and knowledge we need in order to do this are vital. We need to know we have a community, the law and others on our side.

Wellbeing is also related to our relationship with our self, our focus, how we nurture and replenish ourselves and our inner resources. We can influence the outside world to some extent but obviously not as directly as we can influence our own emotional and psychological life. In this chapter we will consider wellbeing from this latter perspective. This is the R in the SPECTRA of Parent Carer Wellbeing – Replenish and Recalibrate. How we can use activities and psychological tools to create a self-care Swiss army knife which we will always have to hand to help us.

We'll look at what other parent carers and research report as helpful. What works for you will be personal so I'd recommend dipping in and out of the ideas – try them and see what you like. Don't worry: I'm not going to tell you that having a massage is the answer to self-care. Although at times it might be. You need to find your individual wellbeing strategy and part of this involves being aware of your own emotions, noticing how you deal with emotional upset and challenges, and being open to trying new approaches if necessary. There is no magic recipe for happiness, but there are suggestions of what might help.

This doesn't mean we can only focus on these strategies once all of the factors in the previous chapters have been satisfied (that would be impossible). In fact some strategies here are helpful even in the face of the previous conditions not being met, e.g., when we feel disempowered in relation to services we can still apply our values to guide our actions; or when we are in the middle of a crisis we can engage in some focused breathing to aid our stress levels. All lives involve adversity and stress. The key is what we do with this and how we make order out of the chaos.

Some strategies involve 'losing' yourself and others 'finding' or 'focusing' on yourself. They involve doing something with your consciousness that can help promote a feeling of wellbeing or contentment (although that is not always the direct aim it is sometimes a side-effect). Consciousness is a slippery thing and it's hard to pin down exactly how it works or benefits us. In many ways it doesn't really matter how or why something works – whether jogging is helpful because of a release of endorphins, being in flow or mindfulness or whether it's a distraction or escape. What matters is we notice it helps our mood, and allows us to recalibrate or re-gain a sense of balance. If it gives us a break from day to day worries and doesn't harm us (in the short or long term), then it can be added to our self-care Swiss army knife.

We can develop and learn coping strategies that not only help us deal with stress, but also enable us to grow in fulfilment, contentment and sense of purpose in life. Sometimes we may have a 'go-to' strategy that helps. Other times it doesn't work so well and we need to shake it up a bit. Self-care shouldn't feel like another thing on our 'to-do' list. Our strategies may change with age (ours and our child's) as well[136]. Noticing what we do and how it makes us feel acts as a personal mood barometer.

---

[136] Gray, D.E. (2006) Coping over time: the parents of children with autism, *Journal of Intellectual Disability Research*, 50, 12, 970-976

Openness and Flexibility

Research consistently shows that taking a flexible and adaptable approach to life is helpful for wellbeing and our mental health. It is the opposite of having a fixed approach that the world, and we, 'should' be a certain way. Acknowledging that fluctuating factors are part of life, and that we need to adapt to the environment and social world, it is probably unhelpful to think of only one self-care strategy as universally beneficial.

In psychology it is recognised that we are biased towards maintaining our world view, so change can be difficult. Yet if we keep hold of old frameworks and beliefs that no longer apply to our lives we will constantly be dealing with disappointment and frustration. By accepting and assimilating new information, different life paths and adopting a growth mindset we can move forward with our lives. It's not always easy but sometimes we need to let go in order to move forwards, and having a flexible approach can help us navigate challenging times.

Psychological flexibility includes:

- Recognising our own emotional responses and having some insight into these

- Being open to new experiences and new ways of seeing the world

- Shifting our responses to something when certain strategies do not work well in particular circumstances

- Maintaining balance across different life domains (i.e. not letting work or your child take over your life) and

- Being aware of, and committed to, behaviours that match our deeply held values[137].

Using our self-care Swiss army knife of tools and strategies means accessing different things at different times. This may be switching our focus from one perspective to another, or sometimes sacrificing something in one life domain for another, for example if we are training

---

[137] Kashdan, T. B. & Rottenberg, J. (2010) Psychological flexibility as a fundamental aspect of health, *Clinical Psychology Review*, 30, 865-878, p. 865

to run a 5k race we may sacrifice our favourite foods. The ability to change 'modes', as it were, will help you navigate the sometimes rough terrain that is special needs parenting. Flexibility doesn't mean that you lose a sense of self; rather you develop a 'spine' to help manage changing situations.

Living with inevitable change: learning to navigate the rough sea

As we already know, life is change. We are in a process of becoming that does not end until our death. Recognising this will help us to live with it. Further, how we perceive stressful events will influence how they affect us. So if we see something as a threat or a terrible thing to happen to us, we are more likely to feel a stress response. Our attributional style (our beliefs about why things happen) will influence whether we blame ourselves for something or see it as one of those things that happens in life. Taking a 'light touch' approach that allows for flexibility and change is helpful.

> *'I kind of have this sense of, if things are good, they might not last, so appreciate them. If things are bad, they won't stay bad, they'll change.'*

> *'It is the "nothing lasts forever" and "this too shall pass"...*
> *Can't change your past, you can't dictate the future.'*

Along with our adaptation to changing life events there may be a realisation that life is not perfect; it is complex and some things are out of our control.

> *'We have an expectation but we don't really have any control over life, it just happens doesn't it.'*

Over time many parents develop what I refer to as a 'helicopter' or birds' eye view of life and their place in it; they can see the bigger picture of the world. I think this perspective has a wisdom to it and helps us to cope with whatever life brings.

Utilising the different dimensions of the SPECTRA will help us navigate the rough sea.

Worksheet

Appendix I includes a worksheet for you to complete, making notes of your preferred ways of looking after yourself and noting down any new strategies or targets to try. How you use it is up to you – some people might like to set goals for each week whereas for others it will be more of a tool to stimulate reflection on how you can gain greater balance in your life, across different dimensions (refer back to Chapter 2 if you need to re-visit this).

It can be as simple as noticing after a day of sitting at a desk working on a computer you need to get out and do something physical in the evening. Balance across different life dimensions. After a particularly difficult day of considering other peoples' needs you can take time to do something that's just for you. You can download and print the worksheet from the affinityhub.uk website to use if you would find that easier.

Remember 'time that is yours' is key to wellbeing. It is the T in the SPECTRA of Parent Carer Wellbeing. This is not a luxury, it is a necessity. Let go of any guilt associated with taking some time for you. Some of the suggestions in this chapter require you to put some effort in and take responsibility for trying to improve things in your life. I confess to sometimes being guilty of dismissing things, despite thinking they may be helpful, without even giving them a proper go. You may need to put the work in – in the same way you would if you went to therapy or engaged in a new exercise regime. It takes time and commitment. Maybe you can start by acknowledging that it's worth a try, that you and your wellbeing are worth making time for.

Small steps

Our first step into self-care, or a new mode of looking after ourselves, can often be small. It's easy to let it go unnoticed or to dismiss these changes, but they are important. It is better to make small steps that we stick to than make huge changes that are hard to embed as part of our everyday life. Instead introduce tiny shifts that are more sustainable. Be mindful of the negativity bias we can display when we take on something new. We notice the risks of something rather than the potential benefits – this is the way we're hardwired. But by gaining greater awareness of this we can be more reflective in our choices and have an openness and willingness to try.

Self-compassion

Another key factor to remember through all of these activities is that of self-compassion – the need to 'tend and befriend' ourselves. Recognising that you might need some extra nurturing is important, allowing yourself and maintaining compassion throughout is vital, especially if you are trying out new activities that might be a challenge and take some practice – keep compassion close. Self-compassion is slightly different from self-care. It's how you talk to yourself in the difficult moments. It's a way of relating to ourselves – kindly – and embracing our whole selves including imperfections and flaws. It's also having the courage to commit to things that may be hard but are ultimately worthwhile.

Self-compassion is an integral part of mindfulness and acceptance and commitment therapy. I think it should also be part of your whole life. The basic way to remember it is to be a good friend to yourself as well as to others. Treat yourself with encouragement, patience and empathy. For some people this comes easily, for others – particularly if you've had difficulties in your childhood or been through trauma – you may need a bit more support to fully embrace this approach. There is more information on Compassion Focused Therapy, as well as some exercises to try, in Appendix I.

Signposts

A note to raise is that this chapter includes a brief overview of some theories, such as Acceptance and Commitment Therapy (ACT) or mindfulness. These are massive topics to cover and there are many books focusing on these approaches in more detail. There is not enough room in this book to cover them fully but I hope to give you a taster. I signpost to further information in Appendix IV.

The rest of this chapter is divided up into different sections, although there is overlap between them. These are:

- The Basics that we all know but often forget!

- Mindfulness and Meditation

- Body Approaches to Wellbeing
  - The Breath
  - The Body

- Acceptance and Commitment therapy

- Positive re-framing and Changed perspective

- Positive Psychology

- Flow

- Coping Strategies
  - Emotional regulation
  - Worry controller (Prioritising or dis-engaging from competing demands)
  - Delaying your own needs
  - Quick wins

- Trauma and Crises

The Basics that we all know but often forget!

Before discussing each of these in more detail we need to acknowledge the basics of wellbeing. We know these but, sometimes – particularly if we're busy or have a large emotional load – they get neglected. Yet much of the later themes build on a solid base of your basic self-care needs being met. If we are exhausted it's very hard to find a sense of purpose and meaning in life. That's not to say it's impossible – it's just harder. And why make life harder when there are some very (usually) simple things you can do to make life easier.

These are:

- Sleep
- Exercise
- Healthy eating and drinking
- HALT
- Nature

Sleep

Sleep is one of the most important aspects of wellbeing. Study after study shows this is the most influential piece of the wellbeing jigsaw puzzle and one which many parent carers find problematic.

> *'For the first few years I was surviving on about three hours sleep a day and to the point where actually I developed such symptoms, they thought I had a brain tumour, and it turned out to be sleep deprivation.'*

If you don't have enough sleep you can't function. It affects your ability to regulate your emotions, to think in a rational way and solve everyday problems. It makes it harder to eat healthily as you crave quick fix foods – like sugar to give you energy – and it changes your metabolism. If you have problems with sleep you need to get support.

One of the most common and earliest symptoms of stress is trouble with sleep. If you are in stressful circumstances then you need to find ways to identify and alleviate these. Using some of the strategies identified later in this chapter to make time for relaxation or mindfulness may help. Finding activities, groups or a meaningful engagement in life can reduce stress and increase wellbeing.

Good sleep hygiene helps:

- No caffeine too late in the afternoon
- Avoid the screen of your phone or tablet within 2 hours of your bedtime
- Keep to a regular bedtime and routine (i.e. bath, read a book)
- Stick to a regular get out of bed time

- Ensure you exercise during the day

- Some foods may be sleep-inducing: e.g. dairy, breads

There are many books and websites dedicated to helping with sleep problems, including on the NHS website (Appendix IV) so I will not go into too much detail here. However, there is a useful strategy in the box below that might help.

Sleep breathing technique

This can help relax your body and prepare your mind for sleep:

1. Inhale through the nose for the count of four

2. Hold your breath for the count of seven

3. Exhale completely through your mouth for the count of eight

4. Repeat four times

Often for parent carers, though, it is not that *we* have a problem going to or staying asleep it is outside factors (often our child) that wake us up. This can be a challenge to remedy as it requires someone else to do the night watch to enable you to sleep. Respite is ideal if you can access it. Speak to your GP, health visitor, social worker or paediatrician about accessing support.

Until that is achieved you and your partner may have to take it in turns. If you are a single parent see if anyone from your wider family or friends can help you – even one night off a week may help you to keep going and re-charge your batteries.

If you are unable to get cover for the nights make sure you grab naps during the day when you can. There is nothing wrong with dozing on the sofa, although you will need to balance it and monitor when this has an adverse effect on your sleep the next day. For example, if a nap on the sofa means you can't go off to sleep until midnight and you know your child will be up at 2am it might be better to skip the daytime nap and go to bed at 9pm.

Rest

'I have to slow it down, I have to slow the pace down.'

Rest is different from sleep but is also valuable. In our busy lives rest seems to have taken a back seat in importance. Busyness has become tied up with status and many people find it hard and frustrating to rest. But a lot of our rushing around may be unnecessary and unfulfilling. Prioritising what is important and learning to rest even when we have an ever-increasing 'to-do' list – childcare, housework, social media, admin, workload – is necessary, particularly in modern life. This may involve learning to say no to some things to protect your precious time.

Restful activities are deeply personal and wide-ranging – they can include reading, solitude or even gardening, if you find that restful. If it's an activity you have to do and don't enjoy then it is not restful. Watching a movie, having a hot bath, 'pottering about' and listening to music are also commonly used restful activities.

The times when we switch off may be because we need to rest our brains. We can't concentrate for longer than a couple of hours and every half an hour it is ideal to look away (especially if looking at a screen). Daydreaming out of the window and letting our mind wander can be due to an overload of concentration and a need to engage in a different type of mental activity.

Rest should be factored into our life, not something we take purely when we are ill or burnt out. Spending time relaxing helps us make better decisions, and it improves our memory and our physical health. Micro moments of self-care and compassion, such as sitting with a cup of tea and a book are valuable and necessary. Time to *be* rather than *do*; sometimes referred to as the fertile void. And your rest time needs to be taken without guilt. Give yourself this moment.

Exercise

But too much rest is not good for us either. Balance is always needed. We know that sitting in front of the television for long periods of time and not getting any exercise has a negative impact on our wellbeing. Our bodies don't thrive on inaction so have a think about what works for you and build it into your life. Walking the dog, swimming, doing a workout at home, getting off the bus a couple of stops early and walking the rest of the way – these are all ways of getting more exercise. It may feel strange at first and we may be more likely to stick to a new exercise regime if we take it up with a friend, or agree a shared commitment to certain goals.

Exercise can also link to other strategies that I discuss later in this chapter – flow, mindfulness, distraction or escape. If we are engaging in the exercise in a conscious, controlled way it can help focus our consciousness in ways that aid wellbeing. There are many different activities – such as yoga or martial arts – that contain a mindfulness element.

Our physical and mental wellbeing are deeply intertwined – the mind-body can be seen as a single unit. Sometimes getting up and moving transforms our feelings. I noticed this recently in my son who was getting very anxious waiting for his school transport following a long time away from school due to Covid-19. I decided to take him out for a walk while we waited and I could see his anxiety reduce and mood lift as we were walking. I don't need to fully understand all the systems that go into this shift to see that it works.

> *'I go to gym... that's the only time I can just like forget about... thinking. I think that's... one of the things that, I'm being really serious, mentally saved me is going to the gym, exercise is... a mental break.'*

My go-to for wellbeing is going for a jog. It releases feel-good hormones, gets me out into the air in nature. I also feel embodied, mindful of each step I take (sometimes painfully aware) and I feel free (physically and mentally). During Covid-19 lockdown it is probably what has helped my mental health the most.

Physical activity can also provide a break if we are stuck in a stress response cycle. When we have experienced stress our body remains in a fight or flight state until it knows we are safe. Moving your body – even having a dance around the kitchen – acts as a 'shaking off' of the negative mood. This is something animals do instinctively, such as when dogs shakes themselves. Here is a quick way to do this:

Drop forward from the waist, relaxing your upper body as you reach your hands towards your feet. Take in a deep breath and as you exhale make an 'ah' sound. Repeat until you feel the tension has left your body.

Healthy eating and drinking

Being aware of what we put in our body and the impact it has on us is a vital part of a healthy life. There is increasing evidence of how 'gut health' affects our moods and our wellness. So the effect of unhealthy eating is twofold.

If we're full of unhealthy food we may feel energised for a while, but it's not going to last. Sugar-filled or carbohydrate-loaded comfort eating is short lived and has a longer term negative affect. It can even lead to missing vital nutrients. We all know about the five fruit and veg a day recommendation. These are tried and tested ways to feel healthier. Setting up ways to succeed – such as having a fruit bowl out in view and not having unhealthy food in the house – will make it easier to develop as a habit.

It is also worth considering how you eat. If you gulp your food down sitting at a desk or in the car then it's probably rushed with little chewing that can create digestive problems. We can get caught up in a cycle of anxiety.

Again use your noticing skills to see how these things affect you. Although caffeine can energise us, if we have too much we become dependent and any slump is magnified. Drinking plenty of water also helps and we need more of it that we often realise – six to eight glasses a day is recommended.

Alcohol can disrupt our gut, as well as our physical and mental health. It adds to tiredness and low mood. If you do drink alcohol make sure it's in a mindful way – notice it, be aware of what you are drinking, the amount, the taste – rather than drinking without thinking. If you are worried it is becoming too much of an unhealthy habit, it is helpful to note your intake and take action. We all know the negative effect of smoking so if you do smoke make steps to quit.

You'll have your own treats and habits. Be aware of them and see how they affect your mood. I am a fan of balance and small steps. So although there is evidence suggesting coffee, chocolate and wine can have some positive impact on wellbeing, it is always with the caveat of small doses and within a broader healthy approach in our life. Making one swap for a healthier choice is manageable and you are more likely to stick to it.

Halt

A useful acronym to remember is HALT – Hungry, angry, lonely or tired – all of which influence our mood and feelings. We are not in the best position to make decisions if we are experiencing any of these states. We are also liable to feel in a negative place and may fall into a 'mood misattribution' (mistaken belief about something) where we misinterpret what we're feeling. So sometimes we may feel low, that life is hard and there are no solutions, when in actual fact we just need to have a snack, or a chat with a friend. We have to learn to read our emotions – and the messages they send us – in their whole context. It's hard to think when you're depleted – you need to replenish.

Nature

One of my favourite wellbeing enhancers is nature. This can be a walk through the woods or a park or even noticing a flower. Research shows how positive nature is for our mental health on many levels – exercise, beauty, mindfulness and a break from our everyday worries. Taking the time to notice what is around you, time away from online activities, breathing fresh air and getting exercise – what's not to love? And it's great for the children too. It provides a connection with something bigger that can feel spiritual for many. It has even been suggested that just watching nature on television or seeing pictures in a book can have a positive impact.

To reiterate – we need the basics to function. These give us a foundation for our life – to live well, to feel well, to be well. Try to ensure they are built into the fabric of your day – every day.

In the rest of the chapter I will consider other factors that are important in looking after yourself. But it's important to remember that everything that is discussed below works alongside the basics, rather than replacing them. They are all key ingredients for our emotional wellbeing.

We'll now turn our focus to mindfulness and other techniques using our body. It is a good place to start as it is something that we always have access to; our body and our breath can help us in any situation.

Mindfulness and Meditation

The benefits of mindfulness are well evidenced. Recognising that thoughts and emotions come and go – they are something that we have, not who we are – can be helpful particularly when dealing with unwanted emotional responses. Rather it is our reactions to them that often causes the problems. The best way to learn about mindfulness is by giving it a go. So here is an introduction.

Mindfulness

Find somewhere you can be still and quiet.

Close your eyes and bring your awareness to the present moment. This may be physical sensations in your body, such as where your back presses against the chair, or your chest rising and falling as you breathe. There's no need to change the way you're breathing, just notice it.

Your thoughts will inevitably drift off into other things but keep bringing it back to the here and now.

By practising this you become more skilled at noticing when you move endlessly from distraction to distraction and it strengthens your ability to be more present in your life moment by moment.

It is like strengthening a muscle – the more you do it the better you will become at it. Try a few minutes each day.

Smell is one of our most powerful ways of connecting to our senses and the here and now. If you like you can find a smell that has positive associations for you – lavender, perfume or spices – and you can smell it at the end of a mindfulness exercise. You can then use it to bring yourself back to the present moment if you get caught up in worries or unwanted memories.

If you find the openness of mindfulness difficult you could start with a grounding technique. This can be useful for those who have experienced trauma or acute anxiety as it brings you back to a 'neutral' place in the here and now. It can be a safe space to return to after trying some of the other activities – particularly if they have brought up difficult feelings or sensations.

54321 Grounding technique

A simple exercise is the 5-4-3-2-1 that helps you stay grounded.

- Focus on five things you can see,

- four sounds you can hear,

- three things you can feel,

- two scents you can smell and

- take a bite or sip of one thing you can taste.

This grounds you in the present, re-focusing a busy mind and gaining perspective.

Thinking self v observing self

Part of mindfulness is developing awareness of the thinking and the observing self. When we have a thought we may place a lot of importance on it – like it is fact or 'the truth' because we thought it. Of course this isn't always the case; thoughts are just a collection of words or images. They may be a belief, an opinion, an ideal or a story.

Often these thoughts may be negative and we can fall into unhelpful patterns – 'this always happens to me', 'I'll never be happy' or 'I'm no good at being mindful.' To be mindful is to choose to pay attention without judgement. You notice these thoughts but don't necessarily buy into them – they're thoughts not facts. Our thoughts and feelings come and go and we can choose whether to listen to them or not.

As we all know, trying to stop our thoughts can be hard. If I say 'don't think about a pink elephant' your mind can't help itself. It can be draining and take up a lot of time to try and control thoughts. Instead you can develop the 'observing self' to notice what the 'thinking self' is doing. The observing self may reflect, 'I notice that I'm thinking x right now.' It's not about trying to change the thought – just noticing it. You can learn to make room for these thoughts in your life as just another part of being a human being. This is called Expansion or Acceptance.

So, an example is that we receive a call from a service about our child's support being reduced. This is unhelpful and we will naturally feel something (strong) in response to this. Our secondary response however may be less helpful if it is along the lines of 'how am I going to cope with this?', 'what will happen to my child in the future if they never receive this service?', 'am I a bad parent for not having stopped this from happening?' If we keep going over and over it the thought process can become depressive rumination.

In this moment it can help to notice what is going on – engage your observing self – 'I notice that I'm thinking "am I a bad parent?"'. These are not facts. They are just thoughts.

Buddhist second dart

There is a useful metaphor in Buddhism of the second dart. The first dart represents the inevitable difficulties that life throws at all of us. We can't do anything about the first dart; stressful events are part of life. The second dart, however, represents the thoughts and habits we get caught up in about the first dart. These aren't always helpful – a secondary emotion or thought about the primary one. It makes our distress last longer and it is self-inflicted. By noticing this process, our awareness of our thoughts provides a greater awareness of ourselves.

This doesn't mean we just sit down and accept negative outside influences – it is not passive resignation. We may decide to appeal, campaign or respond in some way that is in line with our values. We may also decide to save our energy for another battle. But it is important that we choose to *respond* in a more consciously aware state rather than automatically *react*. And it starts by noticing our thoughts and the patterns we fall into.

A key part of mindfulness is also the self-compassion we show ourselves during our practice. It isn't always easy to be self-compassionate but the more you practice the easier it will become. We can be our own worst critic but by learning to be mindful we can choose to recognise these thoughts for what they are – unhelpful mind chatter.

We can bring mindfulness into all aspects of life by focusing on something as simple as our morning shower. What can you see, hear, smell, taste and feel? Engaging in this practice requires commitment and practice. Our minds naturally wander so it takes time to develop new ways of seeing and being. But for many it is life-changing.

[Mindfulness] 'is all about living in the moment and I was spending a lot of my time worrying about the future because I had children who were deteriorating and I didn't know how long they were going to live for, so actually, to find something that offered me the ability to live more in the moment, because I'd worked out that's what I needed to do, I needed to enjoy moments more, instead of being pre-occupied about what was going to happen in the future... Mindfulness is not a technique for me. It's a way of living now, it's a way of being in the world.'

Meditation

Meditation embodies many similarities to mindfulness as well as some differences. Generally meditation involves focusing on something specific – a word, image, concept or the breath. There is usually a set start and finish for the meditation. So, for example, you might engage in a loving kindness meditation or you might meditate on achieving a certain goal. A simple one is the 'I am X' meditation. Simply add your own word or phrase to this. I am strong, I am managing, I am kind. Repeat it throughout the day or at times when you most need it.

'It's like everything isn't quite as hard to deal with when I meditate for half an hour to an hour and I try and do that twice a day.'

Meditations can also take on the form of a ritual which can help you find meaning and purpose; to celebrate the ordinary in life and become more aware of the here and now.

Accessing training

There are many mindfulness and meditation trainings available, although at times the commitment may feel onerous for parent carers to attend in person, when childcare and other factors can make it difficult. Online provision, such as *Be Mindful*[138] or Calm, may help accessibility.

---

[138] Flynn, S., Hastings, R.P., Burke,C., Howes, S., Lunsky,Y., Weiss, J.A. & Bailey,T. (2020) Online Mindfulness Stress Intervention for Family Carers of Children and Adults with Intellectual Disabilities: Feasibility Randomized Controlled Trial, *Mindfulness*, 11, 2161–2175

*'Love the Headspace app, so I try and do that at least
every day and that's helped. I get it to remind me.
Yes, I definitely think breathing really helps.'*

Not a one-size-fits-all

I want to add some reflections as lately there has been a massive increase in the popularity of mindfulness in all areas of life. Generally I think this is a good thing. Yet mindfulness is part of a whole Eastern philosophical practice and it can sometimes feel that, taken out of context, it is a packaged panacea which may lose some of its holistic grounding. To fully embrace it as an approach for life may mean reading widely about the context to the practice. This is sometimes hard to fully embrace in the Western, capitalist society in which we live.

It is sometimes offered as an 'intervention' for situations that wouldn't be a problem if proper input and support was offered earlier. By that I mean if a parent carer is exhausted and receiving little support it may be preferable to remedy these issues with adequate funding and responsive services rather than to place the expectation on parents to become trained in mindfulness. I believe there is a place for both of these aspects in support for parents. But mindfulness shouldn't mean that the other problems are ignored. We need to acknowledge widespread problems within the system that need rectifying.

There is some suggestion that if you are deeply self-critical then mindfulness might not be the best approach for you[139]. Although if this is you then developing your capacity for self-compassion may be the starting point for your wellbeing (there are some ideas on this in Appendix I). It is also the case that for some people who have more complex mental health needs mindfulness might not always be the first choice.

It's important to flag up that there are times when it's increasingly hard to be in the moment and in fact planning for the future is necessary. We have to make arrangements, for example, applying for services or filling out forms to get the support we need. We can be mindful while we do them – noticing our responses, taking a break when we feel it become overwhelming – but no one can fully live

---

[139] Mather, P., Ward,T. & Cheston, R. (2019) Presence and Personality: A Factoral exploration of the relationship between facets of dispositional mindfulness and personality, Counselling Psychology Review, British Psychological Society, 34, 1

in the moment in our current society. Furthermore, findings from research into psychological flexibility, which as we've already seen is a recognised factor for emotional wellbeing, note that being able to adapt our consciousness to different situations is helpful.

> [This research] 'challenges theory and research promoting an ideal to remain consciously aware of ongoing events as they change from moment to moment... sometimes it is beneficial to be immersed in the present to appreciate the array of beauty walking through the neighbourhood... sometimes it is beneficial to be positioned in the future, clarifying values, future goals to link with those values... sometimes it is beneficial to be in the past whether it is savoring [sic] experiences for a mood boost, re-connecting with one's personal history, extracting life lessons'[140].

As we've already noted, it's important to develop your own Swiss army knife of self-care to support you – and this may entail different things at different times.

Body Approaches to Wellbeing

The Breath

Already identified as crucial to mindfulness it's worth considering how we actually breathe. Many of us only engage in shallow breathing which can prevent the full intake of oxygen and re-centring. A quick way to check is to place one hand on your upper chest and the other on your stomach. When you breathe in the hand on your stomach should gently rise up and down. If you need help with this there are many apps or websites that can support you to breathe correctly, and remind you to do regular practice as practice is a necessary part of it. We have to break unhealthy habits and patterns that will have developed over many years so it may take time to change.

Mindful breathing can be a really useful in-the-moment calming exercise and is possible to do even while you're talking to someone else or in a meeting. If something is upsetting you or you find yourself

---

[140] Kashdan, T.B. & Rottenberg, J. (2010) Psychological flexibility as a fundamental aspect of health, *Clinical Psychology Review*, 30, 865-878, p. 868

getting irritated it's a simple strategy. Ensure you don't shallow breathe though as it can lead to panic attacks if you are prone to these. Breathing creates something of a pause before reacting and provides time to consider the response.

> *'When I get really stressed, I just really tense up and my jaw is really clenched and it just helps me to relax and breathe and not snap at things, so if I get a shitty letter in the post, I'll read it, put it down, do a bit of breathing, and then think about what I'm going to do about it.'*

The Body

As we've already discussed, we are embodied, our mind and body connected: we may feel butterflies in our stomach to express our anxiety; we get goose bumps on our skin when we're scared. Research has shown that there is more of the feel-good hormone, serotonin, in our gut than in our brain. Yet many people still focus solely on the mind when they consider wellbeing.

Vagus Nerve

There is considerable evidence for part of our nervous system called the vagus nerve – which connects the gut to the brain – playing a vital part in our wellbeing. This is a complex topic and I include references to further resources on the body and polyvagal theory in Appendix IV.

For the sake of brevity for this chapter I provide a quick 'how to tone your vagus nerve' in the box below for you to try at times when you may need to re-set.

How to tone your vagus nerve:

- Movements – such as sitting on a gym ball or sitting in a rocking chair
- Physical warmth – holding a hot drink, wrapping up in a warm blanket
- Sing, chant or hum
- Breathing techniques which focus on extended exhalation (sighing, blowing bubbles)
- Massage the sides of your neck
- Look after your gut health
- Connect with people that feel safe

Yoga, qi gong or tai chi

For many people yoga or other body-based exercises are a positive way to reduce anxiety and re-gain calm in their lives. They align body and mind and help settle the calming parasympathetic nervous system (often referred to as the 'rest and digest' system). Again, this is linked to the vagus nerve. Qi gong and tai chi tap into similar benefits – combining movement, breathing and meditation which provide emotional benefits. Further, yoga has also been shown to improve overall mood, life purpose and satisfaction[141].

A useful restorative pose is the 'viparita karani' which involves lying on the floor with your legs up the wall, resting your hands on your stomach and tuning into your breath.

Nurturing touch

Physical touch is beneficial for our wellbeing. It soothes and calms the body. Once again it is connected to the vagus nerve and touch can produce oxytocin – often referred to as the 'love hormone'. This is why sometimes a massage may be helpful for wellbeing. You can trigger this response with a cuddle with your child or partner or even your pet. You can also use nurturing touch on yourself. For example, you can place one or two hands over your heart; cradle your face in your hands or cross your arms and give yourself a gentle hug.

Have a good cry

As identified earlier in the book, having a chance to offload can be a useful stress release. Crying is a basic physical reaction and one that provides an immediate way of dealing with an inescapable stressor. As with the venting or offloading it needs to take place in a safe, non-judgemental space to have the most benefit.

Normally when we cry we feel better. It releases chemicals, such as stress hormones, so it's no wonder that many of the parents I spoke to said this was an important coping mechanism. They didn't always like it but at times when they were stuck in crisis mode it sometimes offered the only response that helped them move on.

---

[141] Hefferon, K. (2013) *Positive Psychology and the Body: The Somatopsychic side to flourishing*, Berkshire, UK: Open University Press, p. 209

'Sometimes that would be the darkest of the darkest period for me and I didn't look after myself. I allowed myself to cry a lot. I allowed myself to get angry.'

'It's where I just go for a cry and I just let it all out and then I'm ready to go back and do what I need to do and it can be, you know, it doesn't have to be sitting in the chapel, it can be sitting in the shower, but it's just that ability just to let it out and then dust yourself off and start again... recalibrate a little bit.'

If however you find yourself crying for long periods, for many days on end, then you might be falling into a depression and it would be best to visit your GP to discuss options for support or consider a form of therapeutic counselling.

This has been rather a whistle stop tour of body-based psychology. There is much more to learn so if there is something that has whetted your appetite it may be worth exploring further.

Acceptance and Commitment Therapy

A therapeutic approach that draws on mindfulness as well as ideas from Cognitive Behavioural Therapy (CBT) is Acceptance and Commitment Therapy (ACT)[142]. It has been shown to not only benefit parent carer wellbeing but also positively impact on those around them (e.g. their child)[143]. It encourages parents to build on their existing strengths to develop a new perspective alongside greater self-compassion.

---

[142] Hayes, S. C. (2004) Acceptance and commitment therapy, relational frame theory, and the third wave of behavioral and cognitive therapies, *Behavior Therapy*, 35, 639-655

[143] Reid, C., Gill, F., Gore, N. & Brady, S. (2016) New ways of seeing and being: Evaluating an acceptance and mindfulness group for parents of young people with intellectual disabilities who display challenging behaviour, *Journal of Intellectual Disabilities*, 20, 1, 5-17

ACT has two main processes:

  i)   developing acceptance of unwanted private
       experiences which are out of personal control, and

  ii) commitment and action towards living a valued life[144].

What I like about this approach is that it brings together many different ideas including acknowledging that human beings are meaning-makers. As we've already seen in the section above, being mindful involves consciously attending to the here and now, being aware with openness and interest. This approach also looks at the meaning we make in life. We create stories about our lives and pick up narratives from our society and culture. These influence how we perceive the world around us and how we feel about ourselves.

By connecting with our values – what is important to us – we engage more fully in life. Stop and think about the last time you were totally engaged in something that felt important, purposeful and fulfilling in your life, e.g. helping people or hiking in the mountains. Life can't always feel purposeful and fully engaging but we can increase the number of times we experience that by identifying what is important and meaningful in our lives and working towards doing those things more often. There are some useful resources listed in Appendix IV to help you with this.

Finding your values involves identifying what is important and meaningful to you. It is considering what sort of person you want to be as well as committing to action that reflects these values. This connects to our sense of purpose and meaning in life, which we will discuss in more detail in the next chapter.

It may feel uncomfortable at first and we need to embrace a willingness to allow the anxiety that may arise. Sometimes as a parent carer it's worth feeling out of our comfort zone to re-engage with something that's important to us. For example, it can sometimes feel difficult to let go and trust someone else to look after our child, but the alternative is we never get time to ourselves or to re-engage with another part of our life.

---

[144] Harris, R. (2008) *The Happiness Trap. Based on ACT: A revolutionary mindfulness-based programme for overcoming stress, anxiety and depression*, Great Britain: Robinson

As carers, time for ourselves and time being something other than 'carer' is key to wellbeing. Re-discover what used to be important to you before becoming a parent. This could be in any number of ways – being in nature, painting, coffee with good friends, getting involved in a campaign or something faith-based. The list is almost infinite and it will be personal to you.

Our values determine a life path that we stick to – even when, as we all do at times, we deviate from this track, we come back to it again. I think often for parent carers we become distracted with other things, away from our path, and it can lead to us feeling disjointed from who we are. There are normally ways to incorporate our values in our lives, even if it's in a very small way at first. You will know when you are doing things that you value – as deep in your heart they truly matter to you.

> *'Doing something that isn't just a carer is really important to me. I hated being a stay-at-home-mum and I hated being just a carer. I need to be doing something. I probably am way too busy but it's very rewarding work and you know I get to help people and I really enjoy working.'*

The funny thing is that when you start to live a more meaningful life you will have more positive experiences and emotions, even though this isn't the direct aim of changes we make to live more meaningfully (if we said our aim was to be happier this would rarely work in a direct way – other strategies work better). And, as we engage in a more value-led life, if we continue to act mindfully in the moment we can appreciate things more – the taste of good food, a beautiful sunny day, a smile from a stranger.

Of course there are days when this is easier to do and others when it is harder.

Periods of emotional difficulty are common to everyone at one time or another. This is because we are all human and being alive includes joys, sorrows and challenges. Feeling anxious, stressed, low, confused, frustrated or angry is not unusual. However, often people try to get rid of these responses and that can affect our behaviour. We might avoid situations or activities; we may socially withdraw – just at a time when we need others in our life. So the first step is to be aware of and understand our emotional responses and then to engage in activities and situations that support us.

There is not space in this chapter to cover all the ideas and practices you can develop. I've listed some books and websites with further information on ACT in Appendix IV.

We will also consider identifying values, sense of purpose and meaning in life in more detail in the final chapter.

Positive Re-framing and Changed perspectives

As we saw in Chapter 5, one of the positives for parent carers involved changing their perspective and seeing things in a new light. Psychologists refer to this as re-framing, re-appraisal or restructuring the problem in a positive way. It consists of thinking differently so as to re-evaluate and re-position your values, beliefs and behaviours. It involves challenging less helpful ways of thinking or, if you find yourself in a negative pattern or downward spiral, finding a different way to make sense of your experiences.

This can happen in different ways and on multiple levels.

Changing how you think about something

Let's start by exploring a strategy from cognitive behavioural therapy (CBT) where we challenge our automatic negative thoughts (ANTs). (Appendix IV signposts to further information on CBT).

If you have a tendency to jump to conclusions – for example, if someone didn't say hello to you at the school gates and you immediately engage in catastrophic or all-or-nothing thinking ('she hates me', 'I must have done something wrong', 'what is the matter with me?') – you could practise stopping to reflect. Maybe they did not see you. Maybe they are having a bad day. Not everything revolves around you and there are probably other factors influencing their life.

You can write a list of assumptions or unhelpful thoughts that you have and then ask of each one – is it true? Does it help me? How can I change my response to this?

Here are some other examples of automatic negative thoughts that can be challenged:

I'm a terrible parent	I'm trying my best but this is a difficult situation
I should know what to do	I can't know the answer to every problem I encounter. I've helped my child through other situations and I will work out how to help in time
My child hates me	My child is struggling with something at the moment and is taking it out on the person who they feel most comfortable with

There is a thought record in Appendix I that you can use to challenge some of these thoughts. Imagery and visualisations may also help the re-framing process[145]. We start to see that we can shift our thoughts towards things. So the thought 'I *have* to pick up my child from school' becomes 'I *get* to pick up my child' which in turn can change how we appraise the event. This can take time as we have to stick with it to adjust our automatic thoughts, especially if our situation continues to be challenging. This is often referred to as the need to 'shift *and* persist'.

Developing these skills can come with practise. A parent shared how she'd found a way to cope with the negativity of completing a Disability Living Allowance (DLA) form.

> *'Mostly it was time. And I guess I justified every difficulty with a solution, so yes, he has trouble getting dressed, but we have a system that helps him do that. Yes, he has trouble making friends, but that's okay... he has three good friends, who needs more than three friends? I sometimes think [pause] you know people don't get him and I rationalise it, I say, well it's their loss. So it's like I try and find the opposite positive thing.'*

---

[145] Greenspan, L.C. (2010) Opportunities for personal growth: Counselling psychology and parents and carers of children with learning disabilities (Unpublished doctoral dissertation), *City University*, London, UK

Changing your wider perspective

Parents also adapt their thinking to the wider socio-political landscape, seeing the normative structures that are in place that previously we may have taken for granted. We awaken to the challenges, re-assess our situation, and change the way we look at the world.

It is something that can be supported by therapy but this isn't always necessary. We may gain a wider perspective by looking around at others and internalising different models (or schemas) of how the world is and our place in it. This might be particular people, groups or even a larger movement or community that helps to provide an alternative narrative from the one we previously held.

> *'The [neurodiversity] community really helps with that as... there's a general sense of like I know he's not broken, whereas I think other people think he's broken and not as good as a child that didn't have autism and it's just that not simple.'*

Your sense of life direction can change or your expectations adjust. You learn to appreciate the little things that may have been taken for granted before. The adjustments create a more realistic assessment of life and purpose. You start to see your place in the bigger picture, that things aren't necessarily 'out of place', instead you are on a different pathway. For some parents this involves fully immersing yourself in the special needs world.

> *'I don't even try and shoot for normal any more. I don't think I ever could even if I wanted to, but I used to try and aim for it and then feel short for it and then that would be a bad loop, mental loop, whereas I'm much more accepting.'*

Whereas for others it might mean they need time away from the disability world in whatever way that may be: coffee with other friends, work or activities that are not related to special needs. This helps them return to their family with renewed energy.

Changed personality

The change may be so great that it feels like your personality has changed. There were a mixture of outcomes in my research in relation to this – some parents felt like they'd changed as a person, both negatively and positively.

'I think I know myself better now which is good.'

'I'm mentally stronger but I'm not as happy as I was.'

Changed parenting style

Interestingly for many it had led to a change in parenting style. As the parent gained greater knowledge, understanding and empowerment in their ability to parent their particular child, they'd realised that their inherent parenting style or model was not always the best for their child. In other words, the way that they had been brought up did not work with their child. This involves a level of emotional intelligence to reflect on the dynamic between parent and child and the ability to flexibly change your behaviour; the enhanced perspective taking we identified in Chapter 5. These are all valuable assets for a parent to have.

The majority of parent carers do find skills and strategies that enable them to navigate the ever-changing landscape of special needs parenting. At times it is sitting with paradox and riding the special needs rollercoaster. It can also be transformative, leading to a changed perspective on the whole of life, like accepting that life isn't always easy; things happen without necessarily finding a causal explanation for them[146] and we can survive them.

Changing your life narrative

We all have a life story that we tell ourselves and others. It helps provide a cohesive sense of self, although at times this may need challenging if we get stuck in a particular narrative – e.g. 'I'm an unlucky person' – or if our circumstances change so much that the story no longer fits. No one has a fixed, all-encompassing life story and the process of telling

---

[146] Pakenham, K.I. Sofronoff, K., Samios, C. (2004) Finding meaning in parenting a child with Asperger syndrome: Correlates of sense making and benefit finding. *Research in Developmental Disabilities*, 25, 245-264

and re-telling our personal story to create a meaningful and coherent 'narrative identity'[147] is ongoing.

Reflecting on this can help us to think bigger, wider and more openly about our life. Journaling or actively engaging in a creative process can help shift our narrative and gain new insight and meaning. Research suggests that for some people the act of writing about emotional experiences can make us feel better in the longer term, physically and mentally[148] (sometimes less happy immediately after writing though). Our new life experience can be incorporated into, and help shape and grow, our future self-identity. The important aspect is that our re-telling shifts our story rather than just repeats it in a negative rumination[149] (that is continuously thinking over the same, often sad, thought).

Writing can also help get things 'off your chest' and move on, particularly for those people who are perhaps more reticent in seeking help from others. It can be seen as a brain dump or download – letting go of things that are playing on your mind or when we have too many things going on in our lives (too many 'tabs' open to use the computer analogy). It can help us feel a little more in control of our experience. Sometimes if we hold onto too many things that feel unsayable it can take its toll on our mental health.

Expressive writing is a personal thing and is not for everyone – but it might be worth giving it a go. If writing is difficult (sometimes verbal processing is arduous) you could try using drawings, such as simple stick people, images or voice recording instead. You can use the space on the worksheet in Appendix I for free writing or drawing.

---

[147] Ricoeur, P. (1992) *Oneself as Another*, Chicago: University of Chicago Press

[148] Pennebaker, J.W. (2014) *Expressive Writing: A Guided Journal for Recovering from Trauma and Emotional Upheaval*, London: New Harbinger Publishing

[149] Neimeyer, B. (2019) Making meaning out of loss, *Therapy Today*, 30, 7, 26-29, p. 28

Free writing

Free writing is a tool whereby you write about anything, allowing your writing mind to go wherever it likes. You can start by spending just five to ten minutes a day writing down your experiences. You can buy yourself a nice journal so that it feels special and a treat, dedicated time to you. Don't worry about grammar or spelling – you are not writing for an audience; it's for you alone.

Here are some suggestions of things you can write about if you need help to get started:

Think of an event that happened

- How has it affected you?
- Your relationship with your child?
- With your wider family?
- With society at large?

You might find it helpful to think about what advice you would give to yourself at the time of diagnosis or at a particularly low point in your journey. Often parents find it rewarding to communicate their experiences with other parent carers. If you want to share your advice for other parents please go on the affinityhub.uk website and email your comments for inclusion on the website.

We may also broaden our horizons, re-frame and change our narrative by reading about others' experiences. You can find books on many different topics related to wellbeing under the Reading Well initiative[150] and on special needs parenting in Appendix IV.

Positive Psychology

The strategies in this next section are mainly taken from positive psychology. This movement arose in response to what was considered an overly negative approach in psychology – only focusing on what was 'wrong' or 'lacking' in humans rather than recognising our strengths. The positive approach focuses on what we can do, or may already be doing, to help our wellbeing.

---

[150] www.reading-well.org.uk

The positive psychology movement has been criticised for going too far the other way and overly focusing on positives while failing to acknowledge the negatives which, as we've seen throughout this book, are deeply entwined and overlapping. Yet many of the techniques are really simple and effective so worth covering here. Again balance is key to wellbeing.

This section looks at:

- **Positive thinking**
- **Gratitude**
- **Hope**
- **Joy and play**

Positive thinking

We naturally focus on negative situations – being alert to potential dangers has kept our ancestors alive after all. It means that we often miss the positives. When we're in a negative mood we are also more likely to remember negative things and we get into a downward spiral. However, with practice and a little bit of work we can learn to change that focus. Generally, if we have a positive mood we can cope better with life. Positivity makes us more open-minded, resilient and connected to others. A positive mood can provide a 'stress-buffer'[151], making us healthier and more generous.

There are several ways in which a positive mood provides a buffer against stress:

- It promotes creative problem solving which means we may be able to deal with challenges more quickly and with an increased number of options of how we respond (what is known as the 'broaden and build' theory[152*])

---

[151] Song, J., Mailick, M.R., Ryff, C.D., Coe, C.L., Greenberg, J.S. & Hong, J. (2014) Allostatic load in parents of children with developmental disorders: Moderating influence of positive affect, *Journal of Health Psychology*, 19, 2, 262-272, p. 269

[152] Frederickson, B.L. (2001) The Role of Positive Emotions in Positive Psychology: The Broaden-and-Build Theory of Positive Emotions, *American Psychologist*, 56, 3, 218-226

- It encourages behaviours that are helpful and restore our wellbeing, such as exercise, sleep and relaxation

- These in turn make us less likely to view some of life's stress in an overly negative way

- It improves our self-esteem

- If we are happy we are also less likely to take part in activities we know are not good for us – such as smoking, drinking alcohol or eating unhealthy foods

*in contrast to a narrowing of our focus and attention (which happens when we are feeling negative)

Strategies that help include rehearsing good news to share with others and celebrating little moment of success. They may feel strange at first but can soon become a natural part of your day.

We can find things that have a positive influence on our emotions and cheer us up (unless we are depressed and then it can be hard to find things that make us feel happy – even things that used to*). At times we may need to engage in them more to create an upward spiral in our mood. Other people, particularly positive others, can lift us up and help us see a different perspective. This positivity can be contagious and lead to us seeing things in a new light.

* If you think you are getting depressed speak to a professional to see if you can get help to prevent a further downward spiral.

To get started on practising a positive mindset you can begin with thinking about simple questions with a positive focus. You will already have strategies and coping mechanisms that work for you – these are your strengths and it can be helpful to remind yourself of them.

Positive focus

- What three things have gone well in the last six months and why?

- What is the best thing about you?

- What do you like most about yourself?

- What are you like when you are at your best?

- What, or who, brings out the best in you?

- What is your most significant achievement?

- How have your strengths helped you in the past?

- How can your strengths help you in the future?

- What have you done that's helped elicit positive change in your life?

Keep your answers in mind (you can note them down in Appendix I), particularly if you find you are starting to slip into unhelpful negative patterns. Try to find new ways to use your strengths each week.

Avoid toxic positivity

Feeling positive seems to be self-perpetuating which is why a lot of 'positive thinking' mantras have developed. However, it's important to distinguish between a validating, hopeful positive thinking versus a toxic positivity where there is no room for the inevitable negative aspects of being a human being. Beware of receiving messages that you must be positive at all costs and blaming those that express a negative element in life (sometimes referred to as the 'tyranny of positivity'). Setbacks are part of life and negative emotions inevitable. They are not to be suppressed and denied; rather practising a change of focus, at times, can be helpful.

While acknowledging the inevitable ups and downs that come with being human, research does suggest that seeking the positive in the midst of a stressful event can interrupt a downward spiral into depression.

Gratitude

Gratitude[153] is strongly correlated to emotional wellbeing. Humans have a tendency to focus on what they *don't* have. When we get something we want we soon become dissatisfied and want something else. This stands in the way of our contentment. By changing our attention to the positives, wanting what we have rather than what we don't, our appreciation grows. This links to the strategy of 'benefit finding'[154] or finding meaning and purpose, which we'll look at more in the next chapter.

> *'She was here and we got to have her and love her and she was so smiley and so happy and it was sort of the gratitude I felt... the bewildering joy of it, stopped me from feeling sorry for myself, for want of a better word, because there was never that opportunity.'*

I find this useful to do with my children too. A simple way to start is to write down or name three things that you are grateful for right now. The food in the fridge, the weather, family, health, a bird song, a chocolate bar. It can be anything – but really inhabit that feeling of gratitude. Writing them down might help you to keep hold of them and prevent them slipping from our memories. You can use a gratitude meditation, journal or ritual that encourages you to think about things that you are grateful for on a regular basis. Or use the space in Appendix I to jot them down.

---

[153] Seligman, M. (2004) *Authentic Happiness: Using the new positive psychology to realize your potential for lasting fulfilment,* London: Nicholas Brealey Publishing

[154] Pakenham, K.I. Sofronoff, K., Samios, C. (2004) Finding meaning in parenting a child with Asperger syndrome: Correlates of sense making and benefit finding. *Research in Developmental Disabilities,* 25, 245-264

> ### Five minute Gratitude mindfulness
>
> 1. Use your breath to anchor yourself in the present moment. Bring attention to your breath or something in the body as you bring your shoulders down.
>
> 2. Bring to mind a sight you are grateful for. Move through your senses and find one thing to start with that you appreciate – a colour, a shape, a movement.
>
> 3. Now move to your sense of smell – a scent you appreciate. What do you notice?
>
> 4. Tune into any sounds around you. On an in-breath, shift your attention to your ears and what it is like to really listen.
>
> 5. Next move to touch and texture – having someone near to touch, gratitude for human contact or something soft to stroke.
>
> 6. Shift to noticing and appreciating objects around you. The effort that went into making something in your life.
>
> 7. As you end this practice, carry an attitude of gratitude with you.

Make it small and realistic – think of something you're grateful for when you put toothpaste on your toothbrush. Glance at a photo that makes you happy. When you go to sleep think of one thing you're grateful for that day.

Awe

Another form of gratitude can be grouped under the description of awe or wonder. These are the moments where you say 'wow' to yourself. Things that awe us tend to have two aspects to them – a sense of vastness or being out of our ordinary frame of reference, and something that is slightly out of your current mental structures or framework, so is hard to get your head around. It can make you feel part of something bigger than yourself and takes you out of your everyday world. Nature seems to particularly inspire this feeling – a waterfall, a forest. But it doesn't have to be just the big hitters. If you fully immerse yourself you can also experience awe in a plant or a rainbow. You can find a spiritual connection with something larger than ourselves, an element that has been around for thousands of years. Wonder can bring a gratitude for these things and enhance pleasure in our life.

Hope

Holding onto a sense of hope – the belief that we will find a way through – even at our darkest times, may help maintain our wellbeing. Hope includes setting realistic goals, working out how to achieve them (including being flexible if we need to change them) and believing in ourselves.

> *'My attitude was always one of hope and optimism always... I always look for the positive but I think there was part of me that just couldn't conceive of the other option... and I also felt like it gave her a better chance, rather than me being just sad and stressed about it, I had to try and be as relaxed and as positive as I possibly could, because if I was asking this huge thing of her, than I had to also expect it of myself basically, I had to kind of rise to it.'*

One study suggests that the way to maintain hope is by embracing the paradox[155] of mixed emotions – negative and positive. Fostering a hopeful outlook can encourage engagement with your child and the caring role. Losing hope can be devastating and if this is your experience it may help to seek therapeutic support.

Joy and play

Taking a break from 'adulting' can support our mental health. For example, do something playful that makes you laugh, meet up with someone or watch a movie that makes you smile. Run down a hill with the wind in your hair or dress up in a fun outfit. We have a tendency to think of play and joy as childish activities but they're not – they're human activities. Sadly we often replace joyful activities

---

[155] Larson, E. (1998) Reframing the meaning of disability to families: the embrace of paradox, *Social Science and Medicine*, 47, 7, 865-875

with the more mundane things that need to be completed. But there are wide-ranging benefits. If you allow yourself to experience small moments of joy, such as buying yourself a bag of sweets or tickling your child, you're more likely to see the bigger picture and be more creative when solving complex problems. This is part of the 'broaden and build' theory that we discussed earlier.

Joy is an in-the-moment feeling. The more joy we have in our life the more we see other opportunities for joy. Simple things like bubbles, ice cream and hot air balloons. A beautiful item of clothing, the smell of jasmine, the colour of nail varnish or the feel of your child's skin. Soak them up and breathe them in. People can appreciate beauty in other ways too – paintings, music, food. These are experiences that feed and fill our life. There is a spiritual element to it. We 'feast our eyes' on something in a sensuous, embodied way that creates an intense flow experience. You can even build in a 'joy date' in the same way as author Julia Cameron[156] prescribes an artist's date. Book time in for your joyful activity though keep it small and manageable; remember to give yourself permission to do it.

Benefits of negative mood

There may be times, of course, when we have negative emotions: this is part of life. Often a negative mood motivates us to act, for example anger can help you deal with a confrontational goal. Studies also suggest that people in a negative mood pay more attention to what is going on around them and judge others more realistically. Adopting a negative mood can also help brace you for difficult news and people often abandon optimism before receiving potentially bad news.

As we've seen throughout this book, splitting human experience into a neat dichotomy (positive v. negative) is rarely an accurate portrayal of our everyday lives. Our emotional lives involve a mixture of both. Once again balance is crucial. If your life is overly focused on the negatives then practising noticing the positives will help lift your mood. If your life is overly focused on the positives then it may mean you miss signals on areas of your life that need to change.

---

[156] Cameron, J. (2016) *The Artist's Way*, Macmillan: London

Flow

Linked to positive psychology is the psychological state of being in 'flow'. This refers to moments where we are fully engaged in an activity and the full attention blocks out everything else. These moments are strongly correlated with a sense of wellbeing. In moments like these we are so fully engaged in the activity that we become part of something bigger and lose our sense of self.

Another element of flow activities is that they gives us a feeling of being in control – we are architects of our own destiny in that moment. Some people find that engaging in a task that requires concentration helps (e.g. Sudoku, crossword, reading, trying to remember the names of your teachers at school in year order). Studies show that even two minutes of distraction reduce the urge to focus on the negative. Choose something that you need to concentrate on but not so hard that you feel like giving up. One parent reflected on how playing in a band gave her a positive distraction:

> *'It was so absorbing and the only time I don't think about learning disability.'*

Studies suggest that when we are in flow it affects us physically, for example our breathing deepens and regulates, our heart rate slows down and our blood pressure reduces[157]. This illustrates, once again, the intertwining of our physical and mental wellbeing.

Creative process

Flow links to creativity and when you're engaged in something fulfilling the hours can disappear like seconds. Creating something, or losing yourself in it – art, music, a story – can provide a distraction as well as a chance to offload, depending on how each individual uses it. It can act as a way of externalising worries and anxieties and gaining great understanding and control over such feelings. Or it can take us away into another world that gives us respite and calm.

> *'I write music, I write prose, you write it out, there have been some horrendous times that you just write out and you control that world and you can turn it around.'*

---

[157] Hefferon, K. (2013) *Positive Psychology and the Body: The Somatopsychic side to flourishing*, Berkshire, UK: Open University Press, p. 36

Daydreaming can involve a sense of flow and control that supports our wellbeing – playing out an event in our mind with different outcomes. It helps us create emotional order at times when life may be difficult. It also allows us to 'rehearse imaginary situations so that the best strategy for confronting them may be adopted'[158] and gives us space to consider alternative options.

We need to give ourselves permission to engage in the human creative process. If this is something you used to do, but which has fallen by the wayside, try and find a way to bring it back into your life.

Coping Strategies

The next few themes describe strategies that parents found helpful during times of stress. I've grouped them under the heading 'coping strategies' but I acknowledge that is a very broad title that could incorporate much of this book. In fact the literature on coping is huge and conflicting in its categorisations but I hope these make sense in a practical way.

Emotional regulation

In the same way that we need to support our children to learn to regulate their emotions, which in turn helps build resilience and find ways of coping, we also need to develop ways to do this. We will be influenced by the role models in our own life, especially our early attachments, and we may fall into unhelpful patterns in which we get 'stuck'. This may mean taking a step back – responding rather than reacting emotionally. We develop new 'antennae' for what we need.

'Recognise that you're sinking into that a bit and then rationalising why and then pulling yourself back out of it with that rationalisation.'

This involves developing the capacity to shift our focus and prioritise certain problems as well as delaying gratification to avoid being overwhelmed by our, or our children's, emotions. When we are regulated, those around us are more likely to be too.

---

[158] Csikszentmihalyi, M. (2002) *Flow: The classic work on how to achieve happiness,* London: Random House, p. 120

Worry controller (Prioritising or dis-engaging from competing demands)

At times we may need to put something (a worry, a problem, something that needs sorting out) to one side and save it for another time. We compartmentalise, or 'park' problems, if we are facing overload. This can be a useful form of stress coping as it creates a 'psychological clearing' that enables us to focus on the task in hand or provide some downtime.

> *'I have to almost self-police things because one of the things that I do is that kind of that falling asleep time, that time of the night when it's late and that's when all the demons come out, that's when all the things that you're worrying about at the back of your mind come to the forefront and sit there to stop you sleeping. And I have to be very strict with myself not to let that happen, so what I actually do, I do a colouring in app on my phone, you know, just colouring in and it stops my brain from wandering off.'*

Using the analogy of an air traffic controller, the 'worry controller' has an overview of the many planes (worries/issues) under their care. At times they may need to keep a plane in a holding pattern before finding space for it to land. At other times they may need to keep a plane grounded at a gate or make the decision it is not safe to fly. In psychological terms this is like the Executive Function in our brains that helps us to organise things, deciding which issues we will deal with and in which order.

Parents found it helpful to use these mental strategies to wait until they were ready to face something, or until they had more resources to deal with a difficult issue. If it's a conscious choice and you are aware of why and how often you are doing this then it can be beneficial. As with all things to do with the complex human brain it is not always clear-cut when something is a useful distraction – allowing you to relax or take time off from a worry – or when it is an avoidance of something difficult. For example, disengaging behaviourally from your child, or failing to acknowledge or process painful material, may lead to an individual fully dissociating from their experiences which can be problematic. This may be the case with certain traumatic experiences – which can be likened to putting difficult things into a cupboard until at some point the cupboard is full and the door bursts open. If this is your experience, then please seek help from a GP or therapist – there are evidence-based treatments for trauma.

Here I am referring to a benign (non-harmful) conscious disengaging or prioritising of competing demands. Engaging the worry controller requires a healthy re-focusing of attention, or positive distraction[159], away from things that are upsetting, in order to manage your immediate day to day life.

I notice how I can do this in school or team meetings regarding my son. Something in the discussion may make me feel upset but I have developed skills to put those to one side, in that moment, so I can focus on finding the solution or understanding the information provided. It doesn't mean you neglect the feelings, and you may wish to consider them later on.

Having 'worry time' may be helpful, for example, if something is bothering you and taking over every waking moment, setting a limit with yourself – 'I will think about this at 6pm for ten minutes' – may allow you to have a break. It's like a contract with yourself, agreeing when you will think and when you will have a break.

There are also certain things about the future that might not be helpful to dwell on too much. Of course there are times when you need to think about things and pro-actively make decisions but there will be a time to consider this and a time when it's unhelpful.

'[I] try and be mindful of, you know, that's not happening right now, she's six, why are you thinking about when she's fifty-six... think about it when it feels less overwhelming.'

I think this skill – in moderation – is linked to psychological flexibility. There are many activities we may do to change our focus or provide a distraction when we need it – reading a book, talking about something different or having a change of scene, a simple act of walking to the bus stop a different way from normal, doing things in a different order, or telephoning someone you normally text. Daydreaming or using your imagination to exist in a world other than your immediate situation can also help you cope during a difficult or boring time.

---

[159] Aldwin, C. (2011) Stress and Coping across the Lifespan, in S. Folkman (ed.) *The Oxford Handbook of Stress, Health and Coping*, Oxford University Press: New York, p. 22

*'It's okay not to like... how you feel and it's okay not
to feel... connected to what you're currently doing in
life because the reason why you don't feel connected
is because it's really bloody hard and it's not what
you intended for life.'*

Distraction can be useful if our lives become too stagnant and familiar. At other times there is too much distraction and we need to limit what we have to focus on. There is a place for removing, and seeking, distraction, both equally beneficial if they are in equilibrium.

The question to ask yourself is 'how is this helping me right now?' If it is not helping or if this becomes a dominant way of coping, and you find yourself lost in a fantasy world then it might be you need some psychological help to re-gain balance in your life. One study also suggested that if we disengage too much we are less likely to make sense of or find meaning in our situation[160] – and we'll look at this topic in the next chapter. Some strategies are not helpful – such as regular escape using alcohol or activities that take over your life giving no room to think. But if used in a healthy way, prioritising demands, or parking certain worries for a short time, can help manage the day to day (potential) overwhelm of being a parent carer.

Delaying your own needs

Another strategy that parent carers found useful was being able to delay their own needs so as to meet the needs of their child. All parents do this to some degree but it may be more prevalent in parent carers where their child has immediate needs that have to be dealt with, such as behaviours that challenge where they may harm themselves or others, or factors like a child needing medication or tube feeding. The child may continue to need this immediate attention for considerably longer than a non-disabled child.

Developing the capacity (or utilising the capacity you already have) to hold onto your own needs, in the back of your mind as it were, and then ensuring your needs are met later are crucial coping techniques.

---

[160] Pakenham, K.I., Sofronoff, K. & Samios, C. (2004) Finding meaning in parenting a child with Asperger Syndrome: correlates of sense making and benefit finding, *Research in Developmental Disabilities*, 25, 245-264, p. 260

'I'm going to maintain this calm voice and I'm going to look like I'm coping perfectly fine... and when the melt downs were constant, you know, ten a day, or whatever, I would literally get to the end of the melt down and then I know that he would go to his quiet space and he would then watch an hour of TV. So I'd get him to that space, get him to that safety, make sure all of his needs are met... and then I would go outside and have a cigarette. And then I would cry.'

'[knowing] I've just got a couple more hours and then it's bedtime, or she's off to school, or I can go to work and run away... yes, knowing that there's time off coming, really helps.'

Although these regulation strategies may be part of parenting it is important to realise that it takes energy to delay our own needs. Our inner resources may be depleted and in need of replenishing after these events. By being aware of our emotions and recognising when our needs are unmet we will recognise when our cup needs re-filling. This may be resting on the sofa listening to our favourite music at the end of the day, making time for a chat with a friend or a warm bath. Ensure you take this time to re-charge.

Quick wins

We all need a sense of achievement in some area of our life. The feeling of ticking off something on our to do list captures this. The achievement may be in relation to your child, your work or sometimes a different area. Some of the parents I spoke to reflected on the importance of 'quick wins' as other challenges in their life did not provide this.

'The battle that I have looking after [my son] is all long term and you don't get many quick wins, so organising a festival... that's a great sense of achievement.'

This gives us a feeling of control or self-efficacy in our life. Gaining satisfaction in finishing a task could provide a sense of pride although it was acknowledged that the task needed to be manageable:

'I have to set myself very small tasks because there isn't a lot of time to finish it... and most days it's tidying the kitchen.'

Trauma & Crises

In this final section I want to explore traumatic or shocking experiences because often our coping mechanisms are slightly different in these circumstances. Parents were able to identify a few strategies they found helpful during a crisis:

- Going into 'Survival mode'

- Faith

- Quiet, safe space on your own

- Crisis triggers change and solutions

Survival mode

> *'I look back now and honestly I don't really know the answer because the thing I remember is I was so calm, like... sort of just we have to get through this.'*

Many parents described their way of coping in a crisis like a 'zoning out' and feeling 'surreal'. It's also been likened to 'being in a bubble' or 'in slow motion'[161]. Others called it going into 'fire fighter mode' and then moving on afterwards once the crisis had passed. I'm curious as to whether this is a helpful strategy or actually means the difficulty isn't processed or made sense of; one parent talked about 'memory wiping' after a traumatic event.

> *'You don't afterwards remember a lot of what you did or how you did it, because you were in bare survival mode and that's pretty much how I worked.'*

Taking time to recover after a traumatic event is crucial to replenishing our resources.

Unfortunately for some parents the overwhelming nature of the situation does lead to actual collapse.

---

[161] Emerson, A. (2020) 'Room of Gloom': Reconceptualising Mothers of Children with Disabilities as Experiencing Trauma, *Journal of Loss and Trauma*, 25:2, 124-140

'I just completely broke. I couldn't concentrate on anything. I couldn't sleep. My Mum had to come around. She demanded that someone from the crisis team come round, they did, they come round that evening actually... They came round every day, someone come round.'

Faith

For those whose faith was important to them, turning to this at times of crisis was helpful. Parents found sitting in the hospital chapel and praying (referred to 'fire engine prayers') was comforting and one of the only things they could do during the difficulties.

'It felt like the only constructive thing I could do was pray.'

Safe, quiet space on your own

Finding a safe, quiet space enabling you to just be in the moment is an understandable response when we feel under attack. It provides time to re-set and recalibrate.

'I was meant to go to work and I rang the manager and said I can't actually. I can't help anyone, I just can't give anything to anyone, so she gave me the day off and I went and bought this duvet and just sat under it. I think that day I just followed my guts. I just didn't need to think. It was a very visceral kind of reaction that I had... it just kind of cuddled me in a way that you probably get from if you were young and went to a parent. It was just comfort. Go in to a cave and hide. And process it...'

Withdrawal may be helpful in these moments and protect from the risk that other people will fail in their attempts to support you. This suggests that in a crisis it may not always be the best time to access a support group for some people – it could lead to overwhelm.

'So that's when I fall into my research, I guess, that's when I go, right, okay, I'm going back to the internet and I'm going to read and interpret what I need without somebody giving me really rubbish advice. I think it's more like a healing thing as well because it's quite exhausting to be in that state, so... I find it a waste of time to share with other people because it's energy that I haven't got, so it's energy conservation, not to talk to other people.'

'I'm very careful with who I talk to because you are emotionally so vulnerable that you don't have the resilience to sort of bat off the stuff that's unhelpful.'

For other parents, though, the time of crisis may be exactly when they need to lean on others.

Crisis triggers change and solutions

A crisis situation can also trigger change that is helpful in the long term yet very painful to go through at the time. Parents told me that crises had led to the following strategies they'd put in place:

- Taking two weeks off all hospital and other appointments

- Finding support for sleep

- Seeking counselling

- Letting go of the (unrealistic) expectation of how family life should be and making the necessary adaptations to suit the child's needs

- Seeking a residential placement for the child

- Fighting for respite

- Addressing earlier developmental trauma in parents' own life

- Seeing difficult things in the world with more clarity and understanding

What can help you in a crisis

I outline a step by step plan below for those in a crisis, based on many of the strategies outlined in this chapter. A crisis can happen in different ways – shocking news, behaviours that challenge, feeling overwhelmed and unable to cope with the current demands. Connecting with what you've already identified as helpful throughout this chapter will guide you, so perhaps look through any notes you've made in the worksheet in Appendix I and re-visit these ideas.

'Whenever she's hospitalised and things aren't good, I try and get someone to come and sit with her and I go and do a lap outside of the hospital, it's got really good views and just being outside, breathing and giving myself time to think and walk, I find that really, really helpful.'

Try these simple steps:

1. Slow your breathing down. Take a few deep breaths, focusing on the inhalation and exhalation. Feel grounded in your body (i.e. feel your feet on the ground, or your back on the chair). Focus on your senses in the grounding technique outlined above in the Mindfulness section.

2. Notice what you are feeling. Adopt the observing self to see how your emotional response (feeling upset) is taking over and may be influencing your thoughts. Don't mistake your thoughts (thinking self) with facts.

3. Have you experienced anything like this before? What helped? If you need immediate support, what can you do (e.g. telephone helpline, see a friend, go into another room)?

4. Think about small steps that can be taken across different time scales:

   i) immediate (right now)

   ii) short term (even the next five minutes)

   iii) medium term

   iv) long term.

People often start thinking only about the long term which can feel insurmountable at times of overwhelm. Try thinking about small immediate steps like making a phone call, having a cup of tea, going to the bathroom, writing down your thoughts.

5. Even if there is nothing you can do to immediately improve the situation you can take a stance of acceptance and mindfulness. Engage in the present moment; re-connect with your values and things that are important in your life.

6. This may involve acknowledging that life is imperfect and there are certain elements we cannot control. But we can influence our internal responses and how we engage with that part of our life.

7. Remember to practise self-compassion. If this was a friend what might you say to them to support them?

Caring for the carers

As we've seen throughout this book your mental health is at risk if you do not look after yourself. Finding something that nurtures you is important and deserved. It can be hard for some parents of disabled children to acknowledge that they are a carer; but carers need to be cared for. I hope you have found some things that can help you and have been able to use some of the strategies in this chapter.

Another powerful aspect of coping and growing is having a sense of purpose and meaning to guide you throughout life. This, along with looking to the future, is what we will explore in the final chapter.

Key points

- We may need different things at different times to replenish and recalibrate our wellbeing

- We can use activities and psychological tools to create a self-care Swiss army knife which we will always have to hand to help us

- We need to be aware of our emotions in order to recognise when we need some additional self-care

- Taking a position of openness and flexibility enables us to better cope with the inevitable ups and downs of life

- Looking after ourselves includes the basics such as sleep, exercise and eating healthily

- Approaches such as mindfulness, meditation and breathing can help us relax and connect the mind and body

- Strategies from Acceptance and Commitment Therapy (ACT), positive psychology and being in flow are shown to enhance wellbeing

- Parent carers often use the helpful strategy of positive re-framing to develop a changed perspective on life, parenting and themselves. This is linked to making meaning

- Other coping strategies which help to regulate emotions include utilising our worry controller (prioritising or dis-engaging from competing demands), delaying your own needs (but ensuring they are met later) and achieving quick wins in other areas of our life

- At times of crisis we may need a particular type of support or support after the crisis has passed

- Appendix I has a worksheet to help identify areas that can support you emotional wellbeing

9

Meaningful Futures

'Better to lead a rich life with tears than a happy life with no meaning.'[162]

'[I am] hoping against all hope (and not feeling much hope really at all for it), that by the time I do fall down dead, that he [son] will be somewhere where he's happy, content and there's enough people and enough commitment to his future care and the future care of others that he will have a lovely rest of life and it won't be any stress to him.'

In this final chapter we will explore the future – our child's and our own. This will involve looking at some difficult topics – the fight in perpetuity, lack of care and premature death. We will then consider the importance of having a sense of purpose and meaning in our lives, how this can sustain us despite difficulties, and the positive influence it has on our emotional wellbeing.

Our child's future

As is the case for us, our children will also be finding their own sense of meaning and purpose in their life. They will explore and engage in things they enjoy and which make them get out of bed in the morning.

---

[162] Alan Wolfe in Bruckner, P. (2010) *Perpetual Euphoria: On the duty to be happy*, Oxfordshire: Princeton University Press, back cover

The future can look very different for each individual. For some people it could involve studying at college or it may be the delight in the small, but important, everyday things. Saba Salman, who has a sister, Raana, with a learning disability, recalls in *Made Possible*[163]:

> It's 25 December 2005 and an ordinary family moment – the exchanging of gifts – is about to take on an extraordinary significance. Raana, sixteen years old, is back at my parents' house after her first term at a specialist residential college. She's just done her Christmas shopping independently for the first time (without her family but with her support workers), so I know she's hand-picked this present. I rip open the paper to reveal my favourite brand of peppermint tea. I well up immediately and give her an enormous hug.

Part of our path, as a family, involves challenging the 'normative' narrative that exists in society about what makes someone 'productive' and their life valuable. We need to broaden this out – for our child, for ourselves, for society and for the future. My son is unlikely to live an independent life. His will be a life that involves transport, iPads, cooking, trampolines and swimming pools. Making people laugh with his toilet humour jokes, seeing his dog as his buddy and loving and being loved by his family and the network around him – these are meaningful to him and his family. His life has value.

Just writing that makes me tear up as I feel it so strongly but know that some in society would challenge it. We, as parent carers, can help fight against discrimination and negative narratives. It's not easy and sometimes it's tiring but we are in a unique position, with a foot in both the disabled and non-disabled worlds, to remove barriers between them. As most parent carers are new to this world, rather than naturally embedded in it, we may see the problems more clearly, as well as be able to identify, and enable, the solutions. We can encourage society to accept difference and diversity, not as a burden but as part of human existence that makes life richer and fuller. By being open to new viewpoints, perspectives and lives we become better and more rounded human beings.

---

[163] Salman, S. (2020) *Made Possible: Stories of Success by people with learning disabilities – in their own words*, London: Unbound, p. 5

Our sense of purpose and meaning in life will help us even when there are challenges, and next I want to raise some difficult issues about the future.

Preparation for the future

I thought long and hard about whether to include this section. Hope for the future, rather than fear, is the message I would like you to take from this book. Sometimes, though, preparation is helpful; forewarned is forearmed. And fear of the future is a common theme for many parent carers. I'm not saying these issues will inevitably be part of your life – for most of you they won't. But it would be neglectful of me to not include at least reference to some of the rare but tragic elements of some parent carer journeys.

Important self-care – do not read this section until you feel ready to. If you are feeling emotionally overwhelmed perhaps save it for another day and skip to the next section on purpose and meaning. Exercise your capacity to prioritise what you focus on, as discussed in the previous chapter under 'Worry Controller', as you may not feel ready to consider the future at this precise moment.

My work on emotional wellbeing in parent carers started with a focus on the battle of the early years as I believed that these were the hardest. Then I gradually spoke to more and more parents of older disabled children (and adults). I realised that some obstacles continue, new ones may come along and, for some, the unimaginable happens. There is a constant flux and change – some for the better but not necessarily all. There is an ongoing process of new challenges and we continue to adapt and be tested.

'You can be plodding along, really happily, for six months and then something will happen and you've got to process it and deal with it again.'

Whilst this book has focused on emotions, as we've seen, these are inherently tied to the context in which we live. I therefore want to cover a broad overview of some of the potential difficult issues that may arise. This empowers us to act in the face of the new and unexpected.

The themes I am going to cover are:

1. **Economics of care**

2. **The fight in perpetuity**

3. **Health inequality and lack of care**

4. **Teenage and beyond**

5. **Premature Death**

Economics of care

If there is appropriate support from the beginning of a child's life it will provide long-term economic benefits. Early intervention is shown again and again to benefit not only child, but also family, outcomes[164]. If you're a content, satisfied and supported person you'll be a better and more fulfilled parent. Your child will, most likely, be happier and better supported and will therefore cost less in terms of accessing statutory services. The whole family system benefits from timely, quality input.

> *'I think carers are the unsung heroes, like the amount of money we save the NHS just by looking after our children is massive.'*

Without this, the additional longer term costs may include mental health support, prescriptions, social care, respite, emergency fostering, as well as lack of tax from a parent unable to work[165]. But it is not only the economic savings that we need to consider; there is a human cost to families. The importance of short breaks, flexible working patterns and appropriately funded statutory services is of paramount importance to enable parents to continue to care for their child.

---

[164] Sapiets, S.J., Totsika, V.& Hastings, R.P. (2020) Factors influencing access to early intervention for families of children with developmental disabilities: A narrative review, *J Appl Res Intellect Disabil.*, 00, 1-17

[165] Parents Matter: The impact on parents' mental health when a child has a life-threatening illness, *Rainbow Trust*, January 2020, https://www.rainbowtrust.org.uk/support-for-families

The fight in perpetuity

The early years can be difficult for all parents – sleepless nights, toilet training, lack of communication can all add to the pressures. Yet many of the special needs parents I speak to reflect that not only do many of these issues continue in their lives but new challenges emerge as their child grows and develops.

Transitions such as puberty, secondary school, and moving to adult services all bring periods of adjustment. Even hard-won services feel precarious and we may have to continuously fight just to keep the status quo, such as at Annual Reviews for Education Health and Care Plans (EHCPs), adjusting to a high turnover of staff or managing cuts to services. It can be exhausting.

'I go home from those meetings feeling so deflated.'

The fight in perpetuity reminds me of the Myth of Sisyphus. In the Greek legend Sisyphus is condemned by the gods for eternity to repeatedly roll a boulder up to the top of a hill only for it to roll down again. It's a metaphor for the individual's struggle against life but it feels particularly pertinent for parent carers.

I felt like this recently when proposals were made, during the Covid-19 lockdown, to dramatically reduce my son's therapies in his EHCP. We had almost gone to the local authority SEND tribunal last year to get his current plan and levels of support. All that fight and effort and here we are again.

Many parents of older children report feeling that the work is never 'done', in that you get over one obstacle and a new one comes along. We might not experience the feeling of a child 'leaving the nest' and going on to live an independent life. Although the majority of disabled children will, for some parents the worry carries on for longer than it would with a non-disabled child.

So we, as parent carers, continue to learn and develop. Even though our landscape may stay the same, our capacity to cope grows. You will gain skills and strength that you didn't think possible when you first received the diagnosis – I have seen this in parents who couldn't believe they would get through. But they do.

I definitely feel more able to advocate for my son, and my knowledge of our rights and the law have increased. I also realise that sometimes we need to let a battle go in order to win a war. I've learnt to pace myself so that I don't burnout. To return to the Sisyphus analogy, I've found that I can let others push the boulder up the hill with me or for me sometimes. I rest at the bottom when necessary; the struggle can always wait a day or two. Also, I've learnt to enjoy the view at the top for a while as I know it may be short lived.

Health inequality and lack of 'care'

Despite improvements in care for people with disabilities the picture can still look concerning in some areas. The Learning Disabilities Mortality Review (LeDeR)[166] records all deaths of people with a learning disability and on average people die at a considerably younger age than those without learning disabilities. In fact they are four times more likely to die from treatable conditions. This is not an inevitable part of having a learning disability – sadly it is due to other associated difficulties, including lack of care and accessibility and untrained staff.

The pandemic, Covid-19, has unfortunately highlighted the impact of cuts to care packages, structural inequalities and discrimination that disabled people experience. There have been difficulties with accessing support and increased isolation. Support from schools and associated therapies have disappeared and we realise, once again, that caring is up to us parents and us alone.

Improvements are on the horizon that look promising, such as the #OliverMcGowan[167] mandatory learning disabilities and autism training for all health care professionals – campaigned for tirelessly by his parents after Oliver's tragic, and preventable, death. Raising awareness of disabilities and improving services is a key role for disability charities – such as *Scope, Mencap, National Autistic Society, Contact* and the *Challenging Behaviour Foundation* (see Appendix III). But change can be slow so it is best that you are aware that not all staff in the health, education and social care sectors understand disabilities. You may need to spell things out or fight a bit harder to get your child's needs acknowledged and treated appropriately.

---

[166] http://www.bristol.ac.uk/sps/leder/

[167] https://www.hee.nhs.uk/our-work/learning-disability/oliver-mcgowan-mandatory-training-learning-disability-autism

These problems are well documented[168] so I will not linger on these but will just say there is, sadly, some way to go (for more information see #Asklistendo #treatmewell).

Teenage and beyond

Puberty can be a crucial, and tricky, point in any person's life. As our children grow and develop it may create different challenges to which we need to adapt. As well as the typical changes in hormones, we may start to notice a difference in how our child is perceived by others. Society is less forgiving of an adult who displays behaviours that challenge in the supermarket than it is of a child. The looks are more noticeable.

Networks of support may change or fall away in an inevitable part of children growing up. Teenage years can involve families being more disparate – a child travelling further to school, no contact at school gates and no coffee mornings or groups provided for parents. Our need for emotional support will remain, though, so finding other communities or groups to support us can be helpful. As family members become older, or pass away, our close circle of support diminishes.

> *'The needs of the child constantly change, I think, so that's true with any child, you know, when they go through age stages and you face those challenges but you face them in a different way because having a teenager with a disability who is non-verbal and who has got really complex needs is very, very different to having a teenager that's not got those things.'*

There may be an increase or change in behaviours and as our child grows it inevitably makes us think about the future. We know, on some level, this should be a time of increasing independence for our child and a 'letting go' for parents, but when we do not trust services to support our child it can make this a challenge.

Approaching adulthood takes planning and preparation, whether or not your child will live independently. If your child needs support from social services you may feel like you lose many of your rights to

---

[168] Ryan, F. (2019) *Crippled: Austerity and the demonization of disabled people,* Verso: London

influence their care. There can be complicated processes to navigate the legal system. It's worth reading about this and gaining expert advice if your child is nearing this time. Schools and services can signpost you in the right direction.

Premature Death

Sadly, the future can look limited for some of our children. They may be more at risk of hospitalisation, illnesses and even early death because of a life limiting illness, such as rare degenerative disorders. And as we've already seen there can be increased risks for those with learning and/or developmental disabilities due to the quality of care they receive. There are tragic examples of neglect and preventable deaths[169] (see the powerful but heartrending campaign by Dr Sara Ryan, mother of Connor Sparrowhawk who died under NHS care, #justiceforLB).

We are more likely to be exposed to these difficulties than parents of non-disabled children; even if it doesn't affect your child directly you may hear about children in your online groups or at special school who have died. You may be exposed to experiences that the non-disabled world rarely have to face.

This awareness disrupts something huge in terms of the natural course of events and how we would normally be outlived by our offspring. Humans have an adaptive ability to *not* think about our own mortality and this is challenged, heartbreakingly, by having a child who is seriously ill or vulnerable. It goes against a very deep evolutionary system.

When a disabled child or adult dies the impact on parents, siblings and wider family can be complicated. At times the loss may not always be fully acknowledged by society, turning it into a disenfranchised grief.

As each experience is so personal and this book is not primarily focused on bereavement (and there are many good books and charities that do offer support in this area) I am not going to write much more on this topic. I will leave it to the words of one mother and her daughter's story. This is difficult to read so, again, if you need to, skip to the next section and you can come back to this when you feel ready.

---

[169] Ryan, S. (2017) *Justice for Laughing Boy*, London: Jessica Kingsley

In memory of Claire

I went into labour with my second child feeling confident after a healthy pregnancy. They changed shift and the new midwife wasn't really engaged. I needed to vomit and she just pointed and said 'bowl's there'. She was reading a book and I remember thinking she'd fallen asleep.

Another midwife came in and the monitoring machine had the volume turned down so they hadn't noticed the baby was in distress. After a forceps delivery I heard them willing the baby 'breathe baby breathe'.

The baby was taken away and I was left for the whole day. Finally I heard my husband outside saying 'does she know?' I thought the baby was dead. He came in and said 'we've got a baby girl'. We called her Claire. I was taken to see her in the incubator but then she started having seizures and started turning a dark colour. I couldn't watch. I was told 'if she gets an infection we won't treat her'. I felt unsafe and rang my GP to say I wanted to go home.

Once home I was in shock, staring out of the window.

The next day I called the hospital and was told she's awake. I immediately returned and tried to feed her but she couldn't latch on. Her third day alive was the first day I held her.

I was allowed to take her home after five days but the poor little thing screamed day and night. I was walking the streets at 9pm to try and calm her down. I didn't know what was wrong and no one talked to me. I was too drained and still in shock. I took her to the GP again who telephoned to say she had to go back into hospital. They did tests but I was told nothing.

In the end I contacted a private paediatrician recommended by my friend. He was my saviour. He listened to me. He helped me treat our very sick child. He never charged us as he saw what a state we'd been left in. Claire was put on medication to help with her brain irritation. She calmed down and I could visit to care for her every day in hospital over the next six months.

Gradually they let me take her home and I felt more confident overnight. Having her home helped me with the shock and my focus became looking after her. I had no help at home. I knew something had gone dramatically wrong during the labour so a friend helped me find a solicitor and he got hold of the notes. The strong motivator was that I needed help for Claire. And I needed the truth. It turns out the cord had been wrapped around her neck three times. It made me feel so sad, like she had been hung inside me. She gave me the energy to fight.

Having her home was wonderful. It was just the four of us – my two daughters and our cat. Unfortunately my marriage had not survived.

Claire started in a local school where all the services were provided for her. We had regular respite and I could give my older daughter the time she needed.

As Claire got older though she started to get repeated chest infections and was hospitalised. She spent her sixteenth birthday in hospital. Claire had all the people around her that loved her. Then the consultant told me they would not treat her anymore as it would be 'prolonging things'. This is not what a mother wants to be told, alone, at 9am in the morning. I went back to my saviour consultant who intervened and let me take her home. I trusted my mother's instinct and she lived for another two years at home. I kept her home as I was scared she'd catch something else. The GP trusted me and gave me prescriptions when she needed them.

After this time she became ill and it turned into pneumonia. She was hospitalised again and I knew something was different this time; it was worse. One night I left the hospital to get some sleep and told them to call if there was any change. As soon as I was home she deteriorated and I rushed back to the hospital, ran up the stairs and just made it in time. The nurse commented 'she waited for you'. She died lying in my arms.

I always appreciated when other people treated her as Claire, not felt sorry for her and too scared to hold her. Our respite carer had her own personal experience of having a disabled child and I trusted her implicitly. She knew that Claire was very precious and took great care of her. I couldn't trust others as even the hospital had failed to care for her. Some people focused on 'what should have been' and I felt this was pointing out what she couldn't do, rather than concentrating on her being a person who had survived.

Sometimes people would stare in the supermarket and at times I'd say something like 'do you want something?' It felt nice when people responded to her, she's a human being at the end of the day and deserves respect.

I knew Claire wouldn't make old bones. My focus became the here and now. Giving her everything she needed to make her life the best it could be helped me to be strong.

There are still flashes back even now, so many years later. When my older daughter got married I thought 'Claire should have been here'. My daughter also lost her sister. While she was alive I couldn't let myself go down the path of what should have been but at times I do still go there in my mind.

When my grandson was born it took me back. It was such a relief when the birth was over and both mother and baby were fine. Having him to cuddle and hold was healing. Being around children has always been my life's passion and purpose. Being around my grandson and in my role as a nanny for a family with three boys enabled me to give all the love I had to other children.

The loss doesn't disappear. But you find reasons for living.

Grief can come and go like waves. We can't be expected to 'get over it' in a set amount of time and it will continue to wash in and out of our lives. There will be first anniversaries of things. Connect how you need to; light a candle, bake them a cake, play a piece of music. Acknowledge that it's ok to feel it. And then there will be the realisation that there are no more 'firsts' as time passes and even that can re-open the grief. Do what you need to do to mark the occasion. The loss of a child may involve a loss of role and identity as well which needs to be re-built. Rather than getting easier life grows around the grief.

It is possible to find meaning in the loss though, however impossible that seems when the feelings are raw. Take your time – it's personal to you and there is no one-size-fits-all grief. How has your child shaped your life and who you are? What things are you grateful for that you might have taken for granted before? What have you learnt through your experiences, however traumatic and upsetting they may have been? These suggestions are not intended to lessen the pain. Rather it is the recognition that life goes on. This is your life and you deserve a chance to make new meaning and re-gain a sense of purpose.

Some people find it helpful to have continuing bonds with their child in different ways – speaking to them, writing to them, or keeping some of the care routines. Although this might be seen as denying grief, for many this can help to adjust to the new life in their own time. Grief is the price we pay for love. Meaning doesn't remove the loss and even if meaning is found it won't always feel it was worth the cost of what you lost[170]. But it can be powerful, transformative and comforting.

---

[170] Kessler, D. (2019) *Finding Meaning: the sixth stage of grief,* London: Rider Books

Moving forward

For the majority of our children, though, the future is inclusive, content and fulfilling. Growing up involves increased independence and life skills, along with opportunities for our child to follow their interests and contribute to their community.

Social inclusion starts with being present in society – such as living in your own home, having a job and being able to do everyday things like accessing leisure facilities and going to the shops. Co-production is working with those who are disabled and their families to identify the right support for them to achieve their aims in life. This is underpinned by being given the opportunity to take on valued roles – whether in relationships, work, community or leisure activities. This in turn gives purpose and meaning to life and we've already seen the positive impact this has on emotional wellbeing.

Disabled adults and children need choices, control and to be involved in decisions about their life. Being part of the community and developing a network of relationships with others is crucial. It involves active support, which encourages independence and engagement, rather than everything being done for the person. Sometimes this involves us parents taking a step back, however hard that can be.

Good support is possible

Despite concerns about a minority of poor services, parents must remember that good support is possible and regularly found. Residential placements, short breaks, schools or colleges, supported living and more are all available.

It's useful to bear in mind that even though you have become an expert on your child this does not mean you're necessarily an expert on disability, education or future support. I remember the relief I felt when my son started special school as they really 'got' what he needed, how he learnt and the best way to support him in a way that I struggled to (because of the realities of living at home with other children). It felt like we could share this responsibility.

Of course every situation is unique and for many staying in the family home is the preferred choice for everyone. Although parental guilt can sometimes stop us seeing that for some young adults living elsewhere suits them better.

This is one mother's experience:

'It has been a real struggle coping with my daughter's needs and behaviour over the years. With three other children, the demand has often been relentless and exhausting. My husband (stepdad to my daughter) had been wanting me to find a residential place for some time but I'd always felt too guilty to go through with it. And then lockdown happened. With it, all our support disappeared and I was stuck at home with four children. The pressure was immense and in the end I rang the social worker to say I just couldn't do it anymore. After a short while they found a residential placement for my daughter. Driving there, I imagined I would spend some time helping her to settle in, but when we got there, she seemed happy straight away and turned around to wave me goodbye! I realised then that she'd been ready to leave. We have FaceTimed regularly since and she has settled in well. Looking back, I wish I'd considered it sooner as it's shown that this is what we needed as a family. Us and her. And in a strange way I am grateful for lockdown to help force this to happen.'

Purpose and Meaning

And so now we turn to our own lives. One of the most consistent factors linked to emotional wellbeing is having a sense of meaning and purpose. It increases self-esteem and is a basic human need which has evolved over many years. Parent carers are no different and those who nurture this aspect in their life cope better with life's natural ups and downs. It doesn't mean we avoid struggling or that we never feel unhappy. But these feelings are couched within something larger than us. This is the S in the SPECTRA of Parent Carer Wellbeing – Sense of Purpose and Meaning.

Part of assessing our life purpose and meaning is to reflect on what life is asking of us. Adversity is part of every human life – we cannot control this. We do, however, have some control over our response.

As an existential psychologist I am interested in how people make meaning of their lives. Frankl[171] and Sartre[172] refer to humans

---

[171] Frankl, V. (1962) *Man's search for meaning: An introduction to logotherapy.* New York: Vintage Books

[172] Sartre, J. (1943) *Being and Nothingness.* London: Routledge

as 'meaning making beings', and that meaning is always possible, whatever our situation. Rather than an inherent meaning in life it is personal – we decide what is meaningful to us, acknowledging that our choices are influenced by upbringing and society.

'Personally now I'm in that stage where I'm having to make new meaning, I've got a new project that I'm really excited about that actually draws on all the things that I really love.'

The term 'meaning' may sound like a grand philosophical concept, and in some ways it can be, but it is also small, local and everyday. It includes a feeling of belonging to something bigger than just yourself (a community, a workplace, a family, nature). It also involves having a sense of purpose or direction in your life. Again this doesn't have to be big world-changing aims; it is the feeling that your life is influenced by things that are important to you, your values[173]. These are not static and may change over time.

Defining the precise meaning of meaning can be complicated but it is generally considered to include: coherence, purpose and significance in life[174].

To make it simpler in relation to parent carers I've grouped what I've learnt through my research into three different areas to explore in more detail.

a) Making sense of our experiences

b) Having a sense of purpose or direction

c) Helping others

Making sense of our experiences

Becoming a parent involves a form of meaning-making anyway as we need to integrate the experience into our new life and sense of self. Rather than being a fixed entity, we are always in the process of becoming, changing with our experiences and relationships.

---

[173] https://www.actmindfully.com.au/

[174] Martela, F. & Steger, M.F. (2016) The three meanings of meaning in life: Distinguishing coherence, purpose and significance, *The Journal of Positive Psychology*, 11, 5, 531-545

There may be a slightly more complex journey with a disabled child but meaning-making involves coming to some kind of understanding of your situation, making sense of events that happened and your response to them. We try to understand things as when they don't make sense it can cause a jarring in our experience which is unsettling and uncertain. We create and re-create our own narrative throughout our life.

> *'I mean first you go through that kind of like slightly "'why me?" phase and then the answer we came to that is because we're better equipped to deal with this than a lot of other people would be.'*

> *'The way that I look at it is when people say, why me, I don't ask why me, I ask why not me, so if it's coming, I will tackle it. I've had loads and loads of issues that I've had to be strong and focus. And then the more that I overcome the difficulties the more that I feel comfortable in myself and I'm not really that shaken. It takes a lot to bother me... I suppose I've got the resilience.'*

Other ways of making meaning in life include gaining a sense of belonging through positive others, such as special needs networks. Parents often feel like they are part of something bigger than just themselves – something that transcends our everyday, trivial life. This could be connecting to a wider community, set of beliefs or a moment in history.

Many parents value using their lived experience and skills in their work and home life; recognising that our lives and our experiences are significant and worthwhile.

> *'Most of my personal self I funnel into my public self and that's because my lived experience is a really important aspect of myself.'*

How you experience your caring role will depend on the meaning you attach to your situation. A research study found that parents who identified benefits in their current situation were more resilient and content in their life[175]. Committing to values that have evolved in

---

[175] Pakenham, K.I. Sofronoff, K., Samios, C. (2004) Finding meaning in parenting a child with Asperger syndrome: Correlates of sense making and benefit finding. *Research in Developmental Disabilities*, 25, 245-264

response to our current situation as parent carers is meaning-making in action.

'I believe special needs children just need to be integrated in society all the time.'

One of the difficulties for parent carers is finding the time to process how you are feeling in order to make sense of your situation. It may be hard to think of what you have gained – a new appreciation for life, a focus on doing what is important to you, becoming really good at something or treasuring family life – when you are overwhelmed by the day to day grind. You need time to reflect on this part of your life.

Having a sense of purpose or direction

Our sense of purpose is more of a directional, motivational drive to a certain point. But it is strongly related to what is meaningful, valuable and significant to us. It's like a meandering river that is heading in the right direction (even if we don't ever get to a final destination). We may drift off course at times but we come back to our overall direction, even if we make a few deviations or change destinations, to incorporate new life events, along the way.

In my research there were many ways in which parents found a sense of purpose. There is no hierarchy of purpose where one is 'better' that another. It is personal and each of these ways of finding purpose in life is valid and important.

Having a child, particularly one that may need extra support in life, can be a strong motivator for parents, making them feel fulfilled and purposeful.

'Getting anything for him [son] I'm very confident... I don't give up on it... I feel satisfied, like I'm doing things for him.'

Sense of purpose may be on a local, individual level, such as fighting for the things your child needs and undertaking caring activities, or it may take on a broader perspective – fighting the system and improving provision or services for a wider group. This links to the helping others theme discussed later in this chapter.

Activism for many parents is a way of making meaning, deriving a sense of purpose and creating social change. It can be a natural development from the advocacy on behalf of our child which increases our self-worth, but, as we've seen, battling can lead to burnout and take time and effort. It is preferable that communities support us and it has been proposed there needs to be an 'unmothering'[176] (this study refers specifically to mothers but I suspect is relevant to fathers too) – that is, moving the onus away from parents having to fight; rather it becomes a joint effort or movement. This involves bonding social capital acknowledging that we are in this together. We can help others and be helped in return.

Some parents find ways to use their knowledge to apply to other areas in their life. Much like my motivation for writing this book, parents take their lived experience to apply to a wider context. One father used his experience with his autistic son to add to his creative process.

> *'Music is like diary entries for me... it was venting,*
> *it was a record and it was also a creative thing...*
> *so what can I turn this into?'*

Others notice gaps in service provision and use prior and current skills to develop new support for disabled children and their families.

Finding something that fulfils you doesn't have to be connected to your child or the world of disability – it can come from anywhere in life. This may be work, a leisure activity or being involved in a project of some sort. For example, working with your community to do some litter picking or campaigning to improve the local park, learning a new skill or connecting with friends to watch your team play football might all contribute to your sense of purpose and belonging.

Although it may be hard to make time for this activity it is important that you do, or you can be left feeling like you've lost a part of yourself, along with motivation and enthusiasm for life.

It is clear that when a person's sense of purpose disappears it can be very difficult and may lead to depression and hopelessness.

> *'I could just stay at home, do nothing [but]...I'd be so*
> *heartbroken. Completely heartbroken... [studying]*
> *makes me feel like I'm not wasting my time, I'm doing*
> *something important for me.'*

---

[176] Runswick-Cole, K. & Ryan, S. (2019) Liminal still? Unmothering disabled children, *Disability and Society*, 34, 7-8, 1125-1139

Helping Others

Another strong element that arose from my research is the desire parent carers have to help others. Partly this is to share what they've learnt along the way. At times it is to ensure something is provided that they themselves did not receive and perhaps wish they had. A common theme was wanting to help other parents who were behind them in the disability journey, so that *'no one else feels like I did in the early years'*. I recognise this feeling on a personal level. You don't want your difficulties, struggles or pain to be for nothing. Feeding into something positive and helpful is a value or purpose; making a meaningful contribution to the world.

> *'I've got to be able to turn this into something positive at some stage and even if it's just in a couple of people... I think just being able to use this... to make something helpful.'*

This relates to research showing the benefit to our own wellbeing of undertaking small acts of kindness. There is a sense of connection and gratitude that accompanies giving or receiving kindness and this can ripple out to other people. In helping others we also help ourselves, including our self-worth and value. That's not to undermine the kindness. It is a common theme across many parents which is worth celebrating.

> *'I'm training to help other parents... and that makes me feel happy.'*

By participating in altruistic activities people forget themselves and feel part of a larger context which provides a sense of belonging.

Helping the child helps the parent

Helping our children is deeply ingrained in our genetic makeup and there is a positive effect from seeing them succeed and get what they need. It makes us feel good to help our child.

> *'Overwhelmingly the experience of being a parent carer is positive in most ways... watching them succeed and all the wonderful things that you can facilitate for them, but also what you get from doing that, and... your view of yourself, your self-image, completely changes. Mine certainly did.'*

Knowing that you've done your best for your child can provide a sense of achievement and re-emphasise the love and bond between you. It also removes any feeling of guilt or anxiety that they may not have had all the opportunities you would like for them. I think parent carers often go over and above what other parents may offer their child as we're so keen they don't miss out. Although this can put additional pressures on ourselves it also helps provide a sense of purpose. Many parents don't just want to help themselves or their child; they also want to spread that support out to other parents.

Balance in helping others

There are times, though, when helping others isn't always serving people's best interest. If we are always the helper and never the helped that can have a negative impact on us. Conversely if we're always the helped and never the helper that can feel disempowering as if we have less to bring and our contribution has a lower value. Everyone has something to bring. We all have lessons we've learnt, expertise or perspectives that are valuable and may be the helpful piece of information, or sharing, that someone else needs to hear at that moment. Of course there are times when someone further down the path knows more about a certain aspect than us, but there will also be things we have more knowledge about. There will be occasions when others are down and we are up and vice versa.

> *[Reflecting on a befriending scheme] 'It was the actual befriending that was far more powerful than the person who had been befriended. I'm not saying that they didn't have a positive experience but that to just sit with somebody and listen to another person's problems and suspend your own just for that time being, whilst at the same time, connecting with them that's probably one of the most rejuvenating things you can do and your self-esteem just goes through the roof... so we remodelled it into a non-hierarchical peer support network.'*

Peer support is shown to not only provide social contact with other parents, but also increase self-confidence and expertise and learning from the experiences of other parents[177]. This form of support may be the most equal and empowering type of help – acknowledging that both sides of the interaction benefit.

Drama triangle of connection

There may be times, though, when our relationships with others don't help us and it can be easy to get caught in an unhealthy dynamic. The Drama triangle[178], based on a model of human behaviour called Transactional Analysis[179], can be useful to identify if you get stuck in a particular role, namely Rescuer, Victim or Persecutor. You might recognise that you regularly fall into a certain role with particular people or professionals. Try to stop and notice this. Does it help you? Who's taking responsibility for whom? Are you doing more than half the work? What are you not getting? Remember that the dynamic between people can change and you can influence that through your own awareness, empowerment and personal growth. In 'The Winner's Triangle'[180] there are three positive alternatives: assertiveness, care and vulnerability. Assertiveness involves expressing our interests and needs; caring entails concern for others in a way that empowers rather than rescues them. Finally, vulnerability acknowledges suffering, and the related feelings, without becoming a victim.

Valuing our expertise

Developing this theme further, there is an important conversation to be had about services and professionals valuing parent carers' lived experience. Parent carers are often involved in peer support, mentoring schemes, helplines and as befrienders. While this is an important avenue for many parents, and gives them a sense of purpose and value, too often it is voluntary or there is little supervisory support or chance to develop expertise. These roles would ideally be remunerated by

---

[177] Shilling, V., Morris, C., Thompson-Coon, J., Ukoumunne, O., Rogers, M., & Logan, S. (2013), Peer support for parents of children with chronic disabling conditions: a systematic review of quantitative and qualitative studies, *Developmental Medicine and Child Neurology*, 55, 602-609

[178] Karpman, M.D., Stephen (1968) Fairy tales and script drama analysis, *Transactional Analysis Bulletin*. 26, 7, 39–43

[179] Berne, E. (1966) *Games People Play*, New York: Ballantine Books

[180] Choy, A. (1990) The winner's triangle, *Transactional Analysis Journal*, 20, 1, 40-46

services and charities. Where it is offered for free, appropriate levels of support and care need to be provided so that parents do not feel overwhelmed, taken advantage of or left to pick up the pieces when there is a personal cost.

Furthermore, co-production should be at the heart of family services and we need to be involved in identifying and developing necessary support and training from the start of the process. Collaboration, consultation and seeking feedback ensures that available support provides meaningful outcomes for families. The wealth of expertise we bring as parent carers with lived experience should not be underestimated. Parent carers want to speak to those who have 'walked the walk' and that has value, significance and meaning.

Meaningful endings

So we are nearing the end of this book. We started with a difficult birth and in this final chapter have considered difficult deaths. Meaning and purpose can be found even when you experience the unimaginable. But this doesn't protect you against pain or heartache. Rather it lives alongside it. The positive and negative embedded in one another once again.

We can change our perspective on life – seeing something in a more positive light, making sense of our experiences or finding a new life goal. Believing that things can change, and that we have agency to make those changes, are strongly linked to the meaning we make of life events. We can work alongside community movements (guided by shared values and goals) to improve the system and society. Throughout the process of writing this book I have come to realise how proud I am to be part of the Parent Carer community. We are simultaneously both vulnerable and strong.

I'm also proud of our children for all they endure and their capacity to cope in a world that doesn't always adapt for them (that's probably the start of another book).

We, along with our children, will continue to grow – in our awareness, learning and capacities as parents and people. Our sense of purpose and meaning in life can support us along the way.

Writing this book has also been meaningful – meeting other parent carers and attempting to portray and pull together the many varied experiences of family life has helped me make sense of my own path. At times the journey has been painful. There has been heartache as well as joy. But these conversations are necessary.

I hope that this book can help broaden your own life story and remind you that your own wellbeing is important.

And it all started for me with one beautiful little boy. xx

Key points for your wellbeing

1. Take care of yourself. You are important. Taking time for yourself is a necessity not a luxury.

2. Take things day by day. Develop your emotional awareness to notice what you need at different times.

3. Recognise your own expertise and how far you've travelled.

4. Seek help when you need it. If you are not happy with the response seek help elsewhere.

5. Find your community and positive others – whoever that may be. Belonging, connection and understanding are key to wellbeing.

6. Enjoy and cherish your child. Don't compare to other families – each family and child is unique and will develop and do things differently.

7. Utilise your self-care Swiss army knife, including looking through the worksheet in Appendix I. Try different things – a walk in nature, coffee with a friend, playing tennis, listening to music. Practise noticing the positives – your child's achievements, something you've managed well, little things like a rainbow or a smile from a stranger.

8. Try to take a stance of openness and flexibility to help manage life's inevitable ups and downs. Life is change and keeping hold of narrow beliefs of how things 'should' be can restrict our enjoyment of it.

9. Our changed perspective on life can be a source of wisdom and growth.

10. Engage with your values – find your sense of purpose and meaning in life.

Appendices

Wellbeing Worksheet

This worksheet includes different exercises to try and see what works for you. It is also available to download from www.affinityhub.uk so you can keep a note of how things change over time.

It includes sections on the following:

- Spectra of wellbeing

- Writing to offload

- Short bursts of self-care and longer term values-led action

- Noticing positives

- Challenging negative thoughts

- Self-compassion

Spectra of wellbeing

As discussed in Chapter 2, the 'Spectra' identifies different dimensions to supporting your wellbeing. Try to identify ways in which you can bring balance across the different aspects, keeping in mind the image of the scales. You can write down, or draw, what you currently do or what you would like to do more of in your life, what nourishes you and what depletes you.

You may also find it useful to note down obstacles that prevent you from doing things and ways to overcome these. Some ideas will overlap. For example, you may want to spend more time working on certain projects or activities that give you a sense of meaning in life, but it can be hard to make the time. Prioritising your time over other non-essential activities may be one way of doing this to guarantee your 'time that is mine' and it may involve you being more empowered or assertive to say no to other demands.

I've included some prompts at the top of each but you can use the table however you find most helpful.

Sense of Purpose or Meaning

What is providing purpose or meaning in my life? How can I engage with this more? What's stopping me? (You can use the Acceptance and Commitment Therapy resource listed in Appendix IV to help you identify your values if you are finding this difficult)

Positive Others

How balanced are my relationships with others? Who has a positive effect on me? How can I connect to the positives more?

Empowerment

What makes me feel empowered? What makes me feel disempowered? What is possible to change? Who can change it? What cannot be changed? (see the 'What I can and can't control' chart below)

Child

How balanced is the relationship with my child(ren)? What do I want to do more of? What do I want to do less of? Who can help me achieve this?

Time that is Mine

How balanced is the time for me and time for others? What can help give me more time? What do I need to do, say or be to enable this? What do I want from the time for myself?

Replenish and Recalibrate

Do I engage in activities that replenish and recalibrate me? What helps when? Is there anything new I want to try? How do I feel after these activities? Is it helpful in the long term? (NB some activities help in the short term but not the long term – e.g. withdrawing from social activities)

Awareness of Emotions

How do I feel right now? What can help me when I feel like this? Do I need to sit with this feeling or take action? Do certain physical sensations help me notice how I am feeling or what I need to do?

Writing to offload

Our brains can only focus on a limited number of things at one time and can get overloaded if we have too many things going on (referred to as 'psychic entropy'[181]). Keep it simple. Some people find it useful to write things down and offload their concerns. You can use the space below to note things that are on your mind. As referred to in Chapter 8, you can develop your 'Worry controller' to prioritise, and sometimes dis-engage from, certain activities until you're in a better place to deal with them.

You can also use the space to free write or draw, noting down anything on your mind even if it doesn't make sense at first. It will help to clear the mental clutter so you can focus on what is important right now.

---

[181] Csikszentmihalyi, M. (2002) *Flow: The classic work on how to achieve happiness*, London: Random House, p. 37

Brain dump or space for free writing or drawing
(you can even use stick people or abstract images,
shapes and colours)

What I can and cannot control

Some people find identifying what you can and cannot control is a useful way to note things down and 'park' worries for another time.

Things I can sort out myself	Things that others can help me with
Things I can think about another time	**Things I cannot do anything about**

Short bursts of self-care and longer term values-led action

Committing to acts of self-care, either by writing them down or telling someone else about your plans, can make it more likely you'll stick to them. You can use the space below.

For example:

3 short bursts of self-care

1. Call a friend or meet up for a coffee
2. Focus on something absorbing – yoga, colouring in, nature, reading or a jigsaw puzzle
3. Do something for your senses – have a bath with a face mask, enjoy a delicious chocolate bar, hug your child

1 longer term values-led action

Sign up for an online training course on something of interest that you've been meaning to do for a while or join a campaign that you feel passionately about.

For you to complete:

3 short bursts of self-care

1. _____

_____

_____

2. _____

_____

_____

3. _____

_____

_____

---

1 longer term values led action

Noticing positives

Human beings have evolved a negative bias that has kept us safe in the past but which can sometimes mean we are more prone to notice negatives and ignore the positives. With practice, though, we can re-focus on the positives, which is shown to improve our wellbeing (see Chapter 8).

Positive focus

What three things have gone well in the last six months and why?

_____

_____

_____

What is the best thing about you?

_____

_____

_____

What do you like most about yourself?

_____

_____

_____

What are you like when you are at your best?

_____

_____

_____

What, or who, brings out the best in you?

_____

_____

_____

What is your most significant achievement?

_____

_____

_____

How have your strengths helped you in the past?

_____

_____

_____

How can your strengths help you in the future?

_____

_____

_____

Linked to positive psychology is the focus on gratitude.

Gratitude Journal

Write down or name three things that you are grateful for right now,
however big or small, e.g. the smell of a flower, a bird song, family,
health, something nice someone said to you or the tastiest thing you've
eaten today. Try to do this every day. You can also encourage your
children to do this.

_____

_____

_____

Challenging negative thoughts

As highlighted in Chapter 8, sometimes we need to challenge our
Automatic Negative Thoughts (ANTs) to start to see things in a more
balanced light. Below is a thought record for you to make a note of your
thoughts. You can find out more about Cognitive Behaviour Therapy
from the resources listed in Appendix IV.

Situation	Mood	Automatic Thoughts	Evidence that supports the difficult thought	Evidence that does not support the difficult thought	Alternative/ Balanced thoughts	Rate mood Now

Self-compassion

Sometimes people notice that even with their new thoughts or ways of looking at things there is a lack of self-compassion. We may speak to ourselves in a critical voice. Compassion Focused Therapy[182] aims to help us notice how we speak to ourselves and to develop greater compassion – for others and for ourselves.

This can be useful for parent carers who may be particularly prone to self-criticism. Spending time being compassionate to yourself can be de-shaming. We are human beings, with emotions and thoughts that are often out of our control and linked to how our brains evolved. We don't need to blame ourselves. We can take action though.

Some books are listed in Appendix IV if you wish to read more about this approach. I've provided a couple of short exercises below as a brief introduction.

We can develop our own self-compassionate voice by noticing when our self-critical voice appears and changing our self-talk.

Self-critical voice	Self-compassionate voice
Criticises for past mistakes and focuses on punishment 'well you messed that up again didn't you'	Emphasises the desire to improve and grow in the future 'I know this is really hard. That didn't quite work as I had hoped it would, so next time maybe try X'
Can you think of an example of when you have spoken to yourself in a self-critical voice?	*What would your self-compassionate voice say instead?*

---

182   Gilbert, P. (2013) *The Compassionate Mind*, London: Robinson

You can also create a compassionate image in your mind to draw on in times of need. What qualities would your creation have (e.g. wisdom, strength, warmth and absence of judgement)? What would they sound, look and feel like? How would they relate to you?

Different systems

In his book 'The Compassionate Mind' Paul Gilbert illustrates three different emotional regulation systems that influence us:

1. Threat system which focuses on the negatives and notices potential dangers. It can be useful as it keeps us safe and anger can motivate us to act in the face of injustice.

2. Drive system encourages us to seek things out such as excitement and joy as well as to achieve. Our sense of purpose and value in life can be a motivator.

3. Soothing system involves connection with others and taking our time to engage in activities that replenish us.

Sometimes, though, the systems can get out of balance. A useful exercise is to draw circles for each system to illustrate how you are feeling now, or how you've been feeling over the last week. This can help to identify when things need to change.

For example, the circles below would show that stress or anxiety levels are high and more soothing activities are necessary. If this is done over a period of time you may start to identify what triggers any imbalances. This, in turn, enables you to pro-actively engage in more soothing activities prior to a stressful event.

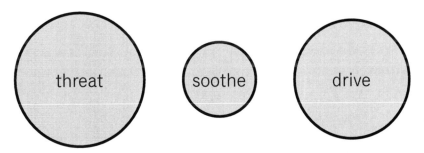

Adapted from P. Gilbert (2009) The Compassionate Mind, London: Robinson, p. 24

It can also be a useful exercise to think about for our children. For example, my son feels very unsettled by loud noises (threat system) and needs time to then self soothe (jump on the trampoline or watch tv). It can help us recognise that if someone is in the threat system it is more likely they will react (negatively) to things like requests or demands on their focus. Having some down time to recover will help them reduce the threat system and re-gain balance.

APPENDIX

Social Model of Disability and Terminology

Social Model of Disability

The social model of disability was developed by disabled people in response to the medical model, which focused on diagnosis and difference as the main cause of disability. The medical model 'looks at what is "wrong' with the person"'[183]. In contrast the social model of disability highlights that whilst the impairment can be a challenge it is often the environment that is disabling. It is not about treating everyone the same; it is about allowing everyone full access and removing unnecessary barriers that cause the inequality. For example, if a disabled person who cannot use the stairs wishes to access a building that has a step at the front, it is the building and lack of adaptation that disables them.

Terminology

The Equality Act 2010 defines someone as disabled if:

> 'you have a physical or mental impairment that has a "substantial" and "long-term" negative effect on your ability to do normal daily activities'.

There are historical reasons for using the term 'disabled' based on the social model of disability.

---

[183] https://www.scope.org.uk/about-us/social-model-of-disability/

Disabilities are often described in the education, health and social care sectors in degrees of severity, so you may hear terms such as mild or moderate learning disability (MLD), profound and multiple learning disability (PMLD) or high/low- functioning autism. These are attempts to categorise the individual's needs for services and sectors but are disliked by some communities[184]. These terms are a very blunt and a rather simplistic instrument for what is an extremely complex area. For example, people can have co-occurring diagnoses and, while an individual may be viewed by services as having a mild condition (e.g. 'high-functioning autism') and live an independent life, they may be severely affected by social anxiety.

There are also different views and discussions around whether person-first or identify-first language is preferable. Some people prefer to say 'I am autistic' (identity-first) and others prefer 'I have autism / I am on the autism spectrum' (person-first). The National Autistic Society, following a survey of their members, is now using the term 'autistic person' as this was preferred by the majority of respondents. Autism is classified as a disability and thereby covered by the Equality Act 2010.

In other diagnoses there may be different preferences, for example, some prefer 'person with a learning disability' or 'learning disabled person'. It's always best to check with the individual what they wish to use.

I'm sure the terminology will continue to change and the language in this book will inevitably be outdated soon. English is a living language and it is empowering that the people who are affected by the language continue to influence and change it according to the social context.

---

[184] https://www.autism.org.uk/what-we-do/help-and-support/how-to-talk-about-autism

List of organisations that provide support to parent carers

There are a number of national charities, listed below, that provide support for family carers.

Services can vary locally so it is also worth asking your GP, paediatrician, Child and Adolescent Mental Health Service (CAMHS), Local Authority and Adult Service. Other local and national services that provide emotional support are listed on the affinityhub.uk website.

Birth Trauma Association

The Birth Trauma Association supports all women who have had a traumatic birth experience. It is estimated that, in the UK alone, this may result in 10,000 women a year developing Post Traumatic Stress Disorder (PTSD). The website offers emotional and practical support to women and also their families. www.birthtraumaassociation.org.uk

Bliss

Bliss offers a wide range of services to provide support to parents and families of babies born premature or sick. www.bliss.org.uk

Carers Trust

Carers Trust is a charity for, with and about carers. It works to improve support, services and recognition for anyone living with the challenges of caring, unpaid, for a family member or friend who is ill, frail, disabled or has mental health or addiction problems. www.carers.org. www.babble.carers.org

Carers UK

Carers UK provides expert advice and information champions carers' rights and campaigns for lasting change and to support carers find new ways to manage at home, work or wherever they are. www.carersuk.org

Cerebra

Cerebra offer a range of different services for families with a child with brain conditions. They have a dedicated Sleep Advice Helpline on 0800 328 1159 or sleep@cerebra.org.uk www.cerebra.org.uk

Challenging Behaviour Foundation

The Challenging Behaviour Foundation (CBF) offers support via email or telephone to families with a relative who has severe learning disabilities. 'Severe learning disabilities' means that the person has no speech or very limited speech, and requires support with everyday tasks like dressing and washing. The CBF provides a range of information resources and can also link families for peer-to-peer support. www.challengingbehaviour.org.uk

Contact

Contact is the charity for families with disabled children. Contact supports families with the best possible guidance and information, brings families together to support each other and helps families to campaign, volunteer and fundraise to improve life for themselves and others. www.contact.org.uk

Crisis Mental Health Teams

Crisis resolution and home treatment (CRHT) teams can support those who have a mental health crisis outside of hospital. They're often called crisis teams for short, although local services can be called something different.

www.mind.org.uk/information-support/guides-to-support-and-services /crisis-services/crisis-teams-crhts/ www.nhs.uk/service-search/mental-health/find-an-urgent-mental-health-helpline

Disabled Children's Partnership

The Disabled Children's Partnership is a major coalition of more than seventy organisations campaigning for improved health and social care for disabled children, young people and their families. www.disabledchildrenspartnership.org.uk

Family Fund

The UK's largest charity providing grants for families raising disabled or seriously ill children and young people. www.familyfund.org.uk

Gingerbread

Gingerbread provides information and advice for single parents, including those with disabled children. Local support groups provide the opportunity to talk to other single parents. Some run drop-in centres or offer home visits. Your local group may also publish a newsletter covering activities in your area or providing help with organising respite care. www.gingerbread.org.uk/

KIDS

An established national charity, KIDS provides support to disabled children and their families to thrive, not just survive. KIDS ensures disabled children from birth to twenty-five have the opportunity to learn, play, build friendships, gain confidence and improve their wellbeing. Kids provides vital time, emotional and practical support to parents and siblings. www.kids.org.uk

LAPIS

London Accessible Psychotherapy and Inclusive Supervision (LAPIS) provides specialist counselling and psychotherapy to people affected by disability and life changing health issues. LAPIS offers an affordable service to disabled people, their family and carers. A sliding scale is in operation so you can pay according to what you can afford and therapy is available on an ongoing basis. www.thelapis.co.uk

Mencap

Mencap's helpline offers free advice and information about learning disability and helps to find the right support and Mencap services in your area. The online FamilyHub is always available for parents and family carers of people with a learning disability. It's a place to share triumphs and challenges with people who really understand. www.mencap.org.uk

National Autistic Society

NAS are the UK's leading charity for people on the autism spectrum and their families. Since 1962 they have provided support, guidance and advice, as well as campaigning for improved rights, services and opportunities to help create a society that works for autistic people. www.autism.org.uk

National Society for the Prevention of Cruelty to Children (NSPCC)

The National Society for the Prevention of Cruelty to Children is a charity campaigning and working in child protection in the United Kingdom and the Channel Islands. www.nspcc.org.uk

Peeps – HIE Awareness and Support

Peeps – HIE Awareness and Support are the only UK charity dedicated to supporting those affected by HIE (hypoxic-ischaemic encephalopathy) or brain injury caused by oxygen deprivation. The nature of HIE means that outcomes can vary greatly, and the impact on parents, siblings and the wider family can be huge. The charity offers practical, financial and emotional support, wherever a family may be on their HIE journey including specialised counselling (over the phone, so no travel required), with a trained therapist, and ensure that no HIE parent feels they are on their own. www.peeps-hie.org

Rainbow Trust

Rainbow Trust pairs each family with a dedicated expert Family Support Worker to help them face and make the most of each new day. Family Support Workers support the whole family with whatever they need so that families don't have to manage alone. There is also guidance on supporting parents' mental health when a child has a life-threatening illness. www.rainbowtrust.org.uk/support-for-families

Relate

Relate provides relationship support, including talking to a trained relationship counsellor online for free via Live Chat. Parents can find a Relate counsellor near them at www.relate.org.uk/find-your-nearest-relate and request a counsellor with experience of working with parents of disabled children.

Respond

Respond offers therapeutic help to people with learning disabilities and/or autistic spectrum disorders who have experienced abuse or trauma and support to their families. Often distress in people with learning disabilities does not attract a helping response until they behave in ways that are potentially harmful to others. Respond recognises this situation and is unique in offering therapy to both survivors and perpetrators of abuse in the same location. The Family Support Service seeks to help by means of individual or group support, encouraging peer support, and advocacy in limited circumstances. Family or individual therapy may be available. www.respond.org.uk

Scope

Scope have a service called Navigate which is a national mentoring service that provides emotional support for parents of disabled children who are finding out about their child's additional needs. Parents can find out more about this service by going to their website: www.scope.org.uk/family-services/navigate

Sibs

Sibs supports brothers and sisters of disabled children and adults. It is the only UK charity representing the needs of over half a million young siblings and over one and a half million adult siblings. There is useful information for parents here: www.sibs.org.uk/supporting-young-siblings/parents

Together for Short Lives

Together for Short Lives is a UK wide charity that, together with its members, speaks out for all children and young people who are expected to have short lives. They help children and their families to access specialist children's palliative care services when and where they need it. The website is a hub where families and professionals can find information and resources. www.togetherforshortlives.org.uk

YoungMinds

YoungMinds offer free, confidential online and telephone support, including information and advice, to any adult worried about the emotional problems, behaviour or mental health of a child or young person up to the age of twenty-five. www.youngminds.org.uk

IV

Resources

Social media:

You can follow my work on #parentcarerwellbeing here:

Instagram: affinityhub.uk

Twitter: affinityhub_uk

Facebook: affinityhub.uk

Recommended books:

Bartram, P. (2007) *Understanding your young child with special needs*, London: Jessica Kingsley Publishers

Newbold, Y. (2014) *The Special Parent's Handbook*, UK: Amity Books

Ryan, F. (2019) *Crippled: Austerity and the demonization of disabled people*, London: Verso

Ryan, S. (2020) *Love, Learning Disabilities and Pockets of Brilliance: How practitioners can make a difference to the lives of children, families and adults*, London: Jessica Kingsley

Ryan, S. (2017) *Justice for Laughing Boy*, London: Jessica Kingsley

Salman, S. (2020) *Made Possible: Stories of Success by people with learning disabilities – in their words*, London: Unbound

Solomon, A. (2013) *Far from the Tree*, London: Chatto & Windus

Resources for further information:

Acceptance and Commitment Therapy

Harris, R. (2008) *The Happiness Trap. Based on ACT: A revolutionary mindfulness-based programme for overcoming stress, anxiety and depression,* Great Britain: Robinson www.actmindfully.com.au

Hayes, S.C., Strosahl, K.D. & Wilson, K.G. (1999) *Acceptance and Commitment Therapy: An Experiential Approach to Behavior Change,* New York: Guilford Press

Anger

NHS – www.nhs.uk/conditions/stress-anxiety-depression/controlling-anger/

Mind – www.mind.org.uk/information-support/types-of-mental-health-problems/anger/managing-outbursts/

Anxiety and Stress

National Health Service (NHS) – www.nhs.uk/conditions/stress-anxiety-depression/understanding-panic/

Anxiety UK – www.anxietyuk.org.uk/

Mind – www.mind.org.uk/information-support/types-of-mental-health-problems/anxiety-and-panic-attacks/about-anxiety/

Butler, G. (2016) *Overcoming Social Anxiety and Shyness: A self-help guide using cognitive behavioural techniques,* Robinson: Great Britain

Body and Polyvagal Theory

Dana, D. (2020) *Polyvagal Exercises for Safety and Connection: 50 Client-Centered Practices,* London: W.W. Norton & Company

Van Der Kolk, B. (2014) *The Body Keeps the Score,* Great Britain: Penguin Books

Porges, S. (2011) T*he Polyvagal Theory: Neurophysiological Foundations of Emotions, Attachment, Communication, and Self-Regulation,* London: W.W. Norton & Co.

Chronic Sorrow

Roos, S. (2002) *Chronic Sorrow: A Living Loss,* New York: Routledge

Cognitive Behavioural Therapy

Greenberger, D. & Padesky, C. (2015) *Mind over Mood: Change how you feel by changing the way you think* (2nd ed.), New York: The Guilford Press

Mind – www.mind.org.uk/information-support/drugs-and-treatments/cognitive-behavioural-therapy-cbt/about-cbt/

NHS Catch It app - www.nhs.uk/apps-library/catch-it/

NHS – www.nhs.uk/conditions/cognitive-behavioural-therapy-cbt

Compassion Focused Therapy

Gilbert, P. (2013) *The Compassionate Mind*, London: Robinson

Gilbert, P. (2010) *Compassion Focused Therapy: CBT Distinctive Features Series*, London: Routledge

Creativity

Cameron, J. (2016) *The Artist's Way*, London: Macmillan

Depression

NHS – www.nhs.uk/conditions/clinical-depression/

Mind – www.mind.org.uk/information-support/types-of-mental-health-problems/depression/about-depression

Rethink Mental Illness – www.rethink.org/advice-and-information/about-mental-illness/learn-more-about-conditions/depression

Blurt: Increasing awareness and understanding of depression – www.blurtitout.org/resources

Exercise

NHS – www.nhs.uk/live-well/exercise/free-fitness-ideas

Walking for Health – www.walkingforhealth.org.uk

Flow

Csikszentmihalyi, M. (2002) *Flow: The classic work on how to achieve happiness,* London: Random House

Grief

The Compassionate Friends – www.tcf.org.uk/content/helpline

Care for the Family – www.careforthefamily.org.uk/family-life/bereavement-support/bereaved-parent-support

Cruse Bereavement Care – www.cruse.org.uk

The Good Grief Trust – www.thegoodgrieftrust.org

Sibling Loss

DeVita-Raeburn, E. (2004) *The Empty Room*, New York: Scribner Book Company

Gill White, P. (2008) *Sibling Grief: Healing After the Death of a Sister or Brother*, iUniverse

Healthy Eating

Carers UK – www.carersuk.org/help-and-advice/health/nutrition/eating-well

NHS – www.nhs.uk/live-well/eat-well

Meaning

Frankl, V.E. (1985) *Man's search for meaning*, New York: Washington Square Press (originally published in 1946)

Kessler, D. (2019) *Finding Meaning: the sixth stage of grief*, London: Rider Books

Vos, J. (2018) *Meaning in Life*, London: Palgrave

Mental Health and Learning Disabilities

Resources on mental health and learning & developmental disabilities which includes a section on Family Carers: www.minded.org.uk

Mindfulness

Heaversedge, J. & Halliwell, E. (2010) *The Mindful manifesto: 'How doing less and noticing more can help us thrive in a stressed out world'*, UK: Hay House

Kabat-Zinn, J. (2013) *Full Catastrophe Living: How to cope with stress, pain and illness using mindfulness meditation,* London: Piatkus

NHS – www.nhs.uk/conditions/stress-anxiety-depression/mindfulness/

Mental Health Foundation – www.mentalhealth.org.uk/a-to-z/m/mindfulness

Positive Psychology

Action for happiness – www.actionforhappiness.org

Positive Psychology – www.positivepsychology.org.uk/gratitude/

Ehrenreich, B. (2009) *Smile or Die: How Positive Thinking Fooled America and the World,* London: Granta Books [Interesting critique of positive psychology]

Hefferon, K. (2013) *Positive Psychology and the Body: The Somatopsychic side to flourishing*, Berkshire, UK: Open University Press

Seligman, M. (2011) *Flourish: A Visionary new understanding of happiness and wellbeing,* London: Simon and Shuster

Seligman, M. (2003) *Authentic Happiness: Using the New Positive Psychology to Realize Your Potential for Lasting Fulfillment,* London: Nicholas Brealey Publishing

Reading Well initiative

www.reading-well.org.uk

Sleep

Family Fund – www.familyfund.org.uk/tired-all-the-time

Contact – Helping Your Child's Sleep

NHS:

www.nhs.uk/live-well/sleep-and-tiredness/how-to-get-to-sleep/

www.nhs.uk/live-well/sleep-and-tiredness/10-tips-to-beat-insomnia/

Yoga

Annand, N. (2020) *Yoga: A Manual for Life*, Bloomsbury

Hefferon, K. (2013) *Positive Psychology and the Body: The Somatopsychic side to flourishing*, Berkshire, UK: Open University Press

Glossary

Annual Reviews

By law, Education, Health and Care plans (EHCPs) should be reviewed at least once every year, in a formal meeting known as an annual review.

Carer's Allowance

A government allowance if you care for someone for at least thirty-five hours a week and they get certain benefits.

Carer's Assessment

An assessment undertaken by, or on behalf of, social services to assess what support you may need if you care for someone.

Child and Adolescent Mental Health Services (CAMHS)

CAMHS are the NHS services that assess and treat young people with emotional, behavioural or mental health difficulties.

Children and Families' Act 2014

The Children and Families Act 2014 covers adoption and contact, family justice, children and young people with Special Educational Needs (SEN), child care and child welfare. It introduced EHCPs.

Clinical Commissioning Group (CCG)

Clinical Commissioning Groups (CCGs) were created following the Health and Social Care Act in 2012, and replaced Primary Care Trusts on 1 April 2013. They are clinically-led statutory NHS bodies responsible for the planning and commissioning of health care services for their local area.

***Contact* (see Appendix III)**

Crisis Mental Health Teams (see Appendix III)

Disability

The Equality Act 2010 defines a disabled person as having a physical or mental impairment that has a 'substantial' and 'long-term' negative effect on your ability to do normal daily activities. https://www.gov.uk/definition-of-disability-under-equality-act-2010 (See Appendix II for further discussion on terminology.)

Disability Living Allowance (DLA)

Disability Living Allowance (DLA) is a benefit for disabled people. It's a monthly, tax-free payment. It's gradually being replaced by Personal Independence Payment.

Do Not Attempt Resuscitation Order

A 'do not attempt resuscitation' (DNAR) decision instructs medical staff on whether or not they should attempt to resuscitate you.

Early Positive Approaches to Support (E-PAtS)

Early Positive Approaches to Support (E-PAtS) is an 8-week programme for families raising a young child (five years and under) with a learning and/or developmental disability. It was developed by family carers working alongside professionals (co-produced). www.positiveapproachestosupport.co.uk

Education Health and Care Plans (EHCPs)

An education, health and care (EHC) plan is for children and young people aged up to twenty-five who need more support than is available from within an education setting's own resources. EHC plans are legal documents which identify educational, health and social needs and set out the additional support to meet those needs.

General Practitioner (GP)

General practitioners (GPs) treat all common medical conditions and refer patients to hospitals and other medical services for urgent and specialist treatment.

Improving Access to Psychological Therapies (IAPT)

Talking therapies programme within the National Health Service which aims to increase the number of people who can access support for anxiety or depression.

Local Authority

An administrative body in local government responsible for vital services such as schools, housing and social care.

Local Offer

The SEND Local Offer helps children, young people and their parents to understand what services and support they can expect from a range of local agencies – including their statutory entitlements.

Makaton

Makaton symbols and signs are used either as a main method of communication or as a way to support speech.

Mencap (see Appendix III)

Multi-disciplinary team (MDT)

A Multidisciplinary Team is a group of professionals from one or more clinical disciplines (e.g. paediatrician, psychologist, physiotherapist, occupational therapists, speech and language therapist) who together make decisions regarding recommended treatment of individual patients.

National Autistic Society (see Appendix III)

National Health Service (NHS)

The NHS is the publicly-funded medical and health care service in the United Kingdom.

Occupational Therapist

Occupational therapy provides practical support to empower people to facilitate recovery and overcome barriers preventing them from doing the activities (or occupations) that matter to them.

Personal Independence Payment (PIP)

PIP is for people between sixteen and sixty-four who need help at home because of an illness or disability.

Physiotherapist

Physiotherapists help people affected by injury, illness or disability through movement and exercise, manual therapy, education and advice.

Psychologist

Psychology is the scientific study of the mind and how it dictates and influences our behaviour, from communication and memory to thought and emotion. It's about understanding what makes people tick and how this understanding can help us address many of the problems and issues in society today.

Respite

Respite care means taking a break from caring, while the person you care for is looked after by someone else.

Scope (see Appendix III)

Short breaks

The term 'short breaks' is used to describe the time off that family carers and disabled people receive. These breaks come in different forms.

Some families access short breaks at centres, others are part of schemes involving placements with families. Some receive direct payments to buy their own support.

Social model of disability (see Appendix II)

Social services

Social care is the provision of social work, personal care, protection or social support services to children or adults in need or at risk, or adults with needs arising from illness, disability, old age or poverty.

Special Educational Needs and Disabilities (SEND)

A child or young person has special educational needs and disabilities (SEND) if they have a learning difficulty and/or a disability that means they need special health and education support. The SEND Code of Practice 2014 and the Children and Families Act 2014 give guidance to health and social care, education and local authorities to make sure that children and young people with SEND are properly supported.

Special Educational Needs and Disabilities Information Advice and Support Service (SENDIASS)

Free, confidential and impartial information, advice and support service on issues related to SEND in local areas.

Special Educational Needs and Disabilities (SEND) Tribunal

An independent national tribunal which hears parents' and young people's appeals against LA decisions about the special educational needs of children and young people. It also hears claims of disability discrimination against schools.

Speech and Language Therapist (SLT)

Speech and language therapists provide treatment, support and care for children and adults who have difficulties with communication, or with eating, drinking and swallowing.

Acknowledgements

There are many people I would like to thank for helping me both in bringing this work to fruition as well as ongoing support throughout my life. Firstly, thanks to Alice Solomons for believing in this project and providing patient guidance throughout the process.

Thank you to all of our family who have been there for us through thick and thin and always with love in their hearts. Margaret Woodcock, Roy Woodcock, Nicola Jones, Dave Jones, Richard Woodcock, Mette Sommerfelt, Alan N. Griffin, Janet Scott, Vibeke Egelund, Wenche Egelund, and Dolly Bond. To all the godparents and friends who have supported us as a family.

Particular thanks to Dr Marie Adams, Debbie Austin, Carla Barrett, Leigh Baseley, Jill Bradshaw, Joanna Campion, Bev Burke, Neil Dunford, Cat Essery, Jo Fowler, Claire Garthwaite, Dr Nick Gore, Dr Lisa Greenspan, Dominique Grimaldi, Rasha Hafidh, Dr Emma Johnston, Angela Kelly, Stephen Kingdom, Silvia Laraia, Lizzie Latham, Julie Lewis, Mark Love, James Robinson, Olu Sholagbade, Michelle Stacey, Jane Steeples, Hana Young.

Thanks to Clare Kassa for help with the section on siblings. Thanks for permissions to quote or reference personal experiences: Saba Salman, Paula McGowan and Dr Sara Ryan.

With deep gratitude to all the parents who took part in my research and answered the online survey. To the many parents I've spoken to over the last 13 years and have kindly shared their experiences.

To our therapists who have consistently been there for us as a family: Annick Algar, Heather Holgate, Gill Stern, Virginie Host and Sarah Pressley.

To my husband, Alan, and my precious boys who give meaning to my life.

Index